# *Investigating Mass Media*

Peter Trowler

Collins Educational
*An imprint of* HarperCollins*Publishers*

Published by Collins Educational
An imprint of HarperCollinsPublishers
77–85 Fulham Palace Road
Hammersmith, London W6 8JB

First published in 1996

ISBN 0–00–322438–4

Commissioned by Emma Dunlop
Edited by Susan Millership
Production by Mandy Innes
Cover artwork and design by Derek Lee
Illustrations by Julia Osorno
Typeset by Harper Phototypesetters Ltd, Northampton
Printed and bound by Scotprint Ltd, Musselburgh

# Contents

# *Acknowledgements*

*The author and publisher would like to thank the following individuals and organizations for permission to reproduce material:*

The Associated Examining Board; Daniel Betts pp. 60, 63, 75, 99, 120, 155 and 229; Boddingtons and Bartle Bogle Hegarty Ltd p.193; BFI Stills, Posters and Designs p.113 (Orion), 122 (World Productions Ltd), and 213 (Paramount Television); BMW p.133; Camden Press Ltd p. 40; Johnson and Johnson p. 148; Granada Television p. 210; Professor J. Lull p.219, first appeared in *Media, Communication, Culture: A Global Approach;* News International plc pp.70 (bottom) and 224; Nigel Paige pp. 21, 25, 27, 56, 65, and 124; Pirelli p. 183; Rediffusion p.5; Rex Features pp. 1, 8, 29, 30, 33, 44, 46, 70 (top two), 92, 98, 100, 150, 168, 176, 206 and 232; Scope Communications p. 16; Topham pp. 47 and 186; Shannon C and Weaver W (1949) *The Mathematical Theory of Communication*: University of Illinois Press p. 22; Paul Trowler pp. 105 and 139.

While every effort has been made to contact copyright-holders, the publishers would be pleased to hear from any copyright-holders who have been overlooked.

This book may contain references to fictitious characters in fictitious case studies.
For educational purposes only, photographs have been used to accompany these case studies. The juxtaposition of photographs and case studies is not intended to identify the individual in the photograph with the character in the case study. The publishers cannot accept any responsibility for any consequences resulting from this use of photographs and case studies, except as expressly provided by law.

# Developments in the mass media

Figure 1.1 The power of television?

---

**The mass media**

The mass media can be defined as 'the methods and organizations used by specialist social groups to convey messages to large, socially mixed and widely dispersed audiences'.

---

 *Look at table 1.1. If you can tick each box on the horizontal line next to the examples given they count as part of the mass media. If you can't then they do not meet the definition above and are not part of the mass media. Try it.*

Even since the publication of the first edition of this book in 1988 there has been a remarkable growth in the range of home entertainment items and through them exposure to different aspects of the mass media. This chapter discusses some of the most important developments in the mass media in recent years and is organized by type of mass medium, starting with television. Table 1.2 provides a summary of some of the changes there have been.

 *What are the sociologically most important trends this table reveals? What other information would we need to know before we could make generalizations about the penetration of different aspects of the mass media into society?*

Table 1.1    Types of mass media

| Example | Method or organization? (tick if either) | Specialized social group? | Messages conveyed? | Large audience? | Socially mixed audience? | Widely dispersed audience? |
|---|---|---|---|---|---|---|
| Cinema | | | | | | |
| Film | | | | | | |
| The BBC | | | | | | |
| Fanzines | | | | | | |
| Computer video games | | | | | | |
| Desktop Publishing | | | | | | |
| Graffiti | | | | | | |
| Books | | | | | | |
| Photocopier | | | | | | |
| Music CDs | | | | | | |
| Printed T Shirts | | | | | | |
| Your examples... | | | | | | |

Table 1.2    Summary of changes in the mass media, 1986-93: Media technology in the home

| | 1986 % | 1987 % | 1988 % | 1989 % | 1990 % | 1991 % | 1992 % | 1993 % |
|---|---|---|---|---|---|---|---|---|
| Video recorder | 44 | 55 | 58 | 70 | 75 | 72 | 77 | 80 |
| Teletext | 17 | 23 | 25 | 30 | 41 | 40 | 46 | 49 |
| Home computer | 21 | 23 | 18 | 26 | 22 | 22 | 30 | 29 |
| Compact disc player | n/a | n/a | n/a | n/a | n/a | 22 | 29 | 27 |
| Video games | 10 | 10 | 10 | 11 | 11 | 12 | 17 | 20 |
| Satellite TV dish | n/a | * | * | 2 | 4 | 8 | 10 | 12 |
| Video camera | 2 | 1 | 2 | 3 | 4 | 5 | 9 | 10 |
| Nicam digital stereo television set | n/a | n/a | n/a | n/a | n/a | 5 | 6 | 7 |
| Cable TV | 1 | 1 | 1 | 2 | 1 | 3 | 3 | 3 |
| Video disc player | 1 | 1 | 1 | 2 | 2 | 2 | 3 | 2 |
| Prestel/Viewdata | 1 | 1 | 1 | * | 2 | 1 | 2 | 2 |
| Cable phone | n/a | n/a | n/a | n/a | n/a | n/a | n/a | 1 |
| Have one or more of these | 57 | 65 | 67 | 77 | 81 | 80 | 83 | 86 |
| Have none of these | 43 | 35 | 33 | 23 | 19 | 20 | 17 | 14 |

Base: All TV viewers

Notes: *Less than 0.5%; n/a Not asked

*Source: Gunter et al., p. 11, table 2.2.*

When a sociologist researches developments in the media s/he looks at them from a particular perspective which prompts particular sorts of questions. Try to bear those listed below in mind as you read this chapter:

● How will the development impact on different social groups (e.g. different classes, ethnic groups, men and women)?

● What do the developments tell us about the changing patterns of power in the media (e.g. ownership of companies, control over content)?

● What impact will the developments have for the individual in society (e.g. the extent of choice, access to information by them or about them, leisure patterns, patterns of interaction)?

● What trends are revealed within and across the media (e.g. globalization, homogenization of content)?

● How might changes affect the nature of culture and the way it is produced and reproduced (e.g. the relationship between 'high' and 'low' culture, and the empowerment of individuals to create their own local cultures)?

*Imagine a middle-class family of husband, wife, son (8 years old) and daughter (14 years old) in 15 years' time. What parts of the mass media will be important in their lives? What will be the main differences from today? Now imagine an unemployed single mother living in the inner city with her 6-year-old daughter and answer the same questions. What is the sociological significance of your answers?*

Table 1.3    Critical points in the history of broadcasting in Britain

| | |
|---|---|
| 1922 | First public broadcasting begins (by private companies) |
| 1926 | BBC set up and begins its radio broadcasts |
| 1936 | BBC TV starts broadcasting. World's first public TV service |
| 1951 | 600,000 TV viewers in Britain |
| 1954 | Independent Television Authority (ITA) set up by Television Act |
| 1955 | First ITA programmes begin transmission |
| 1956 | 6 million TV viewers |
| 1967 | Radios 1, 2, 3 and 4 replace old BBC radio channels |
| 1972 | ITA becomes Independent Broadcasting Authority (IBA). Commercial radio permitted locally by Sound Broadcasting Act. Independent Local Radio (ILR) begins |
| 1981 | Broadcasting Act permits setting up of Channel 4. BBC gets new Charter until 1996 |
| 1982 | Channel 4 starts broadcasting |
| 1984 | Cable and Broadcasting Act sets up Cable Authority and Satellite Broadcasting Board |
| 1984 | Sky Television reaches 1.6 million European homes |
| 1986 | BSB awarded satellite franchise by IBA |
| 1986 | Peacock Report published (see below) |
| 1989 | Sky TV starts broadcasting from satellite Astra |
| 1990 | Sky TV merges with (and essentially takes over) BSB to form BSkyB. Broadcasting Act gives greater freedom to commercial radio stations and allows national and regional stations to be set up. Implements some Peacock recommendations, imposing market forces on BBC in particular (but no advertising or privatization) |
| 1990 | ITC takes over regulation of cable industry from Cable Authority. Radio 5, the fifth BBC radio station, starts broadcasting |
| 1991 | IBA becomes Independent Television Commission (ITC) |
| 1992 | Classic FM, a national commercial station, begins broadcasting. BSkyB breaks even, but still has a huge debt to repay. Broadcasting now concentrates on UK |
| 1994 | BBC Radio 5 Live begins broadcasting, replacing Radio 5. 5 regional commercial radio stations start broadcasting. 150 local and 2 national commercial stations now on air |
| 1995 | Franchise awarded for commercial TV Channel 5 |

## Television

| Table 1.4 | Average weekly viewing time of all TV | | |
|---|---|---|---|
| | BBC 1 and 2 | ITV and Channel 4 | Total |
| 1993 | 10 hrs 9 mins | 11 hrs 31 mins | 23 hrs 8 mins |
| 1994 | 9 hrs 45 mins | 10 hrs 41 mins | 21 hrs 47 mins |

### Top Five programmes (April 1995)

*Coronation Street* (around 16 million viewers each episode)

*EastEnders* (around 14 million viewers each episode)

*Peak Practice* (around 14 million viewers)

*National Lottery Live* (around 12 million viewers)

*The Bill* (around 12 million viewers)

(*Coronation Street* and *EastEnders* are consistently top each year)

 *Children of school age will spend almost as much time watching television each week as they do in the classroom. Does it matter?*

| Table 1.5 | Television viewing by age[1] | | |
|---|---|---|---|
| United Kingdom | Hours and minutes per week | | |
| Age groups | 1986 | 1991 | 1993 |
| 4–15 | 21:06 | 18:20 | 19:12 |
| 16–34 | 21:38 | 22:20 | 22:42 |
| 35–64 | 27:56 | 27:38 | 26:24 |
| 65 and over | 26:32 | 26:04 | 25:41 |
| | | | |
| Reach (percentages) | | | |
| Daily | 78 | 79 | 82 |
| Weekly | 94 | 94 | 95 |

[1] Percentage of the United Kingdom population aged 4 and over who viewed TV for at least three consecutive minutes.

Source: Broadcasters' Audience Research Board; British Broadcasting Corporation; AGB Limited; RSMB Limited

Source: *Social Trends*, vol. 25, p. 216, table 13.3.

 *Summarize what these figures tell us.*
*What explanations could you suggest for this?*

Ninety-nine per cent of the population have a television set. It is the most popular consumer durable; more people have a television than have a telephone. It is also the most popular mass medium in terms of time spent using it. It also tends to be the subject of most attention from academics and politicians. During the 1980s television, particularly BBC television, was the subject of intense scrutiny by politicians. Though

Margaret Thatcher herself did not watch much television, her husband Denis did and it was thought that he gave her the picture that the BBC was left-leaning, over-staffed, union-controlled, under-exposed to the rigours of the market and subversive.

Norman Tebbit, former minister and Conservative party chair, said the BBC was in the grip of an 'insufferable, smug, sanctimonious, naive, guilt-ridden, wet, pink orthodoxy' and that it was a home for the 'third-rate minds of that third-rate decade, the sixties'. A series of programmes and incidents seemed to confirm the Conservatives' view, at least in their minds. Well-known examples were *Panorama*'s 'Maggie's Militant Tendency' (about an extreme right-wing faction in the parliamentary Conservative party), *Real Lives*: 'At the Edge of the Union' (which featured alleged IRA military commander Martin McGuinness interviewed at length in his living room) and *Death on the Rock* (a critical account of the death of IRA suspects in Gibraltar apparently at the hands of the SAS).

In 1985 the government concluded that something had to be done and so set up the Peacock Committee. Professor Peacock, from Edinburgh University, was a known supporter of free markets and presumably was chosen so that the committee would recommend what the government wanted for the BBC: income to be derived from advertising and privatization of the organization. When the report was published in 1986 it contained nothing about advertising or wholesale privatization.

Mrs Thatcher was said to be 'apoplectic' about this and Peacock was later summoned to explain himself to the Home Secretary, Douglas Hurd. The committee did recommend, though, that both ITV and BBC should make fewer of their own programmes and get more from the private sector. This was to be television on the 'publisher-broadcaster' Channel 4 model, which commissions or buys programmes from other companies, making none of its own. Peacock's recommendations were largely incorporated into the 1990 Broadcasting Act. In the end BBC and ITV managed to cut the percentage of programmes that they had to buy rather than make to 25%, phased in over 5 years.

The committee had also recommended that ITV licences should be sold to the highest bidder, rather than on a judgement of merit, but the Act included a 'quality threshold' that bidders had to meet. In this way the Act introduced some measure of privatization and market forces without going all the way down that road. Companies now have to

Figure 1.2

bid periodically for the licence to broadcast in their local region. Even well-known stations like Granada are in danger of losing their licence to a rival each time this happens, in theory ensuring that market forces keep their standards and efficiency high.

## Radio

Commercial radio now has over 45% of all listeners and recent years have seen the decline of Radio 1, once the most popular national radio station. BBC radio saw a period of intense internal conflict beginning in 1993. That year saw several Radio 1 DJs resign on the air. Dave Lee Travis told the nation that he resigned because of changes at the BBC which are 'against my principles, and I just cannot agree with them', and Gary Davies did the same thing: 'It's not the Radio 1 it used to be. They don't care about the audience like they used to.' By 1994 the number of listeners had dropped from 16 million to 14 million.

The discontent was not confined to Radio 1. All the members of Radio 4's *Gardeners Question Time* moved to Classic FM in protest at BBC changes in 1994 and senior foreign correspondent Mark Tully resigned after being 'gagged' for his criticisms of changes at the BBC. Michael Grade, the controller of Channel 4 and ex-BBC 1 and 2 controller, gave a speech to media people in Edinburgh in 1992 and said that in his view the BBC generally was now 'in terminal decline', that it had 'pseudo-Leninist' management. There was much personal antagonism within the BBC towards the Director General, John Birt. He was said to account for every minute of his day on his personal computer, to have a 'mechanistic' way of talking and interacting to people. This earned him the nickname of 'Dalek' – a nickname which stuck.

Despite the success of commercial radio in terms of listener numbers it still does not attract much advertising revenue, only £170m or about 2% of the total advertising spend.

*Using the newspapers from that time, research the issues that were causing such discontent at the BBC and present a written summary and analysis of them to the group, if you are working with one. You will also find the following sources helpful: Horrie, C. and Clarke, S. (1994) and O'Mally (1992). (See further reading for full references.)*

## Cable TV and other services

Table 1.6    Interest in receiving satellite or cable television stations

| | Satellite television | | | | Cable television | | | |
| | 1990 % | 1991 % | 1992 % | 1993 % | 1990 % | 1991 % | 1992 % | 1993 % |
| --- | --- | --- | --- | --- | --- | --- | --- | --- |
| Interested | 19 | 16 | 20 | 17 | 13 | 10 | 13 | 11 |
| Not interested | 79 | 77 | 72 | 70 | 82 | 80 | 76 | 73 |
| Don't know | 3 | 7 | 8 | 13 | 4 | 9 | 11 | 16 |

Base: Respondents who do not currently have a satellite dish or cable television.

*Source*: Gunter *et al.*, 1994, p. 21, table 1.5.

*What could explain the trends revealed in Table 1.6?*

Cable operators provide channels to homes and businesses via cables which run in ducts below roads. They radiate from a central point (called the 'headend') in a town or group of towns. Current cable systems can carry between 30 and 45 television channels. Cable operators need two licences; one for the system and one for the programmes. There is no competition within an area; only one set of licences is awarded, usually to the highest bidder who can prove they are 'fit and proper' operators. Cable operators can deliver the national TV channels, satellite channels, taped films, local productions and non-television telecommunications facilities. Subscribers usually pay around £20 per month. Take-up has been quite low (see Table 1.7).

Table 1.7    Take-up of cable (1994 figures)

Number of homes in Britain: 15 million
Number with cable nearby: 3 million
Number actually connected: 3/4 million
Most connected town: Northampton (50% take-up)
Least connected town: Glasgow (9% take-up)

In the USA, where it is most developed, cable television has not been a huge success either. Howard Stringer of CBS comments on the viewing figures for one night in February 1993 when the four American networks had over 90% of television viewers.

> So for all the cable enthusiasm, and the promotional power they have, and the money they have, and the cash flow they have, what do they have to show for twenty years of achievement? A handful of viewers, all of whom were probably passing through cable channels on the way to something more interesting.
>
> (Murdoch, p. 130)

Figure 1.3  TV audience share, 1991–2

*Source:* R. Negrine (1994) *Politics and the Mass Media in Britain*

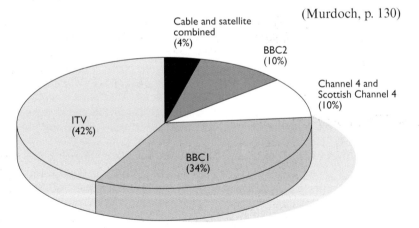

 *What reasons could you suggest for the relatively low take-up of cable TV?*

It seems likely that the fibre-optic superhighway network that is currently being installed across the UK will mean that the distinctions between computers, television, the Internet and other aspects of the mass media will evaporate. The billions of pounds currently being invested will almost certainly result in the computerized TV becoming the centre of the household. It will be used to shop from home, to watch broadcast and cable TV, to play computer games, refer to sources of information on CD-ROM, to access the Internet and talk to other people.

Cable services in the UK are dominated by American industry; 80% of it is owned by American companies. The big three are Nynex, Telewest and Cable Tel UK.

## Satellite TV

Figure 1.4

| Table 1.8 | Claimed share of viewing | | | | | | | | |
|---|---|---|---|---|---|---|---|---|---|
| | Terrestrial only homes | | | Satellite dish homes | | | Cable homes | | |
| | 1993 | 1992 | 1991 | 1993 | 1992 | 1991 | 1993 | 1992 | 1991 |
| | % | % | % | % | % | % | % | % | % |
| ITV | 39 | 39 | 39 | 24 | 26 | 24 | 23 | 25 | 25 |
| Channel 4 | 15 | 13 | 13 | 8 | 9 | 7 | 8 | 9 | 7 |
| BBC1 | 32 | 34 | 34 | 20 | 19 | 19 | 20 | 20 | 19 |
| BBC2 | 15 | 13 | 14 | 8 | 7 | 7 | 7 | 8 | 6 |
| Other | – | 1 | – | 40 | 39 | 44 | 42 | 38 | 44 |

*Base: All giving full details of channels viewed*

Source: Gunter et al., 1994, p. 32

*Why should we be alerted by the title 'Claimed share of viewing' ?*

Satellite TV is best thought of as a medium in two parts: the satellite itself and the programmes which it broadcasts. The company which owns the satellite does not usually provide the services it transmits, it merely leases channels to a programme-supplying company. BSkyB is the dominant service provider in the UK. It is 50% owned by Rupert Murdoch's News International. Many people, including the *Observer*'s television critic John Naughton, think that satellite broadcasting heralds the coming of tabloid TV.

In 1995 there were 32 new satellite channels received from Munich to Melbourne broadcast from the Star satellite. By the end of the century estimates suggest that there will be around 400 TV satellites circling the globe and 5.5 million British households will have satellite TV compared to 2.5 million in 1995. The main players in shaping the future of satellite are Rupert Murdoch (half owner of BSkyB, Chair of Fox TV and Star TV and News International) and Ted Turner, boss of the very successful and rapidly expanding Cable News Network (CNN).

Things may not go completely smoothly for Murdoch and Turner, or for satellite broadcasting in general, though. Cable is cheaper, doesn't require as much equipment and has the potential to be interactive. BSkyB customers are watching satellite channels less than they did (an 18% fall between 1993 and 1994) and are tending not to renew their subscriptions (10% failing to do so in 1994). Moreover, governments are not entirely powerless against satellite and can restrict its penetration.

Some countries like Libya ban satellite dishes altogether while others like Iraq allow only one (it belongs to Saddam Hussein). In the Middle East there is concern about people picking up Israeli programmes while in Britain Red Hot Dutch, a hard-core porn channel, was banned. On the other hand, digital television by satellite could provide very high quality interactive TV services and give satellite a market advantage over terrestrial TV.

The digital television White Paper published in August 1995 proposed at least 18 new digital TV channels and 40 new radio stations, all of higher technical quality than current ones. The Heritage Department minister responsible, Virginia Bottomley, suggested this change was as significant as the move from black and white to colour TV. Digital terrestrial TV could begin in 1997, according to Bottomley, but Andrew Neil, former chair of BSkyB, said that the satellite digital transmission could begin a year earlier and that by 1987 'satellite broadcasters in general and Rupert Murdoch in particular will have the whole market sewn up' (*Guardian*, 11.8.95).

BSkyB has used sport broadcasts as a hook to attract subscribers. In 1992 it signed a surprise deal with the BBC in which they offered £304 million for 60 live football games a year, edited highlights and exclusive rights to FA cup and England games. BSkyB paid most of the money and so could show more full matches. This left ITV sport in the cold and raised the vision of a tripartite future for British television. BSkyB would exclusively provide the premium subscription services such as live sport. This monopoly would ensure it became and stayed profitable. The BBC would slim down to a public-service core and ITV would go further down-market, providing a cheap and cheerful service.

Some have argued that the Director General of the BBC, John Birt, and the Chair of its Board of Governors, Marmaduke Hussey, have been pursuing policies designed to create exactly this situation. The BBC's 'market position' within this future world of terrestrial and satellite broadcasting would be as a high-quality public service provider with a 'mission to explain' but with a small audience (see Horrie and Clarke, 1994) and Table 1.10 on next page.

## Video recording

Table 1.9    Reported use of video recorder, 1993

|  | Viewing programmes recorded off TV | Viewing commercially recorded tapes |
|---|---|---|
| More than once a week | 63 (61) | 12 (13) |
| Once a week | 16 (15) | 14 (14) |
| Less often | 10 (9) | 35 (37) |
| Hardly ever/never | 10 (15) | 37 (36) |
| Don't know | 1 (1) | 1 (1) |

*Base: All who have VCR in household;*
*Note: 1992 figures shown in parentheses.*

Source: Gunter et al., 1994, p. 15, table 2.5.

*What factors may influence how the video recorder is used in homes that have one?*

In the early 1980s when video players became widely available, the major film companies saw video as a threat to cinema box office takings and so refused to release their films on video format. This meant that a small number of independent

Table 1.10    Regulations, duties and obligations of cable and satellite compared to terrestrial broadcasting (1992)

| | BBC/ITV services | Satellite systems | Cable |
|---|---|---|---|
| High quality/standard | Yes | No | No |
| Information, education, entertainment | Yes | No | No |
| Proper balance and wide range of subject matter | Yes | No | No |
| Secure showing for programmes of merit | Yes | No | No |
| Programmes must not offend good taste or decency | Yes | Yes (but difficult to control | Yes |
| Must be sufficient time for news and current affairs | Yes (ITV companies no longer required to show them during peak viewing hours) | No | No |
| News programmes must be impartial and accurate | Yes | No | Yes for UK news |
| 'Due impartiality' in matters of controversy | Yes | No (but British origin programmes may be required to) | Yes (if programmes are of British origin) |
| Must be suitable material for the regions | Yes | No | No |
| Independent producers must provide 25% of output | Yes | No | No |
| Programmes covered by Obscene Publications Act | No | No | Yes |
| Control of operations must be in British hands | Yes | No | No |
| Must carry a majority of programmes of European origin | Yes | No (for categories of programmes such as news or sport) | No |

*Source*: adapted from R. Negrine (1994) *Politics and the Mass Media in Britain*, Routledge.

companies were able to specialize in the video market, making low-budget films of poor technical (and usually artistic) quality. Once the battle between the Betamax and VHS standards was won by VHS and video player prices came down, allowing ownership to grow, the big companies like MGM and 20th Century Fox began to realize the market potential of this medium.

By the mid to late 1980s video had become fully integrated into the mass media market, with cinema films later released for ownership or rent on video in the same way that publishers release a book in hardback version first and then in the cheaper paperback format. Increasingly there is a symbiosis between films and other products such as the music of the film, and video helps this happen.

Since the passing of the 1985 Video Recordings Act, which introduced censorship to video films, the British Board of Film Classification have been more concerned about sex and violence on video than on cinema films. The ability to use slow motion and freeze-frame, to replay scenes repeatedly as well as the easy availability of films of all types to children are the reasons for this. As a result they cut video versions of films more than cinema versions: it took them two years to permit the release of *Reservoir*

*Dogs* on video. Viewing bought or rented video films seems to have declined in popularity between 1986 and 1988 from an average use of 6.07 hours per week to 4.38 hours. Only 30% of video users watch hired films at all. Despite this the video industry is a huge one. More than £1 billion worth of pre-recorded videos were rented or sold in 1994.

Video films are not just the preserve of large corporations, though. The ability to edit, freeze-frame, use slow motion, skip forwards or backwards means that the distinction between production and consumption becomes a fuzzy one in this medium. The availability of cheap, high-quality video cameras has given individuals and groups the power to use video to put alternative points of view. Environmental groups have filmed conflicts with the police and construction companies and succeeded in getting this onto the national news. In the United States police violence against members of minority ethnic groups has been filmed and again this has become national news, in one case leading to race riots and arson attacks which caused millions of dollars worth of damage.

---

**Alternative media**

Forms of mass communication that are used to deliberately challenge the interpretations of events conveyed by the conventional mass media.

---

The future may see a threat to the video recorder as we know it from the Digital Video Disc (DVD). This is a compact disc-sized format which can hold a full-length film and its soundtrack (in different languages if necessary) on two sides of a high-density disc. It gives a very high quality picture, much better than video, and allows all the functions of video such as freeze-frame and slow motion, only in much better quality. The only thing DVD cannot do, yet, is record, but this will come.

DVD is being heralded as a technology which will replace music CDs and computer CD-ROM drives (DVD players will play these too), bringing unification of technologies to the home and helping media corporations increase the level of 'symbiosis' between film and music sales because of the good technical quality. If DVD follows the example of music compact discs they could take the market by storm. Although only 30,000 were sold globally in their first year, today CDs are the most popular music format, despite their very high price. DVD's inability to record from the television may not prove an obstacle: Sony did market research before bringing out the Walkman which showed that people said they would not buy a player that could not record. Actually it sold 139 million of them between 1979 and 1995.

On the other hand, it may not happen. There is a history of 'ground-breaking' technologies which never really got off the ground. Failure came because the public didn't like them, because there was nothing for them to play (no 'software') or because something better came along. Examples include the 8 track stereo (cassettes were better), the 12 inch video disk (too bulky, not enough software), digital audio tape (CDs more popular) and CDi (too expensive, not enough software). Another problem is the lack of a single standard for DVD. Currently there are two: one backed by the Philips-Sony consortium and the other backed by 'SD Alliance' – a group of companies including Toshiba, Time-Warner, Thomson, Matsushita, MGM and other Hollywood studios and electronics companies.

*Will DVD be a market success? Obtain a copy of M. Bell, 'Can digital disk kill video's star?', Observer Business, 4 June 1995, p. 5. Review the arguments and come to a considered conclusion. If you are working with a group, compare your views.*

## Video games

Video games are played on a computer or computer-like console which is connected to a television or monitor. One person can play against the computer, or two people can compete against each other. The earliest game was Pong, an electronic table-tennis game introduced in 1972 by Atari. Today games usually involve manipulating characters via a joystick or other device to avoid obstacles and dangers to achieve a goal. As the game progresses it becomes more difficult and so requires the development of game-playing skills. Games are increasingly linked to Hollywood movies, another example of symbiosis. First characters in the games were based on those in films such as *Indiana Jones* and *Who Framed Roger Rabbit*. More recently film and television have imitated video with characters such as the Super Mario Brothers and stories based on the games.

The current major player in this market is the Japanese company Nintendo. There are over 20 million Nintendo machines in the USA, despite the fact that Nintendo only introduced its hardware in 1986. Total sales in America for video game industry was $4 billion by 1990. The market is very clearly defined; children, especially boys, between the ages of 7 and 16 are the main users. Nintendo and other companies are able to orient their products to this market very specifically because it is so well defined. The problem is that it is highly volatile in terms of fashion and tastes, so companies constantly need to change their products in line with changing tastes. This, plus the ability to upgrade the technology continually, makes the video game industry very profitable, especially as young people in developed economies like the USA and Japan have a relatively large amount of disposable income.

In the UK there has been a lot of concern about video game playing, particularly about its supposed solitary and compulsive nature and the violence and sexism of many games. However, this concern seems to be exaggerated. A 1993 study by Guy Cumberbatch and others showed that video game playing is in the top three preferred pastimes of only 20% of 7–16 year olds, though 66% say they 'often' play the games, with boys between 12 and 16 the heaviest users. The evidence seems to show that they are essentially a time-filler when there is nothing better to do.

*Prepare a report on the current state of the video game market. You could:*

*1. do a survey of what is on sale in local shops;*
*2. interview heavy users of video games about current games;*
*3. search newspaper databases for articles about the video game industry.*

*Questions to be addressed could include the following:*

*1. How big is the market in the UK now?*
*2. Which are the most successful companies and video game titles?*
*3. What have been the trends in the content of the games?*
*4. What are the prospects for the future?*
*5. What issues might be raised by the patterns you have identified?*

# The Press

*Which newspapers are the most class/sex specific? What might be the reasons for this?*
*Comment on and try explaining the change in the readership patterns of the various newspapers since 1971.*

The national newspaper industry in the UK is remarkably stable, with the same names appearing in newsagents year after year. However the 1980s saw attempts to launch new national papers such as the *Independent, Today, News on Sunday* and *Sunday Sport. News on Sunday*, a left-wing broadsheet, quickly died despite trade-union funding. It failed to attract enough advertising revenue or readers. The *Independent* has struggled and was eventually taken over by Mirror Group Newspapers (and so is no longer 'independent'), while the sexy *Sunday Sport* has thrived and is now a daily. There is a constant battle between the papers for market share in their area of the market (broadly divided into the up-market broadsheets like *The Times* and *Telegraph* and down-market tabloids like the *Sun* and *Mirror*). They try various strategies in this conflict, including holding big-prize competitions, price-cutting, television advertising and so on. The current situation is shown in Figure 1.5.

Figure 1.5   Newspaper ownership and percentage of sales in the UK (1994)

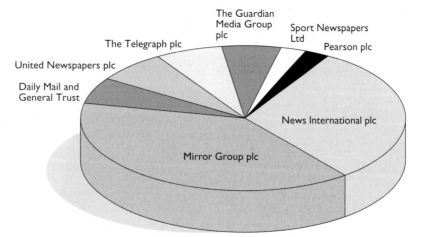

Although the names of the national newspapers tend to change little, what does change is the editorial policy of the paper and its general style. For example the *Sun* shifted from being a Labour-supporting paper to being pro-Conservative in 1974 and under Margaret Thatcher's governments, but then became more critical of the Conservatives under John Major. The *Daily Mirror* was known as the 'Daily Maxwell' (Robert Maxwell was its owner) under editor Mike Molloy (described by another editor, Roy Greenslade, as Maxwell's 'personal public relations officer') but under editor Richard Stott Maxwell was forced to confine himself to editorials only.

The character of *The Times* changed markedly when it was taken over by Rupert Murdoch's News International. Murdoch reportedly thought the Sunday Times was 'a nasty, left-wing radical organ, staffed for the most part by a bunch of left-wing layabouts' (Horrie and Clarke, 1994, p. 84) and after acquisition it became more pro-Conservative and moved down-market. The 'nipple-count' of the *Daily Star* reduced dramatically after its proprietor Lord Stevens took exception to its attempt to compete with the *Sport* by pushing that count up. He was also reported to be

**Table 1.11   Reading of national newspapers by social class and gender, 1993–4[1]**

| Great Britain | | | | Percentage reading each paper | | | | Percentages | |
|---|---|---|---|---|---|---|---|---|---|
| | AB | CI | C2 | DE | Males | Females | All adults | Readership[2] (millions) | Readers per copy (numbers) |
| **Daily newspapers** | | | | | | | | | |
| The Sun | 7 | 18 | 29 | 30 | 25 | 19 | 22 | 9.9 | 2.5 |
| Daily Mirror | 7 | 13 | 22 | 20 | 18 | 14 | 16 | 7.1 | 2.8 |
| Daily Mail | 14 | 13 | 8 | 6 | 10 | 9 | 10 | 4.5 | 2.5 |
| Daily Express | 9 | 10 | 8 | 5 | 8 | 7 | 8 | 3.5 | 2.5 |
| The Daily Telegraph | 6 | 6 | 2 | 1 | 7 | 5 | 6 | 2.6 | 2.6 |
| Daily Star | 1 | 4 | 7 | 7 | 7 | 3 | 5 | 2.2 | 2.9 |
| Today | 3 | 4 | 5 | 3 | 4 | 3 | 4 | 1.8 | 3.1 |
| The Guardian | 8 | 3 | 1 | 1 | 3 | 3 | 3 | 1.3 | 1.4 |
| The Times | 8 | 3 | 1 | 1 | 4 | 2 | 3 | 1.3 | 2.9 |
| The Independent | 6 | 3 | 1 | 1 | 3 | 2 | 2 | 1.1 | 3.5 |
| Financial Times | 5 | 2 | – | – | 2 | 1 | 2 | 7.4 | 4.2 |
| Any national daily newspaper[3] | 61 | 58 | 64 | 59 | 65 | 56 | 60 | 27.4 | – |
| **Sunday newspapers** | | | | | | | | | |
| News of the World | 11 | 23 | 36 | 36 | 29 | 26 | 27 | 12.4 | 2.6 |
| Sunday Mirror | 9 | 16 | 24 | 21 | 19 | 17 | 18 | 8.1 | 3.1 |
| The Mail on Sunday | 18 | 17 | 11 | 6 | 13 | 13 | 13 | 5.9 | 3.0 |
| The People | 6 | 12 | 16 | 15 | 14 | 11 | 12 | 5.6 | 2.8 |
| Sunday Express | 13 | 13 | 9 | 5 | 11 | 10 | 10 | 4.6 | 2.8 |
| The Sunday Times | 21 | 8 | 3 | 2 | 9 | 7 | 8 | 3.7 | 3.0 |
| Sunday Telegraph | 11 | 4 | 2 | 1 | 5 | 4 | 4 | 1.9 | 3.1 |
| The Observer | 9 | 4 | 2 | 1 | 4 | 3 | 4 | 1.6 | 3.2 |
| Independent on Sunday | 7 | 3 | 1 | 1 | 3 | 2 | 3 | 1.2 | 3.5 |
| Sunday Sport | 1 | 2 | 3 | 3 | 3 | 1 | 2 | 9.0 | 3.5 |
| Any Sunday | 69 | 68 | 72 | 65 | 70 | 66 | 68 | 30.9 | – |

[1] Data relates to the 12 month period ending June 1994.
[2] Defined as the average issue readership and represents the number of people who claim to have read or looked at one or more copies of a given publication during a period equal to the interval at which the publication appears.
[3] Includes the above newspapers plus the Daily Record, Sporting Life and Racing Post.
[4] Includes the above newspapers plus the Sunday Post, Sunday Mail and Scotland on Sunday.

Source: *Social Trends*, vol. 25, p. 218, table 13.6.

embarrassed by the character of the paper he owned when he mixed with such high-society figures as the Princess of Wales, a personal friend.

*Buy copies of the national dailies for one day. Try to pick a day where there is some contentious news (avoid Mondays in general, when news is thin). Compare the papers' treatment of the same items:*

1. Do they give the items equal 'weight' (e.g. front page treatment in one paper, page 3 in another)?
2. Does their interpretation of the items differ in any way?
3. Does the general way in which they handle the items differ, and if so how?
4. How does the general content of the various papers differ, one from another?

The 1980s saw great changes in the way newspapers are produced, both in terms of the technology used and the number of people employed and what they do. In the past print unions were very strong and 'chapel fathers' (local officials) ensured that the interests of the workforce were maintained. Many people felt that this had led to over-staffing, out-of-date production methods and unnecessary expense. Rupert Murdoch, head of News International, was determined to tackle this issue as early as 1975 when he bought land in Wapping with a view to moving newspaper production out of Fleet Street. When he bought *The Times* and *Sunday Times* in 1981 the troubled industrial relations which had existed under the previous owners, Thomson, continued. The paper had ceased production for several months during a bitter dispute and things did not improve after the change of ownership. Murdoch decided to move the production of *The Times*, *Sunday Times*, *News of the World* and *Sun* to Wapping.

Using modern technology journalists would, for example, input text directly, thus avoiding the 'double keying' that unions had insisted on in the past. This change would lead to many redundancies. A heavily fortified building was prepared on the Wapping site and the necessary computer and other equipment put into place in the utmost secrecy. Murdoch's company was making what he called a 'dash for freedom' and by the end of 1985 everything was ready. The unions were still ignorant about what was going on. When the transfer from Fleet Street took place they were powerless to do anything about it.

On 24 January 1986 negotiations between News International and three unions – SOGAT, NGA, AEU – broke down and the workers went on strike. As they left work to start the strike, members of the three unions were handed letters telling them that they had effectively dismissed themselves and production at Wapping started in earnest. Though violent demonstrations took place outside the plant there, with thousands of protestors involved, this was effectively the end of the old practices and the dawn of a new era of newspaper production. Murdoch's hand had been considerably strengthened by changes to industrial relations law since 1979. These had progressively weakened the trades unions' powers to take and enforce strike action.

## The Internet

The Internet began as a military project in the USA in the late 1960s. It aimed to set up communication links which could survive nuclear war. Computers link to each other across a spider's web of cable and telephone links. If one link is broken messages are automatically re-routed to their destination via another route. The academic community quickly adopted it and it spread as universities throughout the world linked their computers to the Net. Today the Internet is on the verge of a very rapid expansion in the number of people who use it and the ways in which it is used. The reasons for this expansion are:

- user-friendly software: in the past only the computer-literate could use the communications software; today programs like Mosaic and Netscape mean that 'surfing the net' is as easy as using a word-processor;

- cheap connection to the Internet: for around £12 per month anyone with a telephone, a computer and a modem can get connected;

- faster communication software and hardware: telephone lines can be used to communicate at much greater speeds today so that visual images and sounds can be quickly transmitted across them. Digital communications across ISDN lines allow even more computer data to be transmitted more quickly still, so that video-conferencing is possible. ISDN stands for Integrated Services Digital Network, though at one time technical people said it meant It Still Does Nothing.

Currently the Internet reaches 75 countries directly and 146 countries indirectly, involves 3 million computers and 40,000 sub-networks. There are about 30 million users world-wide and 1 million in Britain, though most limit their use to e-mail.

Figure 1.6 Video-conferencing in action – but does it count as a mass medium? Go back to page 2 to find out.

*Using the Internet: you can join a discussion forum on the mass media if you are on e-mail by sending a message to mailbase@mailbase.ac.uk. The message should just say 'join media-watch' and you should then insert your first name and your last name. If you want to leave the list, do the same thing but replace the word 'join' with 'leave'. The list is described as follows: 'MEDIA-WATCH is for information & discussion on the pleasures & politics of the media in Britain …'.*

*If you have access to the World Wide Web, academic and educational resources on all aspects of media studies and communications can be found at: http://www.aber.ac.uk/~dgc/media.html. There is also a directory to the British media on the World Wide Web at: http://www.mcc.ac.uk/~jcridlan/. A wide variety of diverse material is available here, with many links to other sites. Information about courses concerning the mass media can also be found at the University of Central Lancashire's web site at http://www.uclan.ac.uk/*

### The social significance of the Internet: liberating technology or corporate control?

At the time of writing the first edition of this book in 1987 the big media debate was about 'the Satellite Revolution' and whether it would result in unlimited choice for viewers or 'wall-to-wall Dallas'; in other words mostly soap opera, old programmes, quiz shows and sport. In 1995 a glance at the daily schedule of satellite channels in any TV listings magazine answers that question immediately. It has become clear, too, that satellite TV has had less of an impact than imagined then; its penetration into the population is still quite limited, those who have it don't use it much and even the major satellite broadcasters have difficulty making money.

Debate has now moved on to the future of the Internet and the effects of the 'digital revolution' on our use of the medium and on society as a whole. Again there are essentially two opposing hypotheses; 'digital liberation' or 'digital corporatism'.

## The 'digital liberation' hypothesis

Computers will become cheaper and easier to use. In a few years they will be as common in the home as televisions. In fact they will replace the television, telephone and hi-fi system as these technologies merge. Nearly everyone will be computer literate, though using computers will in future be extremely easy to use as they will be able to understand normal speech and respond appropriately. Many of the daily tasks such as shopping and attending school, college, university and even the office will be done from home via the computer and telephone or cable link. 'Tele-working' from the 'tele-cottage' will be increasingly the norm, reducing pollution and saving travel time as people no longer 'go' to work. In our leisure-time use of this technology the following trends will occur.

● Broadcasting will become 'broadcatching' as people are empowered to pick what they want from an almost unlimited amount of information available on the Internet, including radio and television programmes. People will be able to consume any piece of 'software' (films, programmes, audio tracks etc.) whenever and wherever they want.

● 'Users' and 'producers' will merge: the computer can send as well as receive messages so each user will add their articles, news and views to the many digital voices on the Internet. Films on CD-ROM can already be interactive and this will be the norm in the future, so the 'viewer' will also be the 'director' and 'author' of the film they are watching.

● People will be able to interact directly ('synchronously') with others anywhere in the world if they wish or, if it's easier, leave messages for each other ('asynchronous communication'). The sophistication of the technology means that it serves people rather than their serving it.

● The idea of copyright will become a thing of the past. Information will be the property of everyone because enforcing copyright law will become impossible.

● The amount of data in circulation will also make it impossible for governments to control or censor it. They will eventually give up trying.

● 'Serial delivery' – the chained nature of a story, argument or evening's viewing –

will disappear. Users will follow their own interests and whims by mouse clicks on things that interest them, forming their own unique paths through the data. We will become media surfers.

● Ascribed characteristics such as skin colour, gender and physical attractiveness will become irrelevant in the virtual world of the Internet. Everyone will have an equal voice and the ability to create interesting messages will be the only criterion for success.

The keywords of this vision of the virtual future, then, are empowerment, democracy and equality. This vision is perhaps most coherently expressed in Nicholas Negroponte's book *Being Digital* and Dale Spender's *Nattering on the Net*.

An example of this practice can be found, ironically, within the BBC. Staff who were unhappy with management methods and the way the news was going put a file called '*The Nine O'Clock News is Crap*' on the internal computer system. Anyone could read or write to this file and it was particularly full of highly critical comments about the news from staff on a day when the Queen's speech and continuing talks on Northern Ireland were put above the deaths of 13 schoolchildren in a minibus crash on the M40. Those responsible for this scheduling said they were 'contemporary historians' and that motorway accidents had no historical significance while the Queen's speech did.

## The 'digital corporatism' hypothesis

From this point of view the technology of the Internet holds only threat, not promise. Even if the democratization of the Net happened, it would only lead to 'digibabble'': vast amounts of digital junk created by people with limited skills and knowledge. There would be plenty of data but precious little that could be translated into usable information. Any useful material would be swamped by the deluge of rubbish. Perhaps fortunately this will not happen, instead we will see the commercialization of the Internet and its capture by multinational corporations:

● Companies like Microsoft will develop their own sub-sections of the Internet and will charge for access. These will provide efficient computer software, useful information and quality programming to those that can afford it. To get the most from your computer you will need to subscribe to these services. Garnham foresaw this when he predicted the development of 'a two-tier market divided between the information rich, provided with high-cost specialized information and cultural services and the information poor, provided with increasingly homogenized entertainment series on a mass scale' (Garnham, 1986, p. 38).

● Specialist on-line services such as Lexus for lawyers (which gives information about legal precedents etc.) will be available but they will be charged-for services, either by subscription or the equivalent of pay-per-view.

● The large media corporations will gradually take over smaller commercial Internet providers and we will see current patterns of media control reproduced there.

● Those who cannot or will not pay for these sorts of services will still have access to parts of the Internet, but as it increasingly becomes commercialized they will be left largely with digibabble.

- Individuals will become increasingly isolated and 'privatized' as they spend time in their rooms using the computer rather than interacting in person with others. This will mean that political organization and activism will decline. Jerry Mander in *Four Arguments for the Elimination of TV* suggests that 'television isolates people from their environment, from each other and from their own senses'. Michael Medved agrees:

> A fearful attitude makes it far more likely that average Americans will huddle protectively together in their homes, taking no responsibility for the state of their neighborhoods and their communities'
>
> (Medved, 1993, p. 198).

This is even more likely with the new technologies which, with their interactivity, give the illusion of intimacy and contact.

- Organizations that give access to the Internet, such as universities and commercial companies like Compuserve, will censor what the user can access and say. If they do not do this voluntarily they will be forced into it by legislation, making them responsible for the actions of their users. 'Digital liberation' will never happen; this technology will come under the control of the rich and powerful just as all the others have done.

This vision is perhaps most coherently expressed in Clifford Stoll's book, *Silicon Snakeoil*.

*This chapter has been selective in the areas that it has covered. Let's review it now.*

*1. Which areas of the mass media have been omitted in the chapter? Are these omissions important?*
*2. The 'developments' the chapter has concentrated on have included:*
- *technological change*
- *market characteristics*
- *political change*
- *consumer behaviour*

*Give an example from the chapter under each of these headings. Then give an additional example of your own that the chapter has not discussed. What other categories are there for developments in the mass media?*

## Further reading

*Benn's Business Information Services* (annually).
*Benn's Media Directory.*
*British Film Institute Film and TV Handbook* gives a wealth of facts and figures about film and television.
*Broadcasting Standards Council Annual Reviews*, London: John Libbey & Co. provides a themed annual review by the BSC.

Cumberbatch, G. *et al.* (1993) *Children and Video Games: An Exploratory Study*, The Communications Research Group, Aston University, Aston Triangle, Birmingham B4 7ET.
Davidson, A. (1993) *Under the Hammer: the 1991 ITV Franchise Auction*, London: Mandarin.
Franklin, B. and Murphy, D. (1991) *What News? The*

*Market, Politics and the Local Press*, London: Routledge.

Greenslade, G. (1992) *Maxwell's Fall: The Appalling Legacy of a Corrupt Man*, Simon & Schuster.

Horrie, C. and Clarke, S. (1994) *Fuzzy Monsters: Fear and Loathing at the BBC*, London: Mandarin.

Negroponte, N. (1995) *Being Digital*, London: Hodder & Stoughton.

O'Mally, T. (1992) *Closedown? The BBC and Government Broadcasting Policy, 1979–92*, London: Pluto.

Peak, S. (ed.) (annual) *The Media Guide*, London: Fourth Estate. Probably the best source for up-to-date information about many aspects of the mass media in Britain. Highly recommended.

Provenzo, E. F. (1991) *Video Kids: Making Sense of Nintendo*, Harvard University Press.

Spender, D. (1995) *Nattering on the Net; Women, power and cyberspace*, London: Spinifex.

Stevenson, W. (ed.) (1993) *All Our Futures: The Changing Role and Purpose of the BBC*, London: BFI.

Stoll, C. (1995) *Silicon Snakeoil*, London: Macmillan.

*Television: the Public's View*, London: John Libbey & Co. provides a summary of survey work conducted by the ITC on public responses to their programmes.

*The Annual Review of BBC Broadcasting Research*, John Libbey & Co. gives a summary of the main studies conducted by the BBC each year.

*Willings Press Guide*, London: British Media Publications (annually).

## Useful addresses

**Advertising Standards Authority**
2 Torrington Place
London WC1E 7HN
tel: 0171 580 5555

**Press Complaints Commission**
1 Salisbury Square
London EC4Y 8AE
tel: 0171 353 1248

**Broadcasting Standards Council**
7 The Sanctuary
London SW1P 3JS

**Campaign for Press and Broadcasting Freedom**
8 Cynthia St
London N1 9JF
tel: 0171 278 4430

John Libbey publish a range of useful reference texts and studies conducted for the BBC, BSC, ITC, UNESCO and other bodies. Their media catalogue can be obtained from:
**John Libbey and Co Ltd**
13 Smiths Yard
Summerley St
London SW18 4HR
tel: 0181 947 2777

# 2 Messages, audiences and effects

Figure 2.1 The hypodermic model

## Developments and key concepts in media research

The way researchers study the media is affected by their theories about what is going on when people are exposed to the mass media. As these theories change so the methods change too. We will begin this chapter with a brief overview, broadly chronological, of the different theories about the interaction between the mass media and the audience that researchers have had.

### 1. The hypodermic model

This early and very simple theory imagines that the mass media act like a hypodermic syringe which injects the audience and has an effect on them in the same way that the injection of a medicine or a poison would. The medium itself (television, newspapers, film) is the syringe, the media's message or content is what is injected and the audience is the patient. This medical model of media influence is found in the titles of books, even recent ones. Examples are *The Plug-In Drug* and *Your Daily Dose*.

> ### Narcotization
>
> Political, physical and mental apathy supposedly induced by the mass media. The concept derives from the hypodermic model of the media.
>
> > Increasing dosages of mass communications may be inadvertently transforming the energies of men [*sic*] from active participation into passive knowledge.
> >
> > *(Lazarsfeld and Merton 1948)*

Shannon and Weaver's early model of media effect is essentially a hypodermic model, though they recognize that external 'noise' may introduce differences between the message transmitted and that received:

Figure 2.2    Shannon and Weaver's model of communication

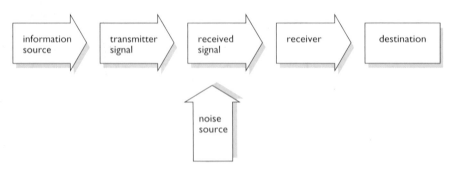

This view of media effects is still found today, despite its many weaknesses. The mass media themselves tend to reproduce it when they report crimes that were supposedly 'caused' by the media, as in the case of the Bulger affair (see p. 110). Politicians and campaigners against sex and violence in the media also hold this model when they argue for greater censorship or complain about particular programmes. Among the academic research community it is now out of favour, but in the early days of study of the media it was at least implicit.

Laboratory studies conducted by psychologists like Bandura, Ross and Ross (see below) looked for a simple cause and effect relationships between media message and audience response ('what happens if we inject *this*?'). In the social sciences, the neo-Marxist Frankfurt School saw the mass media as essentially a drug keeping the working class passive. Marx thought religion was the 'opiate of the masses', but these modern Marxists think it is the mass media. The Frankfurt school's Herbert Marcuse writes in *One Dimensional Man* that 'the hypnotic power of the mass media deprive us of the capacity for critical thought which is essential if we are to change the world'.

The problems with the hypodermic model are many. It ignores:

● the different reasons that people watch, listen to or read the media;

● the amount of attention people give to the media;

● the influence of people's pre-existing attitudes in giving 'resistance' to media 'infection';

● the fact that the media audience consists of very different sorts of people;

- the distinction between short-term and long-term effects;
- the fact that people live in a social world and are not doctors' patients isolated in the surgery being given an injection; they use the media socially;
- the paradox that the researchers identifying the hypodermic-like influence of the mass media are themselves mysteriously immune to it.

A researcher who holds this theory will tend to look for correlations between media content and changes in the attitudes and behaviour of the audience. She will not distinguish between sub-groups in the audience and they will not be very interested in how the audience 'use' the media: their degree of attention, how they respond to it, whether they enjoy it and so on.

 *Although adults may use the media selectively and have quite strong pre-existing attitudes which give them resistance to media messages, it could be argued that the mass media do operate on children in the way the hypodermic model suggests. Would you agree? Why?*

## 2. The normative model

> ### Normative
>
> Related to norms; ways of behaving that come to be considered 'normal' and so regulate social interaction.

This is a more sophisticated *social* theory of media influence than the hypodermic model. It recognizes that 'no man or woman is an island' and that this is just as true of their use of the mass media as in other ways. Studies in the 1940s and 1950s like Robert Merton's (1946) *Mass Persuasion* and Katz and Lazarsfeld's (1955) *Personal Influence* saw that a two-step flow process of media influence was operating. Opinion leaders were found to be important. They can shape how people respond to the media and therefore the effects, if any, that the media have. Katz and Lazarsfeld noted that:

> the influence of mass media is not only paralleled by the influence of people [but] refracted by the personal environment of the ultimate consumer.

> ### Two-step flow model of media influence
>
> The first step is the message reaching a member of the audience, the second is the influence of the social interaction on its interpretation and influence. This concept, developed by Katz and Lazarsfeld, suggests that other people, particularly opinion leaders (whose views are respected and sought) influence how media messages affect you through the comments they make about them. The audience does not passively 'receive' media messages but discusses them actively. An extension of the idea is the multi-step flow model, which recognizes that there are successive stages in the social interpretation of media messages.

An example of how this normative approach works is given by Dorothy Hobson in her study *Women Audiences and the Workplace*. Hobson tells of her research on 'Jacqui', a telephone sales manager for an internationally known pharmaceutical and feminine hygiene company. Jacqui recounted to Hobson how women in her office spent their working day:

> Somebody would say something like 'Who saw *Coronation Street* last night?' and Anita would say 'Oh, I saw it!', and you'd sort of have Mary sitting there going 'Oh, my God!', and making comments about *Coronation Street* and doing some stupid impression beneath the desk and you'd say 'Shut up Mary, shut up!', and everybody would go 'Ssh, ssh, Anita, tell us what happened...' Anita ... would go into great detail about what had happened and ... everybody would sit and listen and if you'd seen it the night before and she missed bits out you'd say 'Er, wait a minute, he wasn't very happy about that', or whatever.

The conversation quickly turned to include topics about their own lives and interests and to discussions of what they would do if they were in the same circumstances as the characters. Women in the office were enticed to watch these programmes just so they could join in the discussions.

- *Discuss whether this happens in your experience.*
- *What programmes do your conversations tend to concentrate on?*
- *Is there a typical pattern to the conversation?*
- *How does your discourse about media messages change your perception of them?*

The problems with this approach are as follows.

- The normative approach sees people as conditioned by their environment too much. People can create and change norms, break them and redefine them.

- It is unclear in this theory whether the norms are based on consensus or whether they are imposed on people by powerful groups within society. The theory is not clear, in other words, about whether it is based on a consensus, functionalist model, or a conflict model of society.

Researchers who adopt this theory will tend, as Hobson did, to study social groups' discussions of media messages, identifying opinion leaders and showing how media messages become interpreted socially.

### 3. The uses and gratifications model

This model stresses that different people use the media in different ways in order to get different sorts of pleasure or fulfil different types of needs through them. Two people may watch the same party political broadcast, for example, but be satisfying very different needs, or getting different gratifications from it. Katz, one of the originators of this approach, said that it:

> asks the question not 'what do the media do to people?' but, 'what do people do with the media?'

(Katz 1959, p. 2)

*Invent a description of the two people and the broadcast media to illustrate the point being made by the uses and gratifications model.*

Dennis McQuail in *Sociology of Mass Communications* (1972) suggested some types of uses and gratifications:

● Diversion – an escape from routine.

● Personal relationships – either through surrogate membership of a community like that in *Brookside* or *Coronation Street* or by enabling us to operate better in a real one, like Jacqui's work mates.

● Personal identity – helping us to explore and confirm our identity through our use of the media; for example the person who sees using the Internet as confirming their self-image as an up-to-date and efficient person. Media use may also challenge and destabilize one's sense of identity.

● Surveillance – the feeling of knowing what's going on.

Figure 2.3    The uses and gratifications model

*Question: Is the corn flakes packet part of the mass media? Go back to p. 2 and find out.*

In his early work (see the earlier articles in Lull 1990) James Lull also adopted the uses and gratifications approach. Like McQuail he develops a list of the social uses of television:

● Structural
● Environmental: background noise; companionship; entertainment
● Regulative: punctuation of time and activity; talk patterns
● Communication facilitation: experience illustration; common ground; conversational entrance; anxiety reduction; agenda for talk; value clarification
● Affiliation/avoidance: physical, verbal contact/neglect; family solidarity; family relaxant; conflict reduction; relationship maintenance
● Social learning: decision-making; behaviour modelling; problem-solving; value transmission; legitimization; information dissemination; substitute schooling
● Competence/dominance: role enactment; role reinforcement; substitute role portrayal; intellectual validation; authority exercise; gatekeeping; argument facilitation

*Select one of these categories and develop examples to illustrate the use and/or gratification.*

It is clear that men and women use the media in different ways and get different types of gratification from it. Some types of media, and media messages, may not be gratifying at all for some women. This is discussed in more detail in Chapter 9, pp. 176–181.

Problems with this approach are:

● it does not raise the important questions about why people have particular needs or why they choose particular forms of gratifications;

● it treats people as asocial and totally self-contained, not recognizing that needs are partly socially created (in this it is different from the normative approach); it focuses on individual differences, personality and psychology, and ignores the cultural context and social background which structures reception;

● it takes a functionalist approach, suggesting that the media perform a function while not recognizing the dysfunctional nature of the media;

● it suggests that 'needs' are pre-existent; in fact the media can also create needs (advertising is based on this idea).

This model changed the focus of research away from the effects of the media on attitudes and behaviour in a simple way to looking at how people used the media and the needs that were gratified by this.

*Reflect on your own use of different media. What different uses and gratifications can you identify?*

### 4. The interpretative model

In this model the audience are seen as a sort of complicated filter mechanism. People not only use the media in different ways: they attend to and receive media messages in a selective way, ignoring or reinterpreting messages according to their particular viewpoint. In short they 'read', or actively interpret, the media 'text', or message. One useful way of thinking about this is in terms of a three-stage process:

● selective exposure: the audience only tend to allow themselves to be exposed to messages in the media with which they agree;

● selective perception: they react to media messages differently, depending on whether they strike a concordant or a discordant note;

● selective retention: they are likely to remember only those messages which they consider valid or true.

James Halloran points out in *The Effects of Television* (1970) that like the uses and gratification model, this approach helped researchers to get away from the habit of thinking in terms of *what media do to people*, and to substitute for it the idea of *what people do with the media*.

---

### Intertextual reception

Fiske (1988) notes that we don't just read one text, but see it in relation to others. We are sophisticated readers of the media. Similarly Pecheux (1982) refers to inter-discourse: the idea that we all exist in a field of different discourses, different message systems.

For example we can watch a soap opera and work at a number of levels, moving between them:

Engagement: 'I felt I was really there with the characters.'

Detachment: 'He will die on this journey because I've heard the actor wants to leave the series.'

Referential: 'That man is very much like my own boss.'

Fiske says 'any one text is necessarily read in relationship to others and … a range of textual knowledge is brought to bear on it'.

 *Think about how you watch a soap opera. How does this intertextuality operate?*

*Figure 2.4 Complete the thought bubbles*

The ways in which people interpret or 'read' the media is partly a result of their level of media literacy. David Buckingham (1993b) suggests that someone with only a low level of television literacy might be able to do the following:

● distinguish between voices on a soundtrack or between figures and backgrounds;

● understand the principle of editing and follow a narrative;

● relate sound and image tracks together;

● grasp elements of 'television grammar' such as camera angles and movements.

This sort of understanding of television might be typical of a child. However, Buckingham suggests, someone with a higher level of television literacy might be able to:

- understand the codes or 'rhetoric' of television language;

- categorize programmes into genres and understand the different conventions the genres use;

- describe different 'story grammars' or models of narrative structure and be aware of the way narrative time is manipulated through editing;

- infer character traits and construct psychologically coherent characters from a few clues;

- be aware of how viewers are invited to identify with characters;

- understand the production process and the circulation and distribution of programmes;

- infer the motivations and intentions of producers.

Clearly these different levels of media literacy will influence how far the interpretation process can go. In some ways they can be thought of as similar to Bernstein's elaborated and restricted codes of language. Elaborated code (high media literacy) allows for greater possibilities of understanding and expression than restricted code (low media literacy) does.

Figure 2.5

Another important finding which added weight to this outlook was that members of an audience differ greatly in the way they react to the same programme:

they reject it . . .

they upstage it . . .

they ignore it . . .

they don't hear it . . .

they switch it off . . .

*Look again at the Blind Date cartoon (Figure 2.4). How would this theory apply in this situation?*

The problems with this approach are as follows.

- Media messages are much more robust than this approach suggests: they carry a dominant and powerful influence. Fiske (1987) argues that there is a semiotic democracy where the message is not very important because the process of viewing can happen in so many ways. Elsewhere (1989) he argues that 'There is no text, there is no audience, there are only the processes of viewing.' This sort of view ignores the power of the media too much.

- The methods associated with this model tend to concentrate on small pieces of media 'text'. However, media messages are not just one-offs but are repeated frequently and reinforced in different formats across different media. The cumulative effect is very strong.

● This approach sees the individual as interpreting messages in a very isolated way. In fact people belong to cultures and subcultures which give them particular ways of looking at the media. The subculture that one belongs to strongly influences whether one accepts the dominant meaning of the message, negotiates the meaning or rejects it and imposes one's own reading.

 *What implications does this perspective have for approaches to research? Compare how the hypodermic approach and the interpretive approach might respond to the following question:*
*'How much influence do the media have over attitudes and behaviour?'*

### 5. The structured interpretation model

Figure 2.6 The Queen Mother meeting war veterans – a polysemic text.

This perspective, which is usually associated with David Morley, builds on the one above. It agrees that the audience can interpret media messages in different ways but suggests that there is a 'preferred reading' or dominant message and that readings are structured by the cultural context of audience. So, for example, a news item about the Queen Mother's birthday may be capable of being interpreted in different ways, but one of these is 'easier' than the others because of the way the story is presented and because of general culture in which the item is produced and consumed ('encoded' and 'decoded' in the jargon). Here the 'preferred reading' is about admiration for a very old woman who still selflessly performs public duties in the national interest.

 *What alternative readings are there? Take an example of any programme on the television. Identify the preferred reading and any alternative readings.*

---

**Monosemy/polysemy**

These concepts refer to the meanings that messages convey. Monosemy suggests that there is only one possible way of interpreting, or reading, a text. Polysemy suggests that a single text is capable of different interpretations or ways of reading it.

---

*Figure 2.7 Lull describes Madonna as 'the queen of polysemy'. Why do you think this is?*

However, the picture is complicated because there are numerous subcultures involved when a single mass media message is received. To understand a text researchers cannot just 'read' it themselves but must understand how the different audiences within different subcultures read it. These could be associated with age, sex, race, class, religion, geography etc. partly depending on the nature of the text. Some of these audiences are sophisticated and have the ability to make multiple readings.

David Morley sums up this approach by paraphrasing Marx:

> audiences produce meanings, but have to work on material which has been pre-selected and organized in particular ways by producers.

Ien Ang in *Desperately Seeking the Audience* notes that audiences have traditionally been seen as an undifferentiated mass, in the same way as we think of 'the population' or 'the nation'. She says that we must avoid this sort of model and instead display sensitivity towards the everyday practices and experiences of audiences themselves. Ethnographic studies of real people in real social contexts are the only way we can understand the role of the media. She refers to this approach as 'methodological situationalism'.

---

### *Methodological situationalism*

Instead of seeing the audience as an undifferentiated mass or even seeing them as divided by class, age etc., we need to see them (and study them) as people interacting with the media in concrete social situations. In this view (which has much in common with postmodernist and post-structuralist perspectives) the same person will perceive and react to the same media message in different ways in different contexts. Because of this it becomes difficult or impossible to make generalizations about 'the audience' as such. What is important is the chain of situations in which television audiencehood is practised and experienced.

The concept comes from Knorr-Cetina (1988) but there is a good discussion in Ang (1991), pp. 162–4.

---

*Imagine a television news story about massage parlours. The theme is usually along the lines of illicit behaviour by a deviant minority. Sub themes typically are sexual exchanges, drug use, organized crime and sexually transmitted disease. However other perspectives are possible, for example 'good health, sexual satisfaction, onerous government regulations, free enterprise and career opportunities' (Paletz and Entman 1981, p. 22). What barriers are there to going beyond the 'preferred reading' to the one suggested by Paletz and Entman?*

The problems with this approach are:

- It takes an over-determined view of individuals, seeing their attitudes and views as largely determined by the social groups they belong to.

- It has serious implications for the researcher, making useful research difficult and complicated. Like the interpretive model, this approach focuses research attention on the audience, but requires the researcher to pay close attention to stratification and diversity within the audience.

# The implications of theoretical approach for research

The above summary shows that more recent theories about the influence of the media have concentrated on the audience and how they receive the message, rather than just on the message itself. Research now tends to concentrate on reception analysis rather than, for example, content analysis.

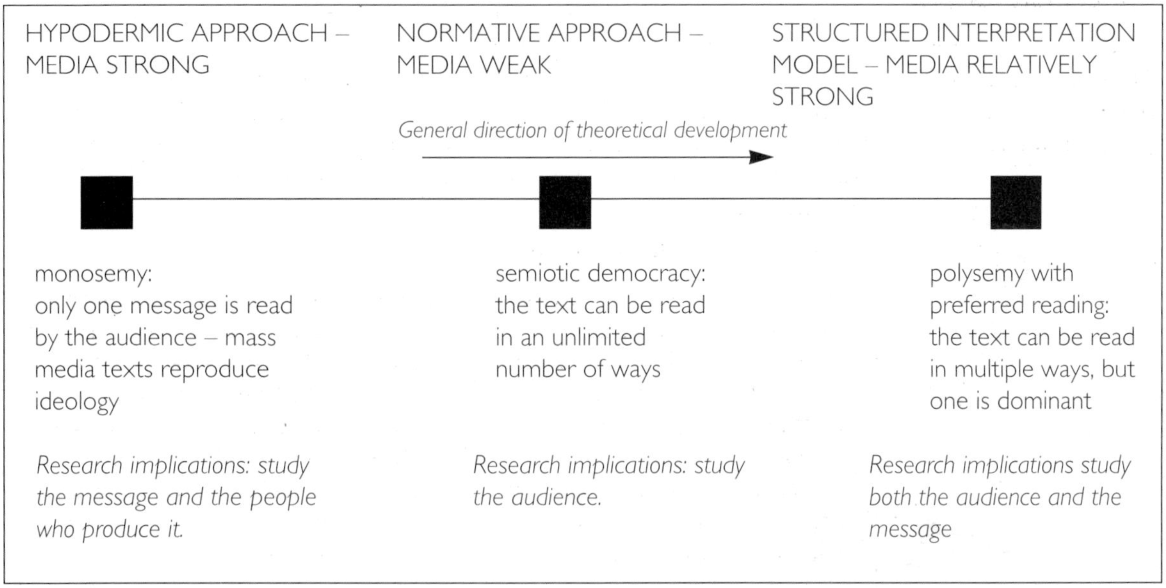

Figure 2.8 Summary of changes in theoretical and research focus

The change in theoretical and research focus is summarized in Figure 2.8. There has been a move from the left hand side towards the right and as a result an increasing focus on audience reception.

| HYPODERMIC APPROACH – MEDIA STRONG | NORMATIVE APPROACH – MEDIA WEAK | STRUCTURED INTERPRETATION MODEL – MEDIA RELATIVELY STRONG |
|---|---|---|
| | *General direction of theoretical development* → | |
| monosemy: only one message is read by the audience – mass media texts reproduce ideology | semiotic democracy: the text can be read in an unlimited number of ways | polysemy with preferred reading: the text can be read in multiple ways, but one is dominant |
| *Research implications: study the message and the people who produce it.* | *Research implications: study the audience.* | *Research implications study both the audience and the message* |

The focus of research is also influenced by other factors. These include:

● what the researcher is interested in/considers important;

● what the funders of the research are interested in/consider important;

● what is a current issue at the time;

● which research technique is most appropriate for the purposes of the research;

> **Fitness for purpose**
>
> Research methods need to be suitable for the purpose of the research. For example it would be inappropriate to use laboratory experiments to study the influence of newspaper preference on voting habits.

● what can practically be done, or what special opportunities are available; for example for many researchers getting access to media organisations may be difficult; however Nicholas Jones was able to do this because he was a BBC journalist;

● the general sociological perspective of the researcher which will incline him/her towards an interpretive or positivist approach involving qualitative or quantitative data collection and analysis techniques.

*If you could study any aspect of the mass media, what would you study?*

 *Compare your answers.*

## Examination questions

Recent (and probable future) 'A' level examination questions have tended to concentrate on reception analysis too:

'Assess the sociological evidence for and against the view that the effects of the mass media vary according to the social characteristics of the audience.'

(AEB Sociology A level (with coursework), June 1992, paper 2, question 8)

'Any sociological explanation of the influence of the mass media needs to take into account the social situation of the audience.'

Explain and evaluate the view expressed in this statement.

(AEB A, Sociology, November 1993, paper 2, question 8)

*(You will find an outline answer to this question in the skeleton answers section of the book.)*

'Although the mass media try to present a single perspective on life, people interpret media messages according to their own situations.'

Critically discuss this statement with reference to sociological studies.

(AEB A, Sociology, winter 1994, paper 2, question 7)

'What are the limitations of "effects" models of audience response to the media?'

(AEB Media Studies, 1997, examination specimen questions, paper 2, question 9)

'How far does the context of consumption affect the ways in which the media makes meaning?'

(AEB Media Studies, 1997, examination specimen questions, paper 2, question 10)

'The important consideration for the analysis of media audiences is not what the media does to them, but rather what they do with the media. How far do you agree?'

(AEB Media Studies, 1997, examination specimen questions, paper 2, question 11)

## Further reading

Buckingham, D. (1993) *Reading Audiences,* Manchester UP

Lull, J. (1990) *Inside Family Viewing: Ethnographic Research on Television's Audiences,* London: Routledge (this is very useful because the series of articles in it show how Lull's methodology has changed over the years as he has moved from, for example, a uses and gratifications approach towards a structured interpretation model).

Lull, J. (1995) *Media, Communication, Culture* Cambridge: Polity Press, has a good glossary of mass-media-related terms at the end of the book as well as giving an up-to-date overview of recent perspectives on the media.

Morley, D. (1992) *Television Audiences and Cultural Studies,* London: Routledge.

# 3 Approaches to media research

Figure 3.1 Doing audience research

Table 3.1 below summarizes the most popular methods available in the study of the mass media. The table separates them according to whether the data they give are more qualitative or quantitative. The previous chapter looked at some of the factors which help in making the choice of appropriate method. This chapter examines each of the methods in turn. Most attention will be given to those methods which are unique to the study of the media, or mostly used in that context.

| Table 3.1 Media research methods: a summary | |
| --- | --- |
| *More quantitative* | *More qualitative* |
| Asking questions | |
| Structured interviews | Semi-structured or unstructured interviews |
| Closed-ended questionnaires | Open-ended questionnaires |
| | Discussion groups |
| Observation | |
| Non-participant observation (can be quantitative or qualitative) | Participant observation |
| Content analysis | Semiology |
| | Ethnography |
| Secondary data | |
| Official statistics | Diaries, letters, autobiographies |
| Experiments | |
| Controlled experiments (in the laboratory) | Uncontrolled experiments (in the field) |

> ### Methodological triangulation
>
> The use of a number of methods to help ensure the reliability of results. For example Radway used structured questionnaires, open-ended group discussion, in-depth interviews and content analysis in her study of women's use of romantic fiction (see p. 203 for more details).

## Asking questions

### Structured interviews

Structured interviews essentially involve the personal administration of a questionnaire. They are rarely used in the academic study of the mass media because they incorporate the disadvantages of two methods. Like interviews they are expensive and yield a small number of responses but like questionnaires they tend to limit the range and scope of the answers given by respondents. They have the added disadvantage of interviewer bias. However, they are sometimes used by audience research or opinion polling organizations such as MORI or BARB. Trained interviewers will stop a structured random sample of people (i.e. a pre-determined number of males and females of given ages, social classes and/or other characteristics) to ask them a series of questions about their viewing or reading habits and, possibly, opinions about what they have seen or read.

> ### Interviewer bias
>
> The effect of the characteristics of the interviewer (clothes, accent, demeanour, skin colour) on the answers given by the respondent.

Structured interviews were used by David Morrison's team from the Institute of Communications Studies, University of Leeds in their study of the Gulf War reporting (in Morrison 1992). The aim of the research was to explore what the viewer thought the role of TV should be in covering the Gulf War and find out how they responded to the images they saw and the information they received. Hour-long interviews were conducted in the homes of around 1,000 adults in the UK in March 1991. They were conducted by trained interviewers and the sample was a stratified random one at 88 sites. Respondents were invited to respond to statements on a scale that ranged from strongly agree to strongly disagree with three intermediate positions (a Likert scale) or given four or five alternative answers. Statements included:

> During war, journalists' impartiality should be suspended and they should emphasise the British side of things.

Questions with fixed choice answers included:

> If a British journalist discovered British troops mistreating Iraqi prisoners of war, which of these comes closest to what you think he should do?
> - Attempt to report it while war is going on.
> - Only report it once war is over.
> - Never report it even after the war.
> - Don't know.

 *What problems can you see with these two interview items?*

*Fitness for purpose is important when choosing a research method. Give three examples each of issues concerning the media which would be most suitably studied using:*

- *structured interview*
- *unstructured interview*

*In each case explain the reasons for your choice. Here is an example for guidance:*
*Issue: preferred channel for watching evening news and reasons.*
*Method: structured interviews with a random sample of people.*
*Reason for choice of method: limited options available so no need for elaboration.*

### Closed-ended questionnaires

The 1994 Television Monitoring Study conducted for the Broadcasting Standards Council (BSC) used closed-ended questionnaires. A total of four weeks' television programming was covered by the audience monitoring study: two weeks in May 1994 and two weeks in September 1994. 2,896 people were contacted by phone and asked to take part. 1,633 agreed to an initial discussion about the study and of these 1,096 agreed to take part. 610 of these were actually accepted and 425 completed their questionnaires.

These 425 respondents, or 'monitors', were provided with a questionnaire to complete about every programme they watched (recorded and 'live') during the monitoring period, which was either in May or September but not both. They also received detailed guidelines in a booklet, which told them for the first time that the research was being done for the BSC and worked through each of the questions on the questionnaire. These asked monitors to rate programmes on a scale from 0 (not at all) to 5 (very much):

- their personal enjoyment of the programme;

- their concern at children viewing the programme;

- the appropriateness of the programme for television;

- the suitability of the programme for the time it was broadcast;

- the extent and justifiability of bad language in the programme;

- the extent and justifiability of explicit sex in the programme;

- the extent and justifiability of violence in the programme;

- whether they were offended by any part of the programme;

- how necessary they felt a clear warning was before the broadcast of the programme.

The full results of this study, and two previous ones, are available from the BSC at £5 per copy.

*What problems can you see with this study? Think about the sample, the questions, the programmes, the viewing patterns of the monitors and any other factors.*

 *Compare your answers and compile a summary list of problems.*

### Semi-structured or unstructured interviews

Andrea Press[1] from the University of Michigan studied women's perceptions of *Dynasty* and in particular how these are conditioned by social class. She says:

> I used snowball sampling as a means of finding my informants. In snowball sampling, one starts with one member of the desired group, and asks that person for a friend, neighbour or relative in order to continue interviewing within the same class group ... I used several snowballs to start off each group.

 *What problems can you see with this method of selection? How could they be overcome?*

> My interviews [with 41 women from different classes and communities] lasted for at least two hours ... and often included follow-up interviews and visits ... I ... left my questions open-ended, and let the interviews travel in directions which seemed most consonant with the women's particular interests and views on the subject. Many interviews I did yielded little information of value for the study, unfortunately, in part because of the open-ended format. However, I am convinced that I would not have gathered the valuable information I did had I created a more closed, structured interview situation ... Interviews were taped and later transcribed. In addition, I wrote notes directly following each interview regarding the general tenor of the interview, my impressions of the informant, and other miscellaneous details. [p. 163] Whether [my] findings can be generalised to apply to the reception of other shows, and other television genres, and their bearing on television reception by other social groups, remains to be demonstrated in future studies. (p. 180)

 *Make a list of the advantages and disadvantages of this approach.*

Chris Richards in Buckingham (1993) wanted to get away from the formality of an interview situation. This is how he tackled it:

> I recorded a conversation with both of my daughters [Cesca, eight, and Fay, four] on a Sunday morning, lying on the living room floor and using what is more often routinely referred to as 'the radio' rather than an unfamiliar tape-recorder. The situation seemed to me very informal, almost haphazard, with no prepared list of questions and no explicit articulation of my expectations ...

However it did not really succeed, as the following dialogue suggests:

[1] Quoted in Brown M (1990) *TV and Women's Culture*, University of Pennsylvania Press.

Fay: But Daddy can we listen to … the radio now? [Cesca sings]

CR: You want to listen to it.

Cesca: Fay but Daddy's interviewing.

CR: I'm not, I'm just chatting to you.

Cesca: Why are you putting on the tape then? (p. 30)

*What are your views on this research approach?*

### Open-ended questionnaires

A form of very open-ended questionnaire was used by Dutch sociologist I Ang to assess people's attitudes to *Dallas*. She put an advert in a Dutch women's magazine called *Viva*. It read:

> I like watching the TV serial Dallas, but often get odd reactions to it. Would anyone like to write and tell me why you like watching too, or dislike it? I should like to assimilate these reactions in my university thesis. Please write to …

There were 42 replies, 69% of which were from women. These form the empirical basis of the research. The book consists largely of these letters and Ang's commentary on the reasons why *Dallas* is so fascinating a programme for viewers all over the world.

*One advantage of such an open-ended question is that the researcher does not restrict answers in any way. Too tight a questionnaire may omit to explore issues which are important to the respondent but which the researcher has not thought to ask about. What other advantages and disadvantages are there to Ang's technique? Why not try a similar advertisement about a recent programme in your local paper, school or college magazine and see what results you get?*

### Discussion groups

David Morley (1986) was interested in how family members used TV differently, for example in the programmes they watch, how they watch them and whether they use the TV for video games, teletext etc. He also wanted to see whether there were differences in their responses to different types of programming, how viewing choices were decided (e.g. who has power over the remote control) and the links between TV watching and other aspects of family life.

The sample was 18 families from one area of south London. Each had two adults living together and two or more children. All were white. Many had lived in the area all their lives, often their parents had done so too. Most were working class or lower middle class.

Each family member was interviewed in depth in their own home, first the parents together and then with the children. The interviews lasted between one and two hours and there was a fair degree of probing by Morley.

Thus, on points of significance I returned the discussion to the same theme at different stages of the interview from different angles. This means anyone 'putting me on' …would have to be able to sustain [their lies] through what could be seen as a quite complex form of interrogation. One powerful safeguard was provided by the presence of other members of the family, who often chipped in with their own queries or sarcastic comments when their husbands or wives seemed to them to be misrepresenting their actions.

The results of this research are set out in Chapter 9, p. 180.

*1. What comments do you have about Morley's sample?*
*2. What are the disadvantages of this form of unstructured discussion in the family context?*
*3. What research design would you have chosen to achieve the aims of this study?*

Morley felt that group interviews increased the reliability of the data produced, but Joke Hermes (1995) used both depth interviews and discussion groups and found individual interviews much more productive and reliable:

For me … compared to the individual depth interviews of the first stage, the group interview was not a very productive method … [The respondents] refrained from giving views they thought would be radically different from the views of the others and … they sometimes overdid statements they thought would make a favourable impression.

David Buckingham (1993a) also used discussion groups and identified further problems with them. His research was concerned with the ways in which children between 7 and 12 *talk* about television. He organized discussions with small groups of between two and five children selected from four schools, two in inner-city Hackney and two from suburban Enfield.

The discussion groups met in the schools and discussion was started by asking questions or setting exercises such as asking the children to re-tell the stories of films they had seen or asking them about their most and least favourite characters on television. The groups met several times over a period of 15 months, with the individuals in them changed as thought appropriate. Buckingham identifies some of the disadvantages of this method:

The data have been gathered in schools, primarily through small-group talk: as I have shown, what individuals say is heavily dependent upon the other children present, and indeed on the role of the interviewer. The data do not necessarily tell us about how children talk about television outside the context of discussion with adult researchers – and indeed, these particular adult researchers. Using audio-tape has meant that non-verbal behaviour and interaction has largely been ignored. Furthermore, the research has not studied the viewing process at first hand … what we have here are individuals' accounts of their viewing, rather than direct evidence of that viewing itself. (p. 265)

*These are the disadvantages. What are the advantages to this method?*

Greg Philo, Director of the Glasgow University Media Unit, used discussion groups in a particularly interesting way in *Seeing and Believing* (1990). Adopting the structured interpretation model, he was interested to see how groups in different social situations would not only 'read' news accounts of the 1984/5 miners' strike, but also construct them. He selected four types of groups (a total of 169 people) and gave them the same exercise to do. The groups were:

1. groups with special knowledge and experience of the strike (senior police officers, miners and women's support groups etc.);

2. occupational groups: groups from solicitors' offices, catering staff and electronics employees; these groups were people who worked together daily;

3. special interests groups: mothers and toddlers groups and an 'activity in retirement' group;

4. residential groups: people living close to each other from the south-east of England.

The task that the groups had to perform was to take a series of photographs of television news reports of the miners' strike and to create a 'news story' about the strike. This enabled Philo to access the ways in which the different groups constructed meaning about the strike.

Philo concludes that direct experience of what the media message is about can have a crucial influence in how new information from the media is understood. This fact means that often the responses of people within these four types of group were not homogeneous. Other factors played a part in conditioning audience response to media messages too, including the beliefs they bring with them, their class experience and the logical processes they use in analysing a message and comparing it with others, either in the media or in their own experience.

# Observation

Observation is most often used to study media content and its production, though audience response can also be observed.

### Non-participant observation

Meehan's study *Ladies of the Evening* illustrates the use of non-participant observation, in which the researcher observes but is uninvolved. She was permitted to 'sit in' on writing sessions for one week by the producers of *The Bob Newhart Show*. A similar opportunity was given to Grant Noble by the editors of *Blue Peter*. They showed him scripts and allowed him to watch rehearsals as well as discussing the production of the show with him. This gave him many insights into the programme: how the illusion of intimacy is created by the nature of the set; the objectives *Blue Peter* has and so on.

Direct observation also has its drawbacks. Here, too, as in other methods of inquiry, there are problems of observer bias, of replication, of subject reactivity, and so forth. No observer, or team of observers, can literally be everywhere at once. A field director must station them according to some strategic plan and instruct them on the setting, the actors, and the transactions on which they should focus as well as on background events. This, by itself, is not enough. The more intimate view that 'getting close' affords is no guarantee of 'objectivity'. Entrapped by the 'insider's' viewpoint, the observer may accept the participants' own common-sense explanations without checking them through. And lastly, insofar as the observer has actually become a participant, there can be effects on the behaviour studied … Turning on … [the] spotlight keeps some things going. To avoid this, social science observers usually keep a low profile, yet, in so doing, forgo data that might be available were they to assume a more active role.

(Lang and Lang 1991, p. 195)

1. *What is meant by 'observer bias', 'replication' and 'subject reactivity'?*
2. *'Insofar as the observer has actually … effects on the behaviour studied'. What name do sociologists give to the phenomenon referred to in this sentence?*
3. *Giving examples from at least one study of the mass media with which you are familiar, how far have the problems with observation referred to here been successfully addressed?*

### Content analysis

Content analysis involves the very careful quantification of the content of media messages. It is able to give a general impression about media content which can be the basis of theoretical work or policy and programme development.

---

**'Hard' and 'soft' content analysis**

The hard approach to content analysis is simply to count the frequency of words or seconds of airtime coverage and other discrete quantifiable bits of data. The soft approach uses trained coders to make a judgement about the meanings of words, phrases or images in context and then allocate them to categories. The resulting data are then quantified.

---

*You are interested in studying (say) the representation of older people in television drama using content analysis. Use the following steps as guidance and conduct your study.*

1. *Decide on the genre of TV drama will you draw on, its country of origin, age etc.*
2. *Decide whether you will study it all or a sample and if a sample how it will be selected.*
3. *Decide whether you would use hard or soft content analysis.*

4. *Construct a coding scheme relevant to the aim of the project*
5. *Observe the sample and code its content.*
6. *Write up your results.*

*Questions:*
- *What methodological issues did this exercise reveal?*
- *How would you do it differently if you did it again?*

The 1994 Television Monitoring Study conducted for the Broadcasting Standards Council included a content analysis component. The research interest was the extent of bad language, sex, nudity and violence on television. It was carried out by Aston University and involved the careful study of one week's television output in the Midlands. All programmes on all channels were video recorded and then subjected to detailed content analysis by trained coders. A schedule of questions was prepared and these were used to categorize the content of output. The questions focused on who did what, where, when, how and why, and comparisons with earlier years were made (see Table 3.2).

Table 3.2    Type of bad language: September 1992, 1993 and 1994

|  | 1992 | 1993 | 1994 |
|---|---|---|---|
|  | % | % | % |
| Serious | 9 | 2 | 3 |
| Genitalia | 8 | 7 | 9 |
| Mild word | 30 | 26 | 22 |
| Other word | 11 | 9 | 12 |
| Religious | 34 | 46 | 40 |
| Minority abuse: women | 5 | 6 | 7 |
| Minority abuse: disabled | 1 | 1 | 3 |
| Minority abuse: homosexual | 1 | 1 | 1 |
| Minority abuse: race | 1 | 2 | 1 |
| Gesture | 1 | 0 | 1 |
| Totals | 101 | 100 | 99 |

*Examples of bad language*
'bollocks', 'bugger', 'pillock', 'knockers', 'bonk', 'git'
*Examples of minority abuse*
'tramp', 'slattern', 'bimbo', 'spasmo', 'nutter', 'spade', 'wop', 'pansy', 'dyke'
*Examples of offensive gestures*
'Two fingers up', 'fist on bicep'
*Examples of violent actions*
'Hit with object', 'poisoning', 'sword fight', 'rape', 'kick', 'slap'

*Source: BSC (1995) p. 142*

*Prepare a detailed critique of this research. If you are working in a group, present your critique to them.*

Earlier content analysis studies include those by the Glasgow University Media group. This group published a series of studies in the 1970s and '80s called *Bad News*, *More*

*Bad News, Really Bad News* and *War and Peace News*. The aim was to give a neutral, statistical account of the output of the news to show the directions in which it was 'biased'.

Their technique was broadly the same in each case, though they switched the focus of attention in each book. They carefully timed each item, noting the number and types of items in each broadcast (crime, industrial relations and so on). The method of presentation was also noted (studio or outside broadcast, interview, newscaster to camera etc.) and details of who appeared and for how long. The resulting quantitative data was analysed by computer.

Table 3.3    Distribution of items by bulletin (weekdays), showing percentage of items in each category.

|  | BBC1 Lunchtime | Early | Nine O'Clock News | BBC2 Newsday | News Extra | ITN First Report | Early | News at Ten |
|---|---|---|---|---|---|---|---|---|
| 10 Political | 21.1 | 22.0 | 21.6 | 23.6 | 25.4 | 23.6 | 22.3 | 21.2 |
| 20 Industrial | 17.9 | 16.6 | 16.6 | 18.6 | 15.3 | 14.3 | 16.6 | 13.1 |
| 30 Foreign | 24.7 | 21.9 | 21.1 | 20.7 | 25.7 | 27.3 | 24.3 | 25.9 |
| 40 Economic | 5.2 | 8.3 | 9.8 | 9.7 | 6.9 | 7.1 | 7.7 | 7.6 |
| 50 Crime | 4.3 | 4.8 | 4.5 | 5.5 | 2.8 | 4.3 | 5.2 | 5.1 |
| 60 Home Affairs | 5.2 | 6.6 | 6.9 | 5.8 | 6.9 | 5.6 | 5.4 | 7.2 |
| 70 Sport | 7.1 | 7.6 | 7.5 | 5.0 | 4.1 | 6.5 | 6.0 | 7.4 |
| 80 Human Interest | 4.6 | 5.3 | 5.4 | 4.2 | 5.1 | 3.2 | 4.7 | 6.6 |
| 90 Disasters | 9.9 | 6.1 | 5.1 | 6.3 | 5.8 | 6.7 | 5.9 | 4.4 |
| 00 Science | – | 0.7 | 1.5 | 0.5 | 2.0 | 1.3 | 1.8 | 1.6 |
| Total % | 100.0 | 99.9 | 100.0 | 99.9 | 100.0 | 99.9 | 99.9 | 100.0 |
| n= | 324 | 685 | 826 | 381 | 393 | 462 | 613 | 942 |

Source: Social Trends, vol. 25, p. 216, table 13.3.

More recently the Glasgow Group have moved on, adopting the structured interpretation model and so studying how different types of audience 'read' the news as well as the preferred meaning of news accounts (see Philo 1990). Philo now says that 'There were two issues which we saw as crucial when we began to develop audience studies. The first was how exactly messages work to convince those who receive them (or not as the case may be). The second question which follows from this is how might a message "work" for some groups but not others?' Glasgow University Media Group and Eldridge (1993) p. 257.

Content analysis is not dead in academic research, however, and is usefully used in conjunction with other methods. A massive content analysis of TV coverage of the 1991 Gulf War was carried out by Aston University and initial results published in Morrison (1992). They recorded the main evening news and current affairs programmes from 14.1.91 to 3.3.91 on BBC1, BBC2, ITV, Channel 4, CNN and BSkyB plus (for comparison) news from German BR2, French TF1, Italian RAI 1 and Russian main service carried on the Gorizont satellite. This resulted in 300 miles of tape recording and a huge analytical task. The other methods used were structured interviews with over 1000 adults and over 200 children described above and group discussions with 10 adult groups and four child groups.

There are some serious problems with content analysis, however. They include the following:

● It concentrates on the message, not the meaning the audience gives it, assuming that the two are the same. Audience reception analysis shows that they are not.

● It implies a hypodermic model of media influence because the assumption is that content is important in affecting attitudes and behaviour.

● The data it reveals are not obvious to the audience – a new 'meaning' has been produced by the research.

● In trying to turn the qualitative into quantitative data the flavour and tone of the original text is lost because this is very difficult to quantify.

*1. Surveys of the public have found that very few people can remember what was on last night's news. Can you?*

*2. Try noting down the news items tonight and then asking friends to recall them tomorrow. How successful are they?*

*3. If they cannot remember much about the news, does this mean that news content is irrelevant?*

*Obtain a copy of K. A. Saucier (1986) 'Healers and heartbreakers: images of women and men in country music', Journal of Popular Culture, 20, 3, pp. 147–66 through interlibrary loan. Critically evaluate this content analysis study of Western country music.*

### Participant observation

Participant observation is usually used in the study of media organizations. An example is Gaye Tuchman's (1978) *Making News*. However it can be used for audience studies. Morley and Silverstone (1990) describe how they conducted participant observation with four different families, each in turn. The object of the study was to research the use they made of communication technologies (TV, VCR, telephone, computer) in the home.

Figure 3.2

They were especially interested in how this use was influenced by the domestic culture of these homes and how the technologies in turn influenced that culture. By observing the families the researchers were able to check the data from other research tools like the diaries they were asked to keep. It was also useful for gaining a picture of the domestic culture, the furnishings in the rooms and so on. However there were some problems:

● participant observation 'would not readily provide ... the basis for a systematic analysis of the key issues of media use';

● nor would it allow 'systematic comparative work between families';

● or 'enable us satisfactorily to contextualise families historically and geographically in relation to their pasts, their futures, and their neighbourhoods'.

*What other problems can you see with this method?*

*Many interesting and readable participant observation studies have been written by journalists and others involved in the media. Examples include Nicholas Jones's* Strikes and the Media *(Jones was an industrial relations and now is Politics correspondent for the BBC) and Stuart Hood's* On Television *(Hood was an editor of BBC news).*
*Other examples include books by Alastair Hetherington (former controller of BBC Scotland), John Whale (a former ITN and Sunday Times journalist) and Roy Greenslade (former Daily Mirror editor).*
*What advantages and disadvantages can you see to this approach?*

### Semiology

---

#### Semiology ( or sometimes 'semiotics')

Semiology is the study of the social production of meaning from signs. 'Signs' include symbolic content which evoke connotations in our minds and

are carried by 'text'. Text need not be written, but could be a picture, a television programme, a film or a piece of dialogue, for example. The Statue of Liberty is an example of a text in this sense. A sign consists of the text (signifier) and its meaning (signified). The meaning includes both denotive codes, what is represented (the picture on the left denotes the Statue of Liberty but is not the thing itself), and connotive code, the images, feelings, responses and connections that are evoked.

The semiological approach to research involves 'reading' text; that is interpreting it and uncovering its meanings. This process is sometimes referred to as 'deconstruction'. This approach is particularly associated with Barthes' (1973) book *Mythologies* and has been widely adopted in the study of the media, for example by Robert Fiske and David Morley. Semiology is closely linked to discourse analysis. See p. 169 for a discussion of this.

---

The best way to describe semiotics is through examples. Fiske and Hartley say that in news broadcasts shots of policing of picket lines or inner city riots are often taken from behind the lines of the police. Thus, the viewer is encouraged to identify with the policemen and to share their fear and anxiety. The viewer sees the massed ranks of the potentially, or actually, violent crowd, perhaps throwing stones and other missiles at his/her vantage point.

The camera shows two or three police officers dragging an injured colleague away, and then pans back to the crowd. The connotations here are: professional, organized but beleaguered police force face the mindlessly ferocious enemy. This interpretation of events is put in the mind of the viewer without the need for commentary. The viewer is usually unaware that he/she has been subtly encouraged to empathize with the police.

Semiology can be applied to any medium; film, cartoons, the printed word and even photographs (a picture is worth a thousand words, as the cliché goes, because of the hidden messages it contains).

Cigarettes provide a good example to illustrate the difference between connotive and denotive codes. We can recognize a picture of a packet of cigarettes for what it represents quite easily, without needing to see the cigarettes inside it or to have any further clues about what the sign (the picture) signifies (a packet of cigarettes). This is the denotive code. Connotive codes are more subtle and could be read in a number of ways. For some people cigarettes, thanks to the power of advertising, have come to be associated with such concepts as masculinity, ruggedness and reliability.

These connotations are encouraged by the regular practice among cigarette advertisers of picturing cigarettes and cigarette packets in the hands of cowboys on the prairie, uniformed officers (presumably airline captains) at the wheel of sports cars and through sponsorship of sports which are thought to require these qualities. Sometimes the required connotive codes are made explicit by advertising copy, though this is usually unnecessary. An example comes from a magazine advertisement. The uniformed sleeve of the helicopter pilot rests on the door of his sports car, the helicopter visible in the wing mirror. The copy runs 'ROTHMANS … WHEN YOU KNOW WHAT YOU'RE DOING'. A sample semiological reading of a photograph and associated copy is given on p. 148.

A combination of semiology and interviewing was carried out by Bob Hodge and David Tripp in *Children and Television*. They asked an experienced researcher to interview 42 children from six different Australian schools after showing them part of an episode of *Fangface*, a cartoon show. The aim was to determine how the children responded to the show and how far they were able to decode it. The findings were that children developed quite sophisticated skills of semiological analysis up to at least the age of 12. There are rules of the cartoon world which children actively learn.

For example, they distinguish between the 'goody-goodies' and the merely 'good', between 'main characters' and 'not-so-main' ones. They know which sort of characters can be expected to solve problems in this type of cartoon, who will drive cars, who will eventually win and so on, even though they had not seen all of the episode in question. The world of the cartoon extends into the real world. Some characters are middle-class, some working-class. Obviously some are male and some female and so on. Thus the children are taking in ideological content, which they have learnt to 'read' from an apparently unrealistic cartoon. However, Hodge and Tripp

Figure 3.4 Graffiti on a
cigarette advertisement.
Benson and Hedges are
the heaviest cigarette
advertisers in the UK.
Sixty-two per cent of
young smokers smoke this
brand.

say that the ideological content is not uniform and it doesn't all go in one direction.
This makes the overall effect difficult to establish.

*Show a similar cartoon, for example* Scooby Doo, *to a child or children
under the age of twelve. Allow them to see five minutes of the episode
only. Ask them which characters are goodies and which baddies, which
will win and which lose, how the programme will finish, and so on (you
will need to prepare your questions carefully in advance). Assess by their
answers how true it is that children have developed a sophisticated
understanding of this genre of TV programme and the universe inhabited
by the characters in it.*

There are numerous critics of semiology. For example, A. Hetherington in *News,
Newspapers and Television* (1985) is critical of the semiological work of Fiske and Hartley:

> Fiske and Hartley, … in analysing an item about Northern Ireland
> in *News at Ten* … say that the images of soldiers on patrol, sand-
> bagged positions and armoured troop carriers were all intended to
> trigger the 'myth' of 'our lads out there, professional, well equipped'.
> Possibly, but it is far more likely that the reporter in London and the
> film editor simply took the best library film available to them to
> illustrate a government decision announced by the Prime Minister in
> the Commons to send extra troops to South Armagh after fifteen
> people (five Catholics, ten Protestants) had been murdered near the
> border in two days. What is more, for those of the audience already
> sceptical about the effectiveness of military operations in Northern
> Ireland or antagonistic to the use of British troops, those images
> would do nothing to diminish their scepticism or antagonism.

The way news stories are presented is thus more a result of technical and other
factors than the encoding of a dominant ideology. The environmental organization
*Greenpeace* was able to influence the news story about Shell's intended sinking of the
oil rig the *Brent Spar* by giving journalists access to their vessel. This access yielded
newsworthy pictures and stories for the media and achieved Greenpeace's aim of
framing the story in their terms. The sinking was cancelled, which had been
Greenpeace's aim, largely due to the public outcry about pollution of the sea which
resulted from the news stories. Also, as the example of the cigarette reading on p.45

indicates, readings are culturally specific. For many people cigarettes now denote anti-social behaviour, danger and death.

- *Try reading these signs.*
- *What alternative readings might there be?*
- *Are there alternative readings of the Statue of Liberty?*

Figure 3.5

An interesting example of one researcher's use of different approaches, including semiology, and how this use has changed over time is the work of Angela McRobbie. Her late 1970s study of the girls' magazine *Jackie* (then Britain's biggest selling teen magazine for over 10 years) showed how the content focused on the personal and emotional side of life: 'romance, problems, fashion, beauty and pop all mark out the limits of the girl's feminine sphere'. McRobbie's 'reading' of *Jackie*, focused on it as a world of romantic individualism in which the Jackie girl is in a constant quest for love. Her main aim is to find a boyfriend as quickly as possible and to escape the 'bitchiness' of other girls' company, though she may occasionally turn to them for support. This message, says McRobbie,

> is immensely powerful, especially if we consider it being absorbed, in its codified form, each week for several years at a time ... if we consider all the other objects and experiences which we recognise as influencing us and shaping our vision of the world, we should not be too quick to dismiss *Jackie* as 'silly, harmless nonsense' ...

Her reading continues:

> *Jackie* boys fall into four categories ... the fun-loving, grinning, flirtatious boy ... the tousled, scatterbrained 'zany' youth ... the emotional, shy, sensitive and even arty type ... and ... the juvenile delinquent ... whom the girl must tame. In every case the male figure is idealised and romanticised so that there is a real discrepancy

between *Jackie* boys and those boys who are discussed on the [problem] page. The central point here is that *Jackie* boys are as interested in romance as the girls, 'Mm! I wish Santa would bring me that for Christmas ... so how do we get together?' and this....simply does not ring true. Boys in contemporary capitalist society are socialised to be interested in sex ... (p. 99)

In a later study, McRobbie reflects on the criticisms that the *Jackie* study received. These can be summarized as follows:

● She admits that she restricted herself to analysing the text of the magazine, not how it was actually *read* (in the semiotic sense) by the girls. We are only given her reading, not theirs. With their different social situations, age and experience their reading would have been different to hers, with different parts of the audience reading *Jackie* in different ways.

● She created an image of *Jackie* as automatically transmitting an ideology in which the girls were imprisoned and subjected to. In other words she used the hypodermic model.

● She did not recognize that *Jackie* was often read lazily or skim-read with readers skipping to the end of stories they did not like (selective exposure).

● She did not realize that girls used several media and that *Jackie* was only one (and probably a lesser one) of a number of possibilities, or that the girls were highly sophisticated users of media, and readers and evaluators of narrative codes.

● She did not recognize that her reading of Jackie imposed a unity on its message which was not there.

In general, then, she was seeing the readers as blank slates on which *Jackie* could write.

In a new study of girls' magazines (*Jackie*, *Blue Jeans*, *Patches* and *Girl* with a detailed reading of these over a three-year period between 1985 and 1988) she notes the following:

● the decline of photo-love stories;

● the replacement of fictional romance with 'true' stories and facts about pop idols, their lives and their music;

● a move from depicting girls as passive, dependent etc. to being assertive and even encouraging them to be more assertive;

● a concern on the part of those working on the magazines to understand their readership and give them what they want; this is reflected in, for example, the maintenance of a panel of 500 readers to test out and comment on the magazine each month, road show events etc.

● treatment of readers as intelligent and discerning;

● the increasing dependence of the magazines on large media companies not only for advertising but for press releases, interviews etc. about the 'stars' – they are locked into a system of consumption;

- a new, open attitude about sex; the problem pages, in particular, take on the role of shaping feminine identity;

- advertising becomes much more important and the distinction between adverts and other content declines. Beauty products, clothes and music are especially important subjects of 'aditorials' and adverts. The cost of greater equality for girls as depicted in these pages is that they are now addressed as young consumers, no less a subject role than the earlier one.

The strange thing is that in her new study she repeats what she says are mistakes in the earlier one. For example she says: 'To resist these rituals [of femininity] is to jeopardise the security of a firm gender positioning. Cleansing, rinsing and all the other beauty routines help teenage girls to work their way towards a clearer notion of their own sexuality ...' (p. 175). Indeed, on p. 183 she says that 'the more sociological questions of readership ... might well be explored in more detail at some later date' just as she had done in the late 1970s. Instead of tackling how *Jackie* is 'read', she now states her conclusions more tentatively than before, putting them as questions not statements and adding riders:

> Is it the case then that the 'cost' of equality in the new girls' magazines is that readers become more strenuously addressed as young consumers? If this is what has happened then it is neither altogether surprising nor does it mean that the readers do as they are required and become 'consuming selves'. (p. 185)

What is clearly needed is precisely a study of the audience's reading of Jackie and other media output.

The disadvantages of semiology include the following:

1. As McRobbie did in her earlier study, there is a danger that researchers impose their readings on text. Current researchers now understand, in the main, that texts are 'polysemic' (see p. 29) and so audiences may read them in a number of ways. This has led to a recent concentration on how audiences read texts, not readings by researchers.

2. It is very labour-intensive; considerable time and effort is often expended on analysing a small amount of text.

3. Changes in context can radically alter the meaning of the same text, so that a reading will only be good for one context. This means that:

4. In order to understand and evaluate a particular reading of a text, the student must be culturally competent – i.e. be able to understand the references and hidden meanings. This excludes some groups from access to the method, its results or its evaluation.

5. The focus of semiology is at the very microscopic level (e.g. a few minutes of airtime, one magazine). This means that getting an overview of media output of a particular type is difficult.

6. The methodology is highly personal and lacks rigour. Results cannot be validated and they are unreliable. Readings of a particular text cannot be generalized.

7. The analyst is assuming that his/her interpretation is the correct one, even if the

text was produced by someone else who may have a different interpretation and even if the text can be read in different ways by different audiences.

*This project is designed to test how far semiology is a viable method of studying media output. The aim is to determine how far the connotive codes of particular 'texts' are read in the same way by different people. Select some people, preferably of mixed ages, social classes and of both sexes. Then select an example 'text' which you can use to explain the principles of semiology to them (a photograph like the one in the Johnson's advertisement on p. 148 would probably be easiest). Explain the ideas behind semiology and give your reading of the example text. Then give a second text (again, possibly a photograph or an advertisement) to the individual and ask them to give their reading of it. This could be tape-recorded for later analysis and comparison with others. Repeat this process with the other people in your sample, using the same texts in each case. You could also ask people for their opinions of this method of studying the media.*

*In your written report describe and give examples of semiology. Comment on how far the various readings of the same text which you obtained were similar and how far they diverged. Assess the implications of your findings for the validity of the method. Describe and discuss people's reactions to semiology as a method. Finally, give a general assessment of the method.*

### Ethnography

---

#### Ethnography

According to Fetterman, ethnography 'is the art and science of describing a group or culture. The description may be of a small tribal group in some exotic land or a classroom in middle class suburbia'.

Hitchcock and Hughes say it involves the following:
1. producing a description of the cultural knowledge of a group;
2. describing the activities of the group from their point of view;
3. describing the key characteristics defining membership of a group;
4. describing and analysing patterns of social interaction that the group experiences;
5. providing as far as possible 'insider accounts';
6. the development of theory (though some ethnographers limit themselves to description).

Ethnography is sometimes confused with participant observation. While ethnography often uses participant observation, it usually involves other research methods too. Also it aims to create a much richer description of meanings, behaviour and norms than participant observation does.

---

An early example of the use of ethnography in the study of the mass media is Timothy Crouse's (1972) *The Boys on the Bus*, an ethnographic account of journalists covering a presidential campaign. However until recently there have been very few examples of the use of ethnography in media research, perhaps because it usually requires an insider's access to do it well. Recent developments in mass media research have led to interest in ethnography as a method. If we have to study in detail what audiences do with the mass media and the influence of culture on this (and it on culture) then we need to use ethnographic methods. In fact, using the media is part of culture and needs to be studied as such:

> the ordinary viewing of television is not an unstructured pastime … media use happens within connected skeins (bundles) of behaviour, accomplished practices, … which constitute and maintain our social realities. Family viewing, for example, is no more casual and sponta-neous than the family dinner. It is accomplished by competent actors with great improvisational skill.
>
> (Anderson 1987).

This means that the researcher has to be with the family in order to understand the role of the mass media in its culture.

*You wish to conduct an ethnographic study of a single family's use of a variety of media. Your aim is to 'explain the presence, functions and influence of the content and technology within the structures, functions, systems and interaction within the family' (Anderson).*
*How might you approach this and what problems would you face?*

Marie Gillespie (*The Mahabharata* in Buckingham 1993b) conducted ethnographic fieldwork in the household of the Dhani family over a three-year period (1988–91). Her intention was to understand how the family create meaning from the epic Indian story *The Mahabharata*. She had taught a daughter of the family, Malati, and got the introduction to the family through her. She asked if she might join the family to watch *The Mahabharata* on television. She told them she knew the story and wanted to learn from the wisdom it contained. She visited the family regularly on Saturdays and during school holidays to watch the series, usually on video. She asked questions about the story and was offered explanations by the family. They

> welcomed me openly into their home and were clearly amused by the teacher who had come to learn from them … We soon became friends … The hospitality of the Dhani family was such that they soon accepted me as a member of the family and thankfully talked to me or ignored my presence as they wished. They got used to my naive and probing questions, my notebooks and my fondness for tea and chapatis. (p. 54)

For her larger work, recounted in *Television, Ethnicity and Cultural Change* (1995), she elaborates on this methodological approach. This work is more fully ethnographic than that done for *The Mahabharata*, drawing on a much fuller data resource. During the period of her fieldwork Gillespie lived in Southall in the house of young adults with a Punjabi background and informally visited other families (including the Dhani family) on a regular basis as well as conducting structured and focused interviews with young people. She had been a teacher in the area since the early 1980s and during the period of fieldwork she taught sociology and media studies part-time, which itself yielded valuable data, particularly during morning registration and informal small-group work.

She supplemented this with a questionnaire survey of 333 young people (12–18 years old) to collect data about how they perceived themselves and their own youth culture in relation to their parents' culture as well as to establish patterns of media consumption. This allowed her to map the patterns of media consumption and to identify important differences in this among sub-groups divided by age, gender, class and religion for example. Through this close contact she was able to investigate 'TV talk', that is the ways in which the young people talked about what they had seen and the constructions they put upon both it and their own lives.

 *Morley (1992), pp. 239–46 offers an ethnographic account of one family's use of technology. Read this section and comment on the usefulness of the findings which this method has produced.*

Ann Gray (1992) describes her research as having 'ethnographic intentions' (though within the text she firmly describes it as ethnographic in at least two places). She examines how women use and make sense of their video recorder. She had conversational interviews with 30 white women, living with a male partner (most were married) in full employment. The interviews were done in their homes, tape-recorded and transcribed. These lasted about one and half hours. She established contact with a video library in Dewsbury, Yorkshire and conducted a survey of people coming into the shop, then selected from these. She also needed to select additional middle-class women many of whom were in education jobs. The results are summarized on pp. 178–179.

 *Compare Gray and Gillespie's studies. Are either or both of them really ethnography? Refer back to the concept box on p. 50. What criticisms do you have of their methodology?*

Ethnography raises many practical issues concerning access to settings, collecting data and analysing the large amounts of qualitative data that are almost inevitably gathered. Many ethical issues are raised, too, about who 'owns' the data and who decides how it should be used after it has been collected. Recently, though, critics of ethnography have questioned the very status of the data which this sort of research collects.

Ang (1989) recognizes that any research project is inevitably 'constructivist' in nature. That is, because of the way it is designed, the assumptions it makes and the methods it adopts will result in a particular, partial, construction of social reality. It does not 'reveal' much about audience culture, their use of the media or the meanings they ascribe to texts. Rather, such research simply reveals the researchers' interpretation of these things. Ang accepts this and sees research as involving the construction of reality from a particular position. There is no question, from her point of view, of establishing 'the truth' because it does not exist. This is a postmodernist position (see Chapter 8 pp. 168–172). Feuer adds to this problem the view that such studies don't really explain anything. In studying the audience and how they interpret media texts, we are simply left with a new text to be interpreted – the audience response.

# Secondary data

> ### *Secondary data*
>
> Secondary data is information which has been collected from another source rather than through one's own primary research. It refers to a whole variety of types of data: from official statistics through to personal letters, from video recording of TV programmes to analyses of film scripts by other researchers.
>
> It has the advantage of being cheap, easily available, often covering large populations and it can be used comparatively (e.g. by looking at other countries' statistics). However, it is often out of date, inaccurate or biased in some way and frequently collected for purposes other than that desired by the researcher using it.

### *Quantitative secondary data, e.g. official statistics*

A study of the media which mixed the use of official statistics with content analysis and questionnaires was conducted by Bob Roshier. He analysed the crime reporting of the *Mirror*, the *Express* and the *Telegraph* together with the *Newcastle Journal* and the *News of the World*: for the month of September in the years 1967, 1955 and 1938.

His finding was that they all consistently over-reported all crimes against the person, robbery, fraud, blackmail and drugs compared with the official statistics on these crimes. Very markedly over-reported was murder. The *News of the World* consistently over-reported sex crimes (about one-third of its total crime reporting, compared to 5% for the other papers).

Crime stories which were serious or whimsical or with sentimental or dramatic circumstances were particularly likely to be reported. How did all this affect public perceptions of crime? Apparently very little. Respondents were closer to the official statistics than to newspaper reports in their estimate of the *amounts* of different crimes and in most other respects it appeared that their perceptions were little influenced by their papers. The main exceptions were that:

● like the papers, respondents tended to over-estimate the amount of cleared-up crime;

● the *News of the World* readers rated sex crimes as being particularly serious and particularly frequent. Whether this is a result of reading the *News of the World* or the reason they buy it in the first place is unclear.

*Roshier's method was threefold:*
*1. a content analysis of newspapers to quantify the nature of their crime reporting;*
*2. a survey of those newspapers' readers on their views of crime, criminals etc.;*
*3. an analysis of the official statistics for comparison.*

*Try carrying out a similar project of your own. First, conduct a content analysis of crime reporting in one or more newspapers for a short period of time. Compare the results of this with the official statistics on types of crime, clear-up rates, types of criminal and so on (these are available in* Social Trends *and in Home Office publications.) Then, construct a questionnaire about these issues. Conduct the survey and collate the results.*

### Qualitative secondary data

Peter Hennessy in *What the Papers Never Said* puts secondary data to good use in the analysis of omissions (and therefore 'bias') in the newspaper reporting of politics and the study of how the press is manipulated by government. The thirty-year rule states that confidential cabinet documents may be released (with some censorship in the interests of national security) after thirty years. Hennessy's technique was to study both the archive material released under this rule and the newspapers of thirty years ago in order to compare what was actually going on in Government with what the newspapers were *saying* about it.

Many examples are cited in the book of manipulation and deception by various governments. One involves the setting up of a cabinet committee, known as GEN 325, to examine the question of immigration to Britain after ministers had become concerned that Britain might 'attract here an undue proportion of the surplus population of the West Indies and other colonial territories'. The work of GEN 325 and the concern of the Government on this issue would have been very newsworthy, but there was absolute secrecy while the committee met and no one even knew of its existence until the records were released in 1982.

## Experiments

---

#### Controlled/uncontrolled experiments

In controlled experiments the researcher tries to control all aspects of the experiment, all the variables involved, so that s/he can accurately establish cause and effect. In the biology laboratory, for example, two identical plants are kept in identical conditions. Temperature, humidity, amount of sunlight, soil type etc. are carefully measured and kept constant for both plants. One variable is then changed for one of the plants, for example it is given more sunlight. The other plant, the 'control', remains as before. Any subsequent differences in the plants (size, speed of growth etc.) should be the result of the differing amounts of sunlight they received as this was the only difference between them. Supporters says controlled experiments are good for establishing cause and effect and they can be replicated to check results too.

Uncontrolled experiments are less rigorous. There is little or no attempt to control the variables involved or to measure effects in quantitative terms. Media studies conducted in the field, rather than in the laboratory, come under this category. An example is a comparison of the behaviour of two groups of children, one with and the other without televisions.

This sort of study is uncontrolled because there are numerous other variables which might affect behaviour other than the presence or absence of a television, but little or no attempt is made to take these into account. Uncontrolled experiments may take the form of experimental field studies (where one or more variables is deliberately changed by the researchers)

---

or correlational studies (where there is no research intervention). The Johnson and Ettema study described below is an example of the first, Belson's study (see p. 114) an example of the second.

### Controlled experiments

Being founded upon a behaviourist model of human learning, controlled experimental studies of the influence of the mass media attempt to identify the ways in which media stimuli influence audience behaviour. They usually disregard what people think about media messages or how they respond to them emotionally. Such studies 'reflect a fundamental neglect of the issue of meaning – both of the "stimulus" and of the "response" it is seen to produce' (Buckingham 1993b, p. 7) The clearest example of this sort of behaviourist experiment is studies of reaction to pornography which have sought only to quantify the degree of erection in men and vaginal lubrication in women (described in Eysenck and Nias (1978) *Sex, Violence and the Media*).

---

### Behaviourism

Behaviourism is a view of learning that concentrates on observable behaviour only: it ignores mental process which cannot be measured. It believes that our behaviour is affected ('conditioned') by stimuli we receive from the environment. We tend to imitate what we see and will repeat any behaviour that is rewarding. Pleasure and pain, reward and punishment are the main influences on us as people in this view.

Behaviourist psychology can be contrasted with cognitive psychology, which is interested in the motivations, emotions and other cognitive processes which go on and influence behaviour. It recognizes that people actively construct meaning from media messages rather than passively receiving a pre-determined meaning.

---

Perhaps the most famous series of controlled experiments are the ones conducted by Bandura, Ross and Ross. They set up the experiment with four groups of children:

- group 1 saw real-life male and female adults attacking a self-righting inflatable doll with mallets;

- group 2 saw a film of male and female adults attacking a self-righting inflatable doll with mallets;

- group 3 saw a TV film of cartoon characters attacking a self-righting inflatable doll with mallets;

- group 4 was the control group. They saw no violent activity.

Following this experience each individual child was deliberately mildly frustrated by being put in a room with a lot of exciting toys but, on beginning to play with them, being told that they were reserved for other children. The child was then put in a room with a doll like those seen by groups 1, 2 and 3. Each child spent twenty minutes in this room being observed by judges seated behind a one-way mirror. They recorded the behaviour of the child, response measures included imitative aggression, partially imitative aggression, mallet aggression, sitting on the doll, non-imitative aggression and aggressive gun play. Bandura *et al.* concluded that:

> aggressive behaviour was sharply higher in each of the model conditions in comparison with the control, and further, that most of this difference was due to the direct imitation of the model's aggressive behaviours. Differences between the various viewing conditions – live, film, and television – were negligible.

Figure 3.6  Ooops!

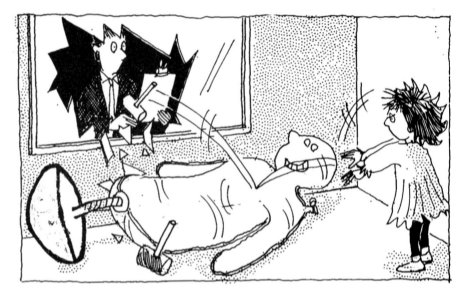

This sort of experiment is out of academic favour today due to its many drawbacks. These include the following.

- A film, viewed in a laboratory, perhaps alone or with a group of strangers, will almost certainly be different in its effects than one viewed at home with the family. The environment itself has an important influence on how one reacts to a stimulus, especially when the environment is as artificial as a university or other laboratory, with film cameras, one-way mirrors etc. The very fact that the subjects are being observed is highly likely to change their behaviour. This is a phenomenon sociologists refer to as the 'Hawthorne effect'.

- Only short-term effects can be studied in a laboratory situation. It is unclear whether any influence remains or fades with time.

- The groups chosen for study are usually unrepresentative, in terms of their social characteristics, of the population at large. Perhaps more important though, is the fact that no researcher has tried to isolate the different personality types and the different ways these may react to a media stimulus.

- The nature of the experiments conducted are usually very artificial themselves. The films shown to subjects are often odd, isolated, violent episodes (adults dressed as cats hitting self-righting dolls with mallets etc.). Then the subjects are put into a room after viewing with the same sort of items seen in the film. Even a young child is likely to get the message that it is expected to repeat the behaviour seen in the film.

- Other people may mediate the influence of films and TV programmes as we saw in the discussion of the normative model.

- The experimental method assumes that the *hypodermic model* of media effect is true. Alternative models are clearly more well-founded. The uses and gratifications, normative and interpretative approaches show us that people watch, listen to and read the media for different reasons, with different amounts of attention and with different pre-existent attitudes and that they interpret media messages in different ways.

 *Using examples of experimental studies reported in Cumberbatch and Howitt (1989), assess the extent to which the following statement is true:*

the 'classic' experiments in this field tend to measure artificial responses to artificial stimuli in artificial situations. They largely ignore the distinction between 'fantasy' and real-life violence, both in the stimulus itself and in the behaviour it is presumed to cause.

(Buckingham 1993, p. 11)

### Uncontrolled experiments

Probably the most famous 'classic' example of an uncontrolled experiment is Himmelweit's early correlational study (Himmelweit 1958). Himmelweit and her colleagues studied 4,500 children from English cities. Some of the children lived in homes with TVs, others without (this was in the early days of television when reception was not possible in much of the country). They carefully matched four groups of children as shown in Figure 3.7.

Questionnaires were given before and after a six-week period and teachers were asked to rate children's behaviour and personality. The influence of TV was found to be:

far less colourful and dramatic than popular opinion is inclined to suppose ... whether TV is good or bad for children depends on the programmes, the amount the child views, the type of child, the type of effects to be examined and the context in which viewing takes place.

Figure 3.7    Groups of children matched in Himmelweit's 1958 study

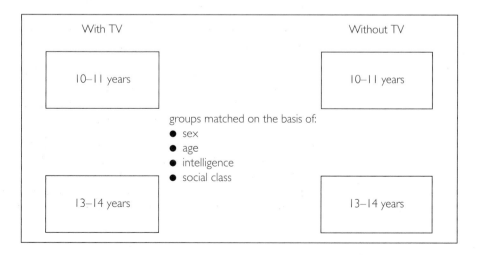

An example of an experimental field study is the one conducted by Johnson and Ettema involving the American programme *Freestyle*. This was created deliberately to be an entertaining way of countering stereotyped images of gender and other roles. Girls were shown displaying independence and being leaders while boys were shown in nurturant roles. Thirteen 30-minute programmes were produced aimed at 9–12 year olds. A large experiment was conducted involving 7,000 children. These were divided into three groups:

1. the 'viewing/discussion group' who watched the programmes at school and then discussed them with the teacher;

2. the 'viewing/school group' who watched the programme at school but with no discussion;

3. the 'viewing/home' group who were encouraged to watch the programmes at home.

The sex-role beliefs, attitudes and interests of the children were measured before and after the series. A sub-sample was re-tested a month after the programmes had finished. The effects were greatest and most long-lasting on the first group with hardly any effect on the third.

 *What are the problems with this study?*
*What advantages does a field study like this one offer over a controlled experiment in the laboratory like that of Bandura, Ross and Ross?*

## The multi-method approach

It seems clear that each method will direct the attention of the researcher to particular aspects of the media: to its content, the audience response and so on. Any one method will thus filter out some aspect of the processes involved in the production, dissemination, reception and influence of the media. David Morley (1978 and 1980) among others has tried to avoid the narrow focus that a single method entails by adopting a multi-method approach. His methodology in the well-known *Nationwide* study incorporated the following elements:

1. collective viewing by a panel of respondents of the television programme *Nationwide* and discussion of it over a period of months;

2. researchers attempt to establish recurrent themes and presentational formats in the programme by content analysis;

3. researchers conduct a detailed analysis of one specific edition of the programme;

4. video of one *Nationwide* programme shown to 18 groups from different social, cultural and educational backgrounds in the Midlands and London; schoolchildren and students in full and part-time further and higher education;

5. video of another *Nationwide* programme shown to 11 groups mainly in London, some with trade union background, others with management background and some students from further and higher education (all groups were in some form of educational setting);

6. subsequent discussion by these 29 groups tape-recorded and transcribed to provide the data for analysis.

The aim was to construct a typology of the range of interpretations ('decodings') made, to analyse how and why they vary and to relate these to other socio-cultural factors like social class.

> While there is some disagreement and argument within the different groups over the decoding of particular items, the differences in decodings between the groups from the different categories is far greater than the level of difference and variation within groups.

(Morley 1992)

 *What problems can you see with the decision to promote group discussion rather than individual interviews?*

> Defining and measuring the effects of television on the public's images of women and men is a complex problem that can only be properly tackled through a multi-faceted research perspective which includes careful study of programmes, audiences, viewing behaviour, and viewers' perceptions of things they see on television. The limitations of much of the research done so far are really to be found in the methods used. Most studies have been uni-dimensional, approaching the subject from one angle, employing one kind of measure and drawing conclusions which their measures do not entitle them to make.

(Gunter 1995, p. 137)

 *Discuss with examples why it is important to take a multi-faceted approach, as Gunter suggests.*
*Take any one study of media influence and assess how far Gunter's theory is true.*

## Problems with media research

To conclude this chapter it is worth reviewing some of the problems that have plagued research on the mass media.

- It tends to take the concepts it uses for granted. For example questions like 'what do we mean by femininity?' or 'what exactly is violence?' are not usually asked by studies on gender representation or violence and the mass media.

- It tends to adopt stereotypical views about the nature of society. For example Morley's research has concentrated on 'traditional' nuclear families and Radway's equates 'woman' with 'housewife'.

- It often adopts simplistic views on social structure. Class and gender are usually proposed as crucial variables, for example, without an appreciation that these are intersected by other factors such as age, sexuality, ethnicity and so on.

- Mass media research tends to be highly gendered. Study of popular culture texts tends to be by and about women while study of news and current affairs tends to be by and about men. For example Jensen looks only at men's reception of the

Figure 3.8

news while Joke Hermes' work on women's magazines looks only at women. This can reproduce stereotypes so that we begin to believe that gender is only constructed in women's media, ignoring the fact that men's gender is constructed in 'their' media too.

● Media research tends, more than other types, to be politically loaded. It stems from the concerns of the researcher – about the representation of women or minority ethnic groups, about the influence of the media on children or whatever. As van Zoonen says:

> Data, whether quantitative or qualitative, do not speak for themselves but are constructed in the research process and the answers to be derived from them are the result of interpretative procedures followed by researchers rather than self-evident, natural knowledge encapsulated in them and waiting to be caught with the appropriate instruments.
>
> (van Zoonen 1994)

An example is the report *Video Violence and Children*, largely conducted by Dr Clifford Hill for the Parliamentary Group Video Enquiry in 1983. Evidence from this was used to support the passage of the Video Recordings Act 1984, especially its conclusion that 'we are priming a time-bomb of violence which will explode on the streets of Britain'. According to the Head of the Television Unit at Oxford Polytechnic (who was close to the report but disassociated himself and the Unit from it) it

> had the feel and used the vocabulary not of a research document, but of a campaigning pamphlet abounding in ... almost hysterical and prophetic assertions and declarations ... It could not be taken as a serious report.

Attempts to clarify the source of the data in the report were largely unfruitful, though the report's claim that 37% of the under-sevens had seen a video nasty seemed to have come from analysis of questionnaire returns from three youngsters. Only 46 returns had been received from this age group at all and only three of these claimed to have seen *any* sort of video film. These three claimed to have seen 17 nasties.

● The media themselves tend to publicize research about sex and violence. However they are highly selective, reporting only what they consider newsworthy. For example Hill's report was carried in great detail in newspapers and TV news. Banner headlines proclaimed the '37% of under-sevens' claim described above. Thus research itself, or at least the way it is reported, can influence the public's perception of the dangers of the mass media and policy about them.

● Researchers take a uni-dimensional approach to the question of the effects of the media. For example in studying the relationship between violence on television and violence in society, they ask 'Does exposure to the first lead to the second?' They ignore other possible consequences of violence on television such as the possibility that witnesses become more likely to report violence or intervene in it, the police become more pro-active, governments take action and so on. Each of these possible effects may in themselves give rise to changes in the actual or perceived level of violence in society. This uni-dimensionality applies to causes as well as effects. Researchers have, for example, concentrated on violent media content as a cause of violent behaviour, but Singer and Singer were surprised to find that heavy viewing of even a prosocial programme like *Sesame Street* seems to have violent effects. They put this down to its 'fast-paced nature', something not previously considered (Singer and Singer 1986).

● Ethnographic studies are dangerous in that they are intrusive and effectively act on behalf of the state in carrying out surveillance of individuals and families:

> It is my proposition that existing accounts of family viewing are deeply regulative, not only in their voyeurism, but also in their claims to tell the truth about the families watched. The knowledge such studies produce needs to be seen as part of the broader regulation of families and the attempt to guard against threats to the existing social and political order presented by the pathological family.
>
> (Walkerdine 1993, p. 74)

*Read Gillespie's study of* The Mahabharata *in Buckingham,* Reading Audiences. *Is this true of that study?*

*Imagine that you have been asked to conduct a study into the portrayal of alcohol and its consumption in television soap opera. The idea is to analyse what messages are conveyed about alcohol and what attitudes towards it might be created or reinforced among the audience. The body funding the research is interested in such details as who is seen drinking alcohol in soaps, why they do it, where and what the consequence of this consumption are. The relevance of alcohol to the plot and stories about the abuse of alcohol are of special interest.*
● *Which methods would you choose and why?*
● *Outline the details of the research – for example, which programmes would you study? what sort of questions would you ask? what sort of people would you interview and how many? what would you look for?*
● *Justify the decisions you have made on these issues. If possible conduct the research.*

### Essays

'The method chosen by the sociologist in studying the mass media will be influenced by both practical and theoretical considerations.'

1. *Discuss this statement, illustrating your answer with examples of studies of the mass media.*

2. *Critically assess any two studies of the mass media.*

## Further reading

Cumberbatch, G. and Howitt, D. (1989) *A Measure of Uncertainty: The Effects of the Mass Media*, London: John Libbey.

Dorothy Hobson 'Women audiences and the workplace', in M. E. Brown (ed.) (1990) *Television and Women's Culture*, London: Sage, pp. 63–4. (Hobson has written extensively on women and is now a full-time writer.)

Gray, A. (1992) *Video Playtime*, London: Routledge.

Gunter, B. and Svennevig, M. (1987) *Behind and in Front of the Screen: Television's Involvement with Family Life*, London: John Libbey.

Haslam, C. and Bryman, A. (1994) *Social Scientists Meet the Media*, London: Routledge.

Jensen, K. and Jankowski, N. (eds) (1991) *A Handbook of Qualitative Methodologies for Mass Communication Research*, London: Routledge.

Miller, N. and Allen, R. (1994) *Broadcasting Enters the Marketplace*, London: John Libbey.

## Useful address

**Broadcasting Standards Council**
7 The Sanctuary
London SW1P 3JS
0101 233 0544

# Perspectives on 'bias' in the media

Figure 4.1

This chapter reviews approaches to bias in the media, examining the answers given by different perspectives on the questions:

● Are the mass media consistently 'biased' in their representations of reality?

● If so, what directions does this operate in?

● What are the reasons for it?

---

**Bias**

The word bias is usually used to mean the deliberate or unconscious distortion or partial reporting of reality so that something is one-sided or incomplete. The problem with the concept is that it assumes:
1. that there is an essential 'truth'; and
2. that it is possible to report this truth in an 'unbiased' way.

Neither is accurate. Even an apparently simple statement like 'the cat sat on the mat' is a partial representation of reality. Despite these problems the word will be used in this chapter to mean consistent and routine distortion through commission or omission. Inverted commas will be used to highlight the problematic nature of the term.

---

'Bias' in the mass media is not very easy to identify. Though it is fairly easy to recognize prejudiced or loaded phrases and questions it is harder to identify *incompleteness* in a news report or a current affairs programme. Sometimes what is *not* said is more important than what is. This was acknowledged by the senior civil servant Robert Armstrong when he admitted that the government had been 'economical with the truth' in their attempts to stop ex-MI5 agent Peter Wright from publishing his revelations about the security service in his book *Spycatcher*. If 'truth' exists then the media, often necessarily, are economical with it.

Studies of routine 'bias' in the media have normally concentrated their attention on news stories. These cover important issues like politics and industrial relations where objectivity is important. This chapter will do the same, though others in the book examine other types of media production.

The chapter examines three perspectives on media 'bias'; the manipulative, hegemonic and pluralist models, first giving an overview of the models, then examining the arguments and evidence in favour of them.

## The manipulative model: an outline

> The class which has the means of material production has control at the same time of the means of mental production ... they regulate the production and distribution of the ideas of their age: thus their ideas are the ruling ideas of the epoch.
>
> (Marx, *The German Ideology*, p. 39)

The manipulative model derives from a crude version of Marxism. It sees the capitalist class and government, who represent their interests according to this approach, acting in a conscious and direct way to maintain the status quo and deny the working class true understanding of its own interests and of how it is being exploited. At the same time, of course, the media are a source of profit to capitalists and are a means of production in that sense too. However, capitalists sometimes buy unprofitable media businesses just to control the means of production of ideas.

The manipulative model says that mass media manipulation is occurring in two senses:

- the content of the mass media is manipulated by those who own and control the institutions of broadcasting and the press, the men (and occasionally women) at the very top and their representatives;

- the hearts and minds of the audience are manipulated through this quite conscious control.

Thus, those at the top of the very small number of companies which own the media institutions use them for their own purposes. The media allow the rich and powerful to become richer and more powerful. The manipulative model is thus based on a conspiracy theory.

---

*Conspiracy theory*

The idea that a small group of individuals knowingly and secretly conspire to promote their own interests against those of the general population. The manipulative model is an example.

---

# The hegemonic model: an outline

Figure 4.2

The hegemonic model is a more sophisticated version of Marxism developed by Antonio Gramsci, the Italian Marxist, and it is also associated with the work of Nicos Poulantzas and Louis Althusser. 'Hegemony' means the dominance in society of one set of ideas. This view sees ideology as more important than the crude pursuit of economic interests. Thus people (journalists and others) act in a genuine way according to their beliefs and these are not necessarily determined by (though they are linked to) their class position. Dominance here is accomplished at the unconscious level. In this view the mass media are part of the 'ideological state apparatus' to use Althusser's term.

The hegemonic model says that the media in Britain help to recruit and maintain support for a single set of attitudes, ignoring others of equal validity. These, then, become seen by most people as 'normal' or 'just common sense'. Such opinions are not spread in a conscious and cynical way. They are simply what those who work in the media consider to be reasonable and true. This is because journalists, editors and so on come from a very small section of society. They tend to be white, male, middle-class and middle-aged. In other words they are a relatively privileged group. Because of this limited social standpoint the attitudes expressed through the mass media tend to involve (among other things):

● approval of business and the creation of wealth;

● condemnation of excessive trade union powers or militancy;

● preference for middle-of-the-road politics;

● support for the monarchy;

● suspicion of feminist women, minority ethnic groups, young people, the working class, radicals, gays, protesters (unless they are middle class), strikers and so on;

● support for parliamentary democracy.

Generating people's approval for these ideas means that things go on much as they always have done. No voice is given to those who wish to change things in a radical way.

So far this sounds quite similar to the manipulative model. The differences between the two are as follows.

● The manipulative model argues that owners control media content. The hegemonic model argues that journalists, editors and managers do.

● The manipulative model argues that media 'bias' is consciously introduced whereas the hegemonic model says that it is unconscious (it stems from the attitudes of the people who work in the media).

● The manipulative model derives from a fairly rigid Marxist position which sees society as divided clearly between the capitalists and the proletariat. The hegemonic model sees society as broken up into an almost unlimited number of groups, each possessing a distinctive set of attitudes thanks to its social position (middle-class professionals, gays, women, the working class, etc.).

● The manipulative model takes a simple approach to 'bias': it is a clear distortion of reality promoted in the interests of a specific group. The hegemonic model acknowledges that all representations of reality are partial and that media representations are no more 'biased' than any other. This model is simply interested in uncovering the particular nature of mass media representations and their effects.

 *Sometimes it is difficult to distinguish between the manipulative and hegemonic models. In the following quote I would argue that Lull is expressing the manipulative model, not the hegemonic one (despite the chapter title 'Ideology, consciousness, hegemony'). Would you agree?*

The ongoing manipulation of public information and imagery constructs a potent *dominant ideology* which helps sustain the material and cultural interests of its creators. Fabricators of dominant ideologies become an 'information élite'. Their power, or dominance, stems directly from their ability to publicly articulate their preferred system of ideas.

(Lull 1995, p. 7)

## The pluralist model: an outline

Pluralism, by contrast to the other two, is based on an approach close to Weberianism and functionalism. Its Weberianism can be seen in its view of society as divided not only by class (itself heavily subdivided) but by status and power. The different parts of the mass media cater for these various fragments of society without operating in or expressing the interests of any one. Its functionalism can be seen in its view that the mass media perform social functions such as socializing people, informing and entertaining them and helping them to communicate with others.

The pluralist model simply says that while there *is* 'bias' in the media this is perfectly acceptable because:

- the nature of the 'bias' is determined by audience choice – that is, what the market wants, and

- there is a large number (a 'plurality') of media outlets, many of them adopting different types of 'bias' for a different audience.

For example, it is quite clear that the popular newspapers over-report sex crimes relative to their proportion compared to other types of crime. However, there is no sinister reason for this. It is simply that this is what its readers want. Sections of the public who don't share that taste can turn to another newspaper (for example the *Independent*). 'Bias', then, lies in the audience, not in the mass media.

Table 4.1 summarizes the process of news production according to the three models:

Table 4.1     Three models of news production

| *Manipulative model* | *Hegemonic model* | *Pluralist model* |
|---|---|---|
| **Hearing about the event** <br> Largely from and about *official* sources: parliament, the church, royalty, official 'diary' events, local government, central government departments. Ordinary people are ignored for 'serious' news. A limited number of capitalist press agencies supply (and virtually monopolize) a large amount of news. These include Reuters, Agence France Presse, United Press International and Associated Press. | **Hearing about the event** <br> Largely from and about *official* sources: parliament, the church, royalty, official 'diary' events, local government, central government departments. Ordinary people are ignored for 'serious' news. Financial, technical and time limitations mean that stories are largely London-based and from sources which are considered reliable and which have the resources to provide useful information quickly. | **Hearing about the event** <br> Casual sources, 'stringers', other media, aggrieved citizens, fire brigade, the courts, the police, the services, press conferences, press releases, companies, unions, pressure groups, local councils, the government, 'diary' events, investigative reporting. In short a variety of sources which lead to a heterogeneous news content. Some sources are using the media to 'axe grind', but these are balanced by other axe-grinders of the opposite persuasion. The media present them all impartially. |
| **Assessing it for inclusion in the news** <br> A considerable amount of self-censorship occurs by journalists who have already been carefully chosen for their views. They will ignore or give a slanted angle on stories which will rock the boat too much (i.e. threaten those with power and influence). They will choose stories which fit the pattern of items on themes such as social security scroungers, 'travellers' trying to organise rock festivals or anti-nuclear protests, football hooligans etc. Newspaper journalists ensure that the tone of the story fits the editorial policy of their newspaper. Proprietors and/or the government will interfere by adding or censoring stories where journalists are thought not to be doing this 'properly'. | **Assessing it for inclusion in the news** <br> It will be included if it is considered newsworthy. Newsworthiness is judged from the journalist's perspective; usually that of a white, middle class and London-based male (or at least what such a person judges other people to to be interested in). | **Assessing it for inclusion in the news** <br> The assessment of 'newsworthiness' will depend on the nature of the medium: <br><br> In the popular press news values relate to scandal, sex and sensation (particularly where personalities and conflict are involved) <br><br> In television, news values relate to visual appeal, balance, audience interest, and conflict. <br><br> In the broadsheet press news values relate to immediacy of the issue with in-depth coverage. <br><br> On radio, news values relate to balance and immediacy. |

| Manipulative model | Hegemonic model | Pluralist model |
|---|---|---|
| **Preparing the story for the media** In the press the story will be angled to fit the editorial policy of the newspaper. Important parts of the story may be left out if they represent a threat to the establishment (for example the reasons behind an industrial dispute, criticism of British political institutions etc.). In television the process of editing news film will result in a version which encourages the viewer to side with the forces of law and order, with the government and the establishment. Dissenting views will be characterized as coming from irrational people bent on destruction. Proprietors and/or the government will interfere in the editorial process if they feel that their interests or views are threatened. | **Preparing the story for the media** The story will be interpreted according to the world view of the person writing the story/preparing the item. This view will be 'encoded' in the language, camera shots, interviews, quotes, questions etc. | **Preparing the story for the media** The most interesting parts are selected and emphasized, these are the ones which are most relevant in some way to most of the people (e.g. the effects of a strike rather than the events which led up to it – people are more interested in the former because it is likely to affect them). |
| **Disseminating the message** The institutions available to disseminate the message are few in number and either owned by capitalists or controlled by the government. Thus the means of dissemination are restricted to established media. Distribution of newspapers to newsagents is virtually a monopoly. Controls on the dissemination of information, such as the Official Secrets Act, D notices etc operate to protect the rich and the powerful. The rich can afford to take out libel actions if they object to media coverage. This option is not open to the average citizen. | **Disseminating the message** The common background of journalists means that a similar message is transmitted no matter what the medium and despite the apparent variety of institutions in the press and publishing media. In order to appeal to the largest number of people the message is aimed at the lowest common denominator. Advertisers demand that the interests of the affluent minority are catered for in a wide range of media aimed solely at them. | **Disseminating the message** Anything can be published unless it is obscene ('liable to deprave or corrupt') or seditious (anything that brings the Royal Family into hatred or contempt or excites disaffection against the sovereign or constitution) or libellous (a false and defamatory statement) or is in contravention of the Official Secrets Act. Anything which displays 'due impartiality' and is not obscene etc can be broadcast by the officially approved media institutions. |
| **Audience choice** Despite the apparent wide variety of media outlets there is in fact little real audience choice. Media ownership is now heavily monopolized in all fields. Public service broadcasting is increasingly being squeezed into a corner by commercial enterprises. Most large circulation newspapers are right wing. | **Audience choice** There is no real audience choice. The same sort of people are involved in all the different types of mass media. As a result there is only one world view propagated through the mass media. This is usually the dominant ('hegemonic') one, though at times and in some media it may differ slightly from what those in positions of political power believe. | **Audience choice** Wide selection is available, particularly in the published media, but also in the broadcast media, especially since the advent of Channel 4, local radio stations (both commercial and BBC), national commercial radio stations, cable TV, satellite TV and video. The franchise for a fifth national television channel has been awarded and the future application of digital television technology will mean that there will be space in the airwaves for many more channels broadcast terrestrially. |

| Manipulative model | Hegemonic model | Pluralist model |
|---|---|---|
| **Effect on the audience** | **Effect on the audience** | **Effect on the audience** |
| With no scope for the expression of dissenting ideas in the media it is hardly surprising if the effect on the audience is to generate attitudes which are both uncritical and supportive of the status quo. | Alternative world views/experiences/ attitudes are undermined. No expression is given for them, their value is denied. The hegemony of the dominant ideology is generally preserved and strengthened. | Selective exposure (to the media) Selective perception (of the message) Selective retention (of the message) The combined effect of these means that the media have little effect other than reinforcing previously held views. |

## The manipulative model: argument and evidence

> God made people read so that I could fill their brains with facts, facts, facts – and later tell them whom to love, whom to hate, and what to think.
>
> (Lord Northcliffe)

> I run the paper purely for the purpose of propaganda, and with no other motive.
>
> (Lord Beaverbrook)

> I think it would be very unlikely that I would have a paper that would support the socialist party. That isn't what some people would call press freedom, but why should I want a product I don't approve of? I believe it is in the best interests of United Newspapers in terms of profits and shareholders to support the Conservatives.
>
> (Lord Stevens, Chair of United Newspapers)

> Rupert Murdoch was an enormous presence in my life. Even when he wasn't there he was this sort of looming presence ... I think that's how he does control things. He leaves you in no doubt that if he's not there in person he's there in spirit and he's watching what you are up to and you've got to stick to the parameters. The idea that he doesn't interfere is nonsense.
>
> (Andrew Neil, former editor of the *Sunday Times*)

The manipulative model states that the rich and powerful class who own or control the media use them in their own political and financial interests and broadly to maintain a status quo which is highly beneficial for them. Radical ideas are suppressed, ridiculed or ignored. Attention is diverted from serious issues by a constant diet of trivia (television personalities, sexy stories and pictures, big-prize games, stories about the rich etc.). The real foci of power are ignored and the attention of the audience is centred instead on institutions where power no longer resides (parliament, the monarchy, local government).

In many developing and socialist countries the media *are* consciously used for social engineering and control by the state. In Britain, though, the press is privately owned and relatively unregulated by the state. Manipulation in this sector of the media is

Figure 4.3

# Key Players in the Global Media

### Lord Hollick

Born 1946, Labour Peer and Chief Executive of MAI. Bought a bankrupted company at 29 while he was working for merchant bank Hambros. Since then has built successful financial services and media company. Took over Anglia TV in 1994 at a cost of £292 million. MAI agreed to merge with United News and Media in February 1996.

### Lord Stevens

Born in 1936, Chairman of United News and Media. Has been a key player in Express Newspapers for 15 years after a career in the City. United News and Media agreed to merge with MAI in February 1996.

### Silvio Berlusconi

Born in 1936, Berlusconi became Prime Minister of Italy after using his Fininvest media empire to promote the free enterprise political party he invented from nothing, Forza Italia (named after a football chant). Later subject to investigation for corruption. Owns three Italian TV channels, newspaper *Il Giornale* and Italy's biggest publisher, Mondadori, which produces between a quarter and a third of Italy's books and magazines. Is said to be fastidious about his personal appearance and will not permit business collaborators to wear a beard or moustache.

### Leo Kirch

The son of a wine-grower and holding a doctorate from Munich University, he is nicknamed Fernsehkirch in Germany (Television-church/Kirch). As the name suggests, he is the uncrowned head of German television, having large stakes in 4 TV channels (SAT 1, PRO 7, DSF and Premiere) and has ambitions to control Springer newspapers and develop a multi-media empire in Germany.

He is a close ally of Chancellor Kohl and oversaw the introduction of *Your Views Chancellor!* on Sat 1.

### Rupert Murdoch

'King of the media moguls'. Chairman and Chief Executive of News Corporation. Born 1931 in Australia with Scottish and Irish parentage. Father, Sir Keith, was a newspaper baron and Rupert inherited the business. Went to Oxford but hated the elitism and is said to dislike establishment institutions and figures. Said to be modest, charming and frugal as a person.

Figure 4.4

# Key Companies in the UK Media

## Pearson
(Lord Blakenham, Chairman)

Financial Times
Penguin Books
Addison-Wesley Longman
Mindscape
Pearson Television
Pearson New Entertainment

## Associated Newspapers
(Sir David English, Chairman)

Daily Mail
Mail on Sunday
Evening Standard
Second largest owner of
regional newspapers
(via Northcliffe Newspapers Group)
Channel One (cable channel)
Stakes in Teletext,
local radio,
West Country TV

## MAI and United News and Media
(merged in 1996)
(Lord Stevens, Chairman and
Lord Hollick Chief Executive):

Control of Anglia and
Meridian ITV franchise stations
Daily Express
Sunday Express
Star
80 Regional Newspapers including the
Yorkshire Post, Lancashire Evening Post
Several magazines
30% stake in Channel 5 (new TV station)
Advertising periodicals, eg Exchange and Mart,
Dalton's Weekly
Business and media information services,
eg NOP, PR Newswire

## News Corporation
(Rupert Murdoch, Chairman and Chief Executive)

News International

Sun
Times
News of the World
Sunday Times
News International (News Corp. subsidiary) has 37% of
UK national newsaper circulation (1995)
HarperCollins
40% of BSkyB
20th Century Fox, including Fox TV
New York Post
TV Guide
49.9% of Vox satellite and terrestrial TV channel
99% of Star TV, covering India, China, Japan, Philippines,
Thailand and Hong Kong
Numerous newspapers and groups in Australia plus 15%
of Channel 7 there

## EMAP
Around 100 regional newspapers
Around 150 consumer and business magazines
Owns or has stakes in Radio City, Kiss FM and other
commercial stations

## Carlton Communications
(Michael Green, Chairman)

**CARLTON**

Carlton London Weekday
Central TV
Stakes in GMTV, ITN and London News Network
Carlton video and film production and processing
Carlton Books
Carlton Cabletime

## Mirror Group
(David Montgomery, Chief Executive)

Daily Mirror
The People
Daily Record
Sporting Life
43% of the Independent and Independent on Sunday
Live TV and Wire TV (cable channels)
40% of Scottish TV

---

Key sources for the current position on media and cross-media ownership are:

| **British Media Information Group** | **Campaign for Press and Broadcasting Freedom** | **Department of National Heritage** |
|---|---|---|
| 7 The Sanctuary Parliament Square London 0171 799 1500 | 8 Cynthia Street London N1 9JF 0171 278 4430 | (Broadcasting Policy Division) 2-4 Cockspur St London SW1Y 5DH 0171 211 6466 |

The current edition of Steve Peak's *The Media Guide*, London: Fourth Estate is particularly useful. As well as giving an overview of the current situation, this book gives addresses of companies. Write for their current annual reports.

done by the 'media barons' like Rupert Murdoch. The broadcasting media, on the other hand, are indirectly controlled by the state. The state and capitalist interest, thus, work hand-in-hand.

Let's look at some of the evidence put forward by supporters of this theory to show that it is true.

1. Ownership of the mass media is concentrated in a few companies and monopolization of the mass media is continuing to occur very rapidly. Time Warner, Sony, Matsushita, Phillips and Thorn EMI are huge organizations operating globally with increasing control over 'hardware' (CD and other technologies) and 'software' (creative work of all sorts including music and the artists who create it). Smaller media organizations have been bought by these mammoths, though their names continue, masking the monopolization which has taken place. CBS was bought by Sony, Virgin Records by Matsushita, for example.

Surprisingly often (and unlike other sorts of business) large media corporations are largely owned and controlled by one person. In the past such people were called 'press barons' (Lord Northcliffe and Lord Beaverbrook are British examples). Today the interests of such people usually extend beyond the press and so they are called 'media barons', though they are less likely to be British and so unlikely to have or receive titles and honours (though Lord Stevens and Lord Rothermere are exceptions). Kirch and Bertelsmann (both based in Germany), Berlusconi (based in Italy) and Murdoch (originally Australian, now a naturalized American) are obvious examples of international media barons.

---

### *Globalization*

Waters (1995) defines this as 'a social process in which the constraints of geography on social and cultural arrangements recede and in which people become increasingly aware that they are receding'. The world has become a very small place as a result of technology, particularly information technology, and the mass media, and people now perceive it to be small. World cultures are becoming increasingly similar and there is a common cultural language. Capitalist monopolization has an important part in this (people sometimes talk about the Coca-Colonization of the world to make this point). See Featherstone (1990) and Waters (1995) for more on this.

---

*Current patterns of ownership in the media can be identified easily by referring to Benn's Media Directory and Willing's Press Guide (see further reading), and by writing to media companies for their current annual report. Their addresses can be found in the above directories. Use this information to establish a database – on a computer if you have access to one – on media ownership.*

2. Media conglomerates now span the globe and are involved in so many aspects of the media that governments are more or less powerless to stop them. Rupert Murdoch's News Corporation is the second largest media conglomerate in the world (after Time-Warner) and is particularly interesting from a British perspective as the British offshoot, News International, is so important here. As well as its British

Figure 4.5 Star TV's footprint

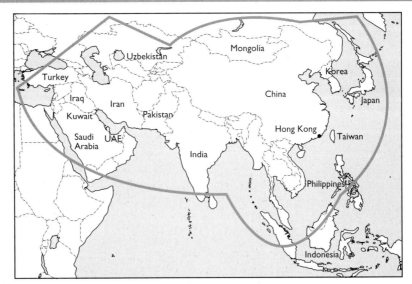

companies News Corporation owns Star TV based in Hong Kong, a satellite which broadcasts five channels to two-thirds of the world's population in Asia and the Middle East, Fox TV, and around three-quarters of Australia's newspapers.

Cross-media laws in Australia make it difficult for News Corporation to get into television there. As this illustrates, Australia is a country where the government has tried more than most to ensure that there is a competitive environment in the media. However even there there is a sense of despondency about what governments can do. Prime minister of Australia Paul Keating expressed his frustration to ABC's *Lateline* in October 1994 about Murdoch and the technologies he controls:

> Star is now actually going to broadcast from the Middle East to the Russian Far East and down to Queensland. Now what are you going to do about that? Poke your tongue out at it? Throw a Bill up in the air? Table a motion in the House?

3. Even if they had the ability to limit the power of media conglomerates and media barons, governments can no longer afford to do so. Such is their power to manipulate public opinion, government leaders know that to cross them can be dangerous. The better course is often to become friends with media magnates and get them, and the media they control, on your side. MP and ex-minister David Mellor says that Mrs Thatcher needed Murdoch's support and so let him dominate the press. Certainly legislation passed during Thatcher's premiership restricted the power of the Monopolies and Mergers Commission to stop his expansion across the British media. Labour has put a hold on its commitment to an inquiry into Murdoch's media interests. *The Times* editor Charles Douglas-Home said that Murdoch was seen as one of 'the main powers behind the Thatcher throne'. In 1984 he said:

> Rupert and Mrs Thatcher consult regularly on every important matter of policy, especially as they related to his economic and political interests. Around here he's jokingly referred to as 'Mr Prime Minister', except that it's no longer much of a joke. In many respects he *is* the phantom Prime Minister of the country.

(Belfield and Hird, 1991)

In America it was the same story. Congressman Jack Kemp said at a dinner in 1981 that 'Rupert used the editorial page and every other page necessary to elect Ronald Reagan President' and Reagan sent Murdoch a presidential plaque thanking him for his help after he was inaugurated in 1981 (Belfield and Hird 1991, p. 114).

4. Extensive media ownership means that political influence can be even more direct than this too. In mid-1994 Italian media baron Silvio Berlusconi, through his company Fininvest, owned three of Italy's 12 channels (Canale 5, Rete 4 and Italia 1), with a 40% share of the audience. His brother owned Il Giornale, but it is effectively controlled by Silvio. After deciding to create a new right-wing political party, Forza Italia, and stand for election he used this media ownership to full advantage. Italy's equivalent of Desmond Lynam, Raimondo Vianello of *Pressing*, a Sunday night sports show, declared on the programme that he was voting for Berlusconi. The coverage of Forza Italia's election campaigns on those channels has been described as 'slavish' (*Guardian*, 30 March 1994).

Though Italy bans political advertising and insists on equal coverage one month before an election, Berlusconi bent the rules with anchormen saying they would vote for him (though two brave souls on Channel 5 said they wouldn't). One young household-name star said, 'God is for Berlusconi and Satan is for Occhetto' (his opponent) and a series of vox-pop street interviews was broadcast in which nearly everyone was planning to vote for Forza Italia (this was banned by the media ombudsman one day before the election). Berlusconi went on to win and become the country's PM, head of a party, predictably enough, which was against state intervention and in favour of business freedom. Its success was achieved despite the fact that it had made no attempt at mass membership and had virtually no representation on the ground. Berlusconi's party has been described as 'a media confection' (Hutton 1994).

 *Use the* British Humanities Index *to find out all you can about Berlusconi. Look under his name under the subject index section of the index.*

5. There is strong evidence that newspaper proprietors always have and continue to intervene editorially with their papers. Such men as William Randolph Hearst (subject of the film *Citizen Kane*), Lord Beaverbrook, Lord Northcliffe and his brother Lord Rothermere were quite open about their desire to manipulate the papers they owned and their ability to do so (examples are given in Cudlipp 1980).

Today's media barons are in the same mould. They remove editors whose point of view they do not agree with. Mike Gabbert, editor of the *Star*, was sacked by Lord Stevens in 1987 for taking it too far down-market. Its increasingly high nipple-count and its nickname of the *Daily Bonk* eventually became too much for Lord Stevens. He felt that its 'girlie magazine' image did not fit with his new status as a peer. Editor Eve Pollard was also allegedly sacked for being too critical of Lady Stevens' friend Princess Diana (see Leapman 1994). The late Robert Maxwell, then head of Mirror Group Newspapers, was interviewing Magnus Linklater for the job of editor of the *London Daily News*, was in the middle of explaining that he did not interfere editorially when the editor of the *Daily Mirror* entered with a proof of page one from that paper for Maxwell's approval! Roy Greenslade, editor of the *Daily Mirror* between 1989 and 1991, tells many stories of Maxwell's manipulation of that paper in his 1992 book *Maxwell's Fall*.

Rupert Murdoch is well known for intervening in editorial policy. He sacked Harold

Evans, editor of *The Times*, and Stafford Somerfield, editor of the *News of the World*, after disagreements over policy. Frank Giles, former editor of the *Sunday Times*, has said that when Murdoch was in London he would make a point of dropping into his office on Saturday evenings just to check on the first copies of the paper as they were being delivered to Giles.

6. A common feature of media content in parts of the media owned by media magnates is their lightweight content: girls, glitter, star prizes and celebrities are the usual diet. This is true of Berlusconi's channels in Italy and the News International newspapers and programmes in the UK. Even *The Times* has moved in this direction:

> Before Murdoch took over the *Sunday Times*, the journalists defined a good story as one that someone, somewhere does not want you to read. This approach is incomprehensible to Murdoch. His journalism is about pap, dressed up as sensationalism. Why try to interpret and understand the world, when a good piece of fiction, a well-turned headline or a carefully cropped photo will do the trick?

> (Belfield and Hird 1991, p. 9)

Figure 4.6 'NO NEWS IS GOOD NEWS'

The same was happening abroad. The American magazine *TV Guide* used to campaign on issues, question why certain issues were ignored by the TV networks and include a considerable amount of serious material. The Murdoch team changed all this when they arrived after News Corporation's purchase of the magazine: 'They just wanted fluff', said one long-serving journalist. What had been critical and investigative journalism became advertorials: a platform for advertising.

7. The *distribution and delivery* as well as the production of the mass media lies in a few powerful hands. Newspaper delivery is concentrated in the hands of two companies, TNT and Newsflow. News Corporation has a 12% share of TNT which delivers 40% of newspapers. Newsflow, a subsidiary of the National Freight corporation, delivers the rest.

Three wholesalers – WH Smith, John Menzies and Surridge Dawson – control most

of newspaper distribution in the UK. WH Smith have 53% of the newspaper wholesaling business, Menzies 28% and Surridge Dawson 19%. Even the poster industry is now strongly monopolized with a contraction from 20 to just four poster site contractors between 1986 and 1990.

8. Evidence of *government* manipulation of the media is not difficult to find. Political correspondents know that prime ministers have consistently sought to use the media to strengthen their own position and to reinforce secrecy of government. 'Spin doctors' such as the Conservatives' Director of Presentation from 1986–91, Harvey Thomas, try to ensure that stories appear in the best possible light.

Tricks are used to try to ensure that the media report stories in the desired way. One example is including sound bites in speeches – short snappy phrases that will make good headlines. One example is Mrs Thatcher's 'You turn if you want to. The lady's not for turning.' When John Major resigned the leadership of the Conservative party in June 1995 he noticeably stressed the phrase directed at his critics 'It's time to put up or shut up', signalling a sound bite to the assembled correspondents. More routinely, lobby correspondents are fed material which makes their job easier, on condition that they do not reveal the source. The prime minister's press secretary is usually referred to as 'sources close to the prime minister' for example.

The government can use its representatives on the 'D' notice committee (D for defence, supposedly looking after national security) to stop the publication of material it believes to be against the defence interests of the country, as happened when the chairman of the committee 'phoned the Reuters news agency and told them not to file a story about the position of the *Canberra* during the Falklands dispute. However, informal (and secret) pressure is usually the most effective. For example, Mrs Thatcher visited the Falkland Islands unexpectedly in January 1983. For security reasons it had not been announced in advance and as a result there was only one camera team there, a BBC one (despite loud hints which had been dropped by the Government to ITN).

Wishing to make as much political capital out of the visit as possible, the PM's press secretary, Bernard Ingham, asked the BBC to share their film with ITN. The BBC refused. There then followed a radio-telephone conversation between Ingham and Alan Protheroe, the assistant director general of the BBC. Fortunately for us it was picked up by a radio ham in the Falklands. Mr Ingham said that there would be 'incalculable consequences' if the BBC did not share its film material with ITN. This seemed to be a direct threat of political repercussions for the BBC. Mr Ingham told Mr Protheroe, 'No film is coming out tonight unless I have your absolute assurance that it will be freely available to ITN and IRN.'

Eventually Mr Protheroe gave in and as a result TV and radio were full of long reports showing the Prime Minister windswept on the rugged island hillsides, joyfully receiving good wishes from Falklanders, and tearfully placing wreaths on the graves of fallen British soldiers. This did wonders for her political image.

The Government has the power of appointment of the BBC's Board of Governors and of the Independent Broadcasting Authority. Such appointments are made by 'the Queen in council', which in effect means the PM with the advice of the Home Secretary and occasionally the cabinet. The Board of Governors is surprisingly powerful; it appoints all the top BBC people, and has considerable powers of censorship, though the Director General and the Board of Management is in day-to-

day control. Bodies like these are highly unrepresentative and out of touch. The Controller of Channel 4, Michael Grade, has described the Broadcasting Standards Council as 'highly unrepresentative, middle-aged, middle class, busybody do-gooders [who] ... talk to people like themselves at dinner parties' (*Sunday Times Magazine*, 6 August 1995, p. 33).

In October 1986, Marmaduke Hussey was appointed Chairman of the Board of Governors, an appointment described as 'outrageous and provocative' by the Labour Party due to his family ties with a cabinet minister, his connections with Rupert Murdoch's union-bashing at *The Times* and the commonly held view that he was appointed to 'sort out' the BBC. Shortly after Hussey's appointment the Director General of the BBC, Alasdair Milne, was sacked. This followed a series of disputes with the government over such programmes as *Real Lives*, *Panorama*'s *Maggie's Militant Tendency* and *Secret Society*, which had culminated in a police raid on BBC offices in Scotland to recover evidence for a possible prosecution of journalist Duncan Campbell and/or the BBC under the Official Secrets Act. Milne was replaced by Michael Checkland, known as an efficient but uncontroversial administrator who was himself replaced by John Birt (see Chapter 1).

Control over the licence fee is another method through which the Government can exercise pressure on the BBC. A. Hetherington, a former editor of the *Guardian* and Controller of BBC Scotland, writes:

> discreet government pressure or informal persuasion is more likely to succeed [than direct pressure], and sensitivity to official attitudes must at times have influenced internal decisions. That has been particularly evident when the BBC's licence fee, its main source of revenue, is about to be settled. The mood of caution in the nine months before [a licence fee] settlement – never made explicit but amounting to 'don't upset Downing Street' – was something that I experienced within the BBC at the time.
>
> (Hetherington 1985)

## The hegemonic model: argument and evidence

> The images on our television screens are the means ... of conveying an ideology: that view of society which has been evolved to provide a seemingly rational and therefore unquestionable explanation of how it works and of the power relationships within it.
>
> (S. Hood, 1980, former editor of BBC TV News)

> the world view of journalists will pre-structure what is to be taken as important or significant ... it will affect the character and content of ... the news.
>
> (Glasgow University Media Group, 1980)

> news naturalises the (fairly narrow) terrain on which sectional ideologies can contend – it constantly maps the limits of controversy.
>
> (Hartley 1982)

The hegemonic model basically argues that the media portray only one view of the world (or *Weltanschauung*). It is the one subscribed to by society's privileged classes and it is the dominant, or hegemonic, set of ideas. The way we think and what appears to be common sense are pre-structured for us by the media so that they are in line with this *Weltanschauung*. Subordinate world views are allowed expression, but greater weight is given to the 'establishment' view. Indeed, allowing this apparent debate between, say, the views of the unions and those of management helps to build consensus in society. However, it is a consensus built around the dominant, hegemonic ideology. Some views are rendered acceptable, normal or common sense. Others are seen as extremist, irrational, meaningless, utopian or impractical.

---

### Cultural reproduction

Associated with the hegemonic theory, this concept relates to the mainte-nance and perpetuation of the norms, values and ways of thinking of a society, including the dominant (or hegemonic) ideology, in this case by the mass media.

---

Hegemonic theorists admit that the media in Britain are not, as a rule, directly commanded and organized by the state, neither do they directly speak for the ruling class. The reason for the 'bias' in the media lies in the media professionals themselves. Media personnel are middle-class, affluent people (usually men) who tend to take a 'reasonable', consensus-oriented view on most issues. Thus they will generally be Liberal Democrats, moderate Conservatives or middle-of-the-road Labour supporters and against extremism in any form. Because they are in the political centre, they have been attacked by both the left and the right (see Norman Tebbit's comments on p. 5).

 *Buy all of today's tabloid newspapers (the* Sun, *the* Star, *etc.). Choose a headline story on the front page of one of them. Identify the elements in it which make it 'newsworthy'. Classify all the stories in the papers into different categories and use these to identify the elements of newsworthiness in general which journalists and editors use. Identify the 'pattern' stories – i.e. one of a type which crop up regularly. Why does the type of story you have identified so regularly appear in the popular press?*

The natural political inclinations of writers, journalists and editors are reinforced by secondary socialization into the culture of the press and broadcasting media. They learn how strikes, for example, 'should' be treated (e.g. on TV it is considered best to use interesting film of the effects strikes have rather than boring talking heads discussing their causes). The content of virtually all the media reflects the perspective of the dominant group in society; white, male and middle-class. Their hegemony is reinforced by media output – other, 'minority' views are seen as odd or peripheral. Sally Cline, once a journalist and woman's editor on a Fleet Street tabloid but now an active feminist, admits that:

> I tried … to be taken seriously. This meant I could not write about women or women's concerns … I followed stereotypes of masculini-ty and femininity. If the women I interviewed broke the pattern, secretly I admired them and in print I lightly mocked them … Each

of my editors assured me that I wrote with what they termed 'sparkle'. This meant I was shallow, predictable and harmless … Then, as now, I recognized that language can be used as a means of changing reality, but as a journalist I rarely tried to use it that way. On the occasions when I did, my copy would be spiked and my column would simply not appear … I learnt to use it competently in order to belittle and betray blacks and homosexuals (these usually by omission), the working classes (these through stereotyping) and women (systematically through all available means).

Hegemonic theorists such as Stuart Hall argue that those involved in the media unconsciously encode the dominant ideology when they create output for the media. This process involves selecting codes which put suitable meanings onto events and stories. The codes embody the 'natural' explanations which most members of their society would accept (that is, which appear naturally to embody the 'rationality' of a particular society). This process of encoding the dominant ideology, of giving weight to the views of the wealthy and powerful, is sometimes masked by professional values (news values, news sense, lively presentation, exciting pictures, good stories, hot news, good jokes). However these values themselves incorporate the dominant ideology. Decoding the messages in the media is a technique referred to as semiology. It is described in detail in Chapter 3 and elsewhere in this book.

Let's briefly look at some of the evidence put forward by supporters of this theory to show that it is true. More detail on studies with this perspective can be found in Chapter 8.

1. Evidence from careful studies shows that the media do set the agenda, set up a hierarchy of access etc. For example, in the pre-Second World War economic depression the peaceful and non-political Jarrow Hunger March was given a great deal of publicity while less 'civic', more political marches such as those organized by the Unemployed Workmen's Association were ignored by the press and cinema newsreels at the time.

2. Journalists are socialized into the culture of the institution for which they work. They quickly come to learn how stories should be presented and which are the important issues that should be reported. When a new entrant to a commercial television company or the BBC begins work he or she quickly learns to think about how their immediate superior will react to a particular story or approach. In case of doubt the policy is always to refer upwards. Newspapers have their own distinct culture too, though in this case also there are clear links with the dominant culture in society at large. In view of this it is not surprising that a past political editor of the *Sun*, Anthony Shrimsley, later became the Conservative Party's press and public relations officer or that David English received a knighthood 'for services to journalism'. As editor of the *Daily Mail* English was responsible for the such front pages as LABOUR'S DIRTY DOZEN in the 1979 election.

 *Choose a news item from tonight's television news. Try rewriting the same story from a different perspective to that adopted by the editors and journalists of the news. For example, a story about inner-city riots from the perspective of the people involved, or a strike from that of the trade unionists involved.*

3. While there are a number of different news organizations even in broadcasting, the content of the news is remarkably similar. It is highly unlikely that this consensus about what constitutes 'news' and how it should be treated would exist if those involved in the media did not share a common world view.

*Watch the news broadcasts at: 6.00 (BBC) 7.00 (Channel 4) 10.00 (ITV) (this may be done only on one night or on successive nights, say for a week).*

*Make a careful note of:*
1. *the type of stories they carry;*
2. *the amount of time devoted to each story;*
3. *how the story was covered (e.g. newsreader, interview, outside broadcast etc.);*
4. *the overall 'tone' of the presentation (favourable, critical, neutral).*

*Then, look for differences in the stories. Are the presentations basically similar, as the hegemonic model argues? Other possibilities for comparison are:*
- *commercial vs BBC radio;*
- *different national BBC stations' news broadcasts, etc.*

## The pluralist model: argument and evidence

The press is predominantly conservative in tone because its readers are. If any substantial number of people seriously wanted the structure of society rebuilt from the bottom, the *Morning Star* would sell more copies than it does.

(John Whale, journalist and former ITN correspondent)

BBC and ITV enjoy a near monopoly, but they too must try to gauge the interest of their audiences if viewing figures are to be maintained ... The daily paper or news bulletin must be packaged or presented in ways that will attract attention and hold its audience. It must strike a responsible chord in the minds of viewers and readers.

(A. Hetherington, former controller of BBC Scotland)

The *Sun* sells more copies a day than any other newspaper ... people enjoy the entertainment ... it's won its place in the marketplace by providing the kind of material people wish to read ... if people wish to read it presumably they enjoy having their prejudices reciprocated.

(R. Greenslade, former journalist on the *Sun*)

Technology has liberated people from the once powerful media barons ... advances in the technology of telecommunications have proved an unambiguous threat to totalitarian regimes everywhere.

(Rupert Murdoch, September 1993)

The pluralist model agrees with the other two in saying that there is 'bias' in particular elements of the media, inevitably so. However, taken as a whole the media cover almost all points of view. The audience need only select what they want to read, listen to or hear. The only consistent selectivity, other than 'bias' which results from catering to audience tastes, is that imposed by technical constraints. These include the difficulties of reporting long-term processes, the problems of getting cameras to unpredictable events, the ease of covering London-based and predictable stories, lack of time and resources to cover stories properly and so on, which all tend to shape the news in certain ways.

Let's look at some of the evidence put forward by supporters of this theory to show that it is true:

1. The results of many empirical studies of the effect of the mass media suggest that rather than changing attitudes, the media serve to confirm those attitudes already held by the audience. As we saw in Chapter 2, the very earliest approaches to the study of media effects treated the message carried by the media as a 'magic bullet' or hypodermic syringe which, on contact with the audience, affected them in a uniform way. Later researchers realized, though, that things were not that simple. Reception analysis began to question the power of the media.

   A study of the effects of media coverage of the Gulf War by Morrison (1992) shows that readers are not taken in by the papers they read or the TV. The *Sun* strongly supported 'the boys in the Gulf' but *Sun* readers were no more likely to demand a pro British stance than readers of any other paper. Similarly while many viewers said they believed the war was really about protecting oil supplies, this was rarely mentioned at all as a cause of the war by any of the TV channels (which most frequently cited 'to liberate Kuwait' closely followed by 'to uphold international law'). Maintaining the oil supply was never mentioned by ITN or Sky and only given as a cause in around 5% of any discussion of causes by other channels (except CNN where it was 10%) so 'the frequency of reasons given for a policy does not necessarily determine how the viewer will order the reasons in terms of primacy ... the number of times a particular person or position is presented does not quantumly affect the attitudes of viewers when the position or reason that is represented runs counter to their understandings of the world' (Morrison 1992, p. 76).

2. Evidence shows that the media in general are quite balanced in their reporting. For example in the Gulf War the various television channels gave access to politicians who were critical of the war and of the government's handling of it (see Table 4.2).

Table 4.2    Reaction by politicians: channel comparisons %

|  | BBC1 | BBC2 | ITV | C4 | BSKYB | CNN |
|---|---|---|---|---|---|---|
| Total support | 74 | 45 | 74 | 68 | 54 | 78 |
| Qualified support | 13 | 12 | 12 | 19 | 4 | 22 |
| Neutral | – | 9 | 3 | – | 18 | – |
| Criticism of war (general) | 10 | 21 | 10 | 6 | 17 | – |
| Criticism of government handling of war | 4 | 12 | 4 | 3 | 7 | – |

*Source: Morrison (1992), p. 79*

The media clearly are gatekeepers, but the gate is relatively open.

3. There is a large range of newspapers and magazines, radio and TV programmes available. Channel 4 in particular uses many small, independent producers of programmes and as a result offers a very varied output to its audience. Indeed, the Act of Parliament which set up Channel 4 requires it to be distinctively different from the others, catering for a whole range of needs and tastes, while the 1990 Broadcasting Act requires the BBC and ITV companies to commission work from outside their own walls.

   The choice available in the future will be even greater when satellite and cable television is more widely disseminated. There are plenty of pro-Labour and Marxist magazines, too. The fact that people are not really interested in them is, however, demonstrated by their circulation figures: in 1987 the *New Statesman* sold only 30,000 copies, the *New Socialist* 13,000 and *Marxism Today* only 15,000. By 1995 the *New Statesman* and *New Society* had merged, *New Socialist* had closed and *Marxism Today* moved to the middle ground of politics to attract a broader readership.

   However, such magazines were and are sold at most newsagents, so there is no conspiracy to keep them off the news-stands. Furthermore, Conservative governments from 1979 have actively promoted deregulation of the media. They promoted legislation to extend the range of media available by assisting in the extension of cable and satellite TV, permitting new national commercial radio stations and providing several hundred new local and community radio stations. Douglas Hurd, Home Secretary in the late 1980s, said 'diversity underlies our whole approach'.

4. New technologies mean that there will be ever greater diversity and everybody who wants to will become empowered to produce their own 'mass medium'. The Internet has shown something of what can be done, but as technology advances this will become thought of as a very primitive form of the popular empowerment to come. Small music groups and companies will sell their music in digital form down the telephone lines, delivered to multimedia personal computers. Television will be delivered in this way too (a consortium was formed in January 1994 between London Weekend Television, Pearson, Kingfisher and BT to develop Video on Demand which will allow this kind of service).

5. The role of the state has diminished as a result of government policy of choice and free-markets. For example the role of the Independent Television Commission, which replaced the IBA, is much reduced and the ITC has far less influence on content and schedules. The IBA 'had direct powers to mandate news, current affairs and other important programming elements such as children's or educational programming' (Williams 1994, p. 41) but these have now gone.

*Compile a list of films, TV programmes, newspapers and magazines to illustrate the range of choice (in terms of political and other perspectives) available.*

*Make a list of your interests/views which are not catered for in the mass media – these might be connected to your hobbies, the ethnic group you belong to, your age, your gender, or simply things you are interested in.*

*Think about your friends and family too. Do the media cover the whole range of interests, and are those they omit left out for good reasons, do you think?*

An example to illustrate the pluralist point of view concerns Greenpeace's success in preventing the disposal of the Brent Spar oil platform in the Atlantic. Earlier in 1995 Greenpeace had captured the headlines on the issue, giving journalists access to their operations and helping camera crews get good footage of their campaign against Shell. However in September Greenpeace admitted that they had made a mistake in interpreting figures about the toxicity of the Brent Spar oil platform and as a result exaggerated the likely environmental effects of its disposal.

At the same time scientific opinion was converging on the view that what Shell had been forced to do by Greenpeace's action (take the Brent Spar to a Norwegian fjord and dismantle it there) was actually more dangerous and damaging than the deep-sea disposal option. This led to a shift in media reporting of these issues. Radio and TV news in particular began to ask whether Greenpeace had too much power over the presentation of events, whether they had in effect 'captured' the media. News reports were given over to explaining how Greenpeace had done this in earlier news reports! This example shows that if 'primary definers' exist they are not only found among the establishment élite. It also shows that their power to define is fragile.

## The case against the manipulative and hegemonic models

Against the manipulative and hegemonic models, pluralist theorists have the following arguments.

1.  Media barons really are not so powerful. Soon after the highly publicized comment by Rupert Murdoch about technology and totalitarian regimes quoted above, the BBC World Service was no longer transmitted by Star (the suspicion being that governments put pressure on them to take it off, though they deny that) and both China and Malaysia banned Murdoch's satellite dishes. He has since backpedalled on his 'unambiguous threat' speech. Governments operate to ensure diversity. Murdoch was excluded from the bids for a fifth national terrestrial channel in the UK, Channel 5, because of his already extensive media ownership. Another example of media companies acceding to state demands is provided by CETV, a rival to Star TV in China. Their programming philosophy is 'no sex, no violence and no news' and they are appealing both to the government and the regime's large and affluent Mandarin-speaking audience. The chief executive, Robert Chua, is frank, describing it as 'a pure entertainment channel so you will not upset any government'.

    These examples show that powerful groups have competing interests and that power shifts around; it is not located only in the hands of one person or group. Often the state is dominant, sometimes popular opinion and sometimes capitalist interest. Examples of the state dominating are provided above. An example of public opinion triumphing with the assistance of the media is Shell's decision not to sink the oil platform, the Brent Spar, after there had been an outcry about the potential environmental damage from the public. There is a plurality of competing interest groups. As issues arise some become active and mobilize their forces to do battle for their interests. The outcomes of these battles are not pre-determined and the role the media plays in them varies from one to another.

2. While there is plenty of evidence to show that the ownership of the media is concentrated in the hands of a few capitalists, their content is driven by market demand, not ideology, in the main. In what ways do *The Simpsons,* for example, further the interests of News Corporation which broadcasts the programme on BSkyB in UK and Fox TV in the USA (other than simply making profits for that company)? Indeed, theorists such as J. Burnham, A. A. Berle and G. C. Means strongly argue that managers, not owners, hold the real power. *Control* rather than *ownership* is the important factor in determining the output of the media.

---

### *Managerial revolution thesis*

Associated with James Burnham, this holds that the rise of the joint stock company in modern capitalism means that the 'capitalist' – the single owner of the company – no longer exists to any important extent. Salaried managers and company shareholders are now the important figures in decision-making. Because they are skilled and technically proficient, managers in particular will be most powerful. Further details on these ideas can be found in most general sociology textbooks.

---

Thus editors and other managers determine the 'line' adopted by newspapers, films, magazines and TV programmes. This they do on marketing rather than political principles. Perhaps the supreme example of the media catering to public tastes is the *Sunday Sport.* Set up in September 1986, it was deliberately intended to offer readers the 'best' bits of other papers, i.e. what the target audience enjoyed most. This was found to consist mainly of two things: sex and sport. Its proprietor, David Sullivan, makes no bones about this. News editor Rab Anderson says that he chooses stories by imagining what a 25-year-old bloke would want to look at before going to the pub.

Indeed, 75% of its readership are males between the ages of 17 and 45 and in classes C or D. A typical lead story is about a part-time nun with an 84-inch bust. This approach seems to work, as the readership of the *Sunday Sport* was 9 million in 1993/4, second only to the *News of the World.* Angela McRobbie shows in *From Jackie to Just Seventeen* how the publishers of girls' magazines nowadays go to great lengths to identify and then cater to the tastes and wishes of their readership.

News Corporation puts profit before ideology too. Murdoch bought Fox Television in the mid '80s and it became successful by broadcasting anti-establishment programmes like *Married … with Children* and *The Simpsons* which confronted traditional family values, in sharp contrast to bland programmes on other channels such as *The Cosby Show.* Fox's output was dubbed 'guerrilla television' and 'counter-programming'. Profits rose and Fox did well, beating the powerful and well-established CBS on viewing figures for 18–49 year olds in 1993 for example. Conversely Fox Films has been one of News Corporation's disaster areas. Profits have collapsed and, apart from hits like *Home Alone, Edward Scissorhands* and *Sleeping with the Enemy,* there have been many failures. *For the Boys, Shining Through, Hoffa* and *Toys* are some examples. Consumer power is important, even when films are heavily hyped by wealthy multinational conglomerates.

The power of the audience is also shown by BSkyB's failure to attract pan-European advertising (and therefore revenue). News Corporation intended the satellite channels to be beamed across Europe, funded by advertisements which would reach everyone. However audiences want adverts attuned to their own culture and tastes. Advertisers know this, showing different adverts in different countries or changing the dialogue as well as the language when showing the same advert in different countries. In the end BSkyB had to withdraw to broadcasting only in the UK because its pan-European advertising strategy failed in the face of consumer demand.

---

### *Cultural discount*

This is the idea that a particular programme is rooted in a specific culture and so is most attractive in that environment. It will therefore have a diminished appeal elsewhere as viewers find it difficult to identify with the style, values, beliefs, institutions etc. in question. When this happens there is 'cultural discount'. Different types of programme will have different levels of cultural discount.

The concept comes from Hoskins and Mirus (1988).

---

 *Will cultural discount be higher for entertainment or informational programming?*

3. While it is clear that ownership of the mass media is being concentrated in fewer and fewer hands, this is not the important point. More important is how much exposure the audience has to mass media from the same source. One way of looking at this is by audience share (see Table 4.3).

| Table 4.3 | Media concentration (TV, newspapers and radio) by audience share, 1993/4 |
|---|---|
| *Media group* | *% Share of audience* |
| BBC | 19.7% |
| News International | 10.6% |
| ITV network (all companies combined) | 9.4% |
| Daily Mail Trust | 7.8% |
| Mirror Group Newpapers | 7.6% |
| United Newspapers | 5.7% |
| Carlton Communications | 3.1% |
| Channel 4 | 2.9% |
| Total as % of newspaper, TV and radio markets | 57.4% |

*Source: adapted from Congdon et al. (1995).*

While this, worryingly, still puts Rupert Murdoch's News International near the top, if we then ask how much time people spend consuming the content of media from these sources, News International is quickly displaced (see Table 4.4).

This shows that terrestrial television is the most consumed medium in this sense. People spend seven times longer watching TV as reading newspapers in general. From a pluralist perspective this is reassuring. TV is precisely the medium over

| Table 4.4 Media concentration by time use | |
|---|---|
| *Media group* | *% of time spent consuming* |
| BBC | 44.1% |
| ITV network (all companies combined) | 25.4% |
| Carlton | 6.9% |
| Channel 4 | 6.2% |
| Granada | 4.1% |
| Capital Radio | 3.4% |
| News International | 3.4% |

*Source:* Congdon et al. (1995).

which government, regulative bodies like the Independent Television Commission and Broadcasting Standards Council as well as pressure groups like the Viewers and Listeners Association have the most democratic control.

4. Supporters of the manipulative model complain about the 'synergy' that ownership of several media can bring. Hird argues, for example, that the *Sun* gives BSkyB favourable treatment.

---

### *Synergy*

The use of one aspect of the mass medium to promote its own or others' interests through links between and within companies. Examples include merchandising, for example of Power Ranger figures and equipment, product promotion through placement within films, the promotion of a company's broadcasting interests through its publishing interests and so on. An example is BSkyB's heavy use of the highly successful *Simpsons* during its launch and afterwards. *The Simpsons* was popularized by Fox TV. Both BSkyB and Fox are News Corporation companies. The Simpsons are also heavily merchandised.

---

If true, however, this can be very limited. The American magazine *TV Guide*, paid few favours to Fox TV, also owned by News Corporation. *TV Guide* needs advertising from other television network companies and so *has* to be neutral. If the magazine rubbished their programmes this crucial source of income would quickly evaporate.

5. Although *some* journalists and editors may feel that a certain amount of manipulation is going on from above, the vast majority do not. The quality and audience-appeal of work are what determine whether or not it is included in media output. Journalists do not usually feel that any form of political censorship or manipulation is occurring. On the rare occasions when they do, they are willing to stand against it to maintain their professional integrity. This occurred in the *Real Lives* affair when TV journalists went on strike in support of editorial freedom. Editors and proprietors know very well that any attempt to interfere with the work of journalists will result in all kinds of problems. Usually it leads to their best staff going elsewhere.

6. Many journalists are far from sharing the dominant ideology. A number of them are involved on a day-to-day basis with attempting to expose the unacceptable

sides of capitalism. McRobbie (1994) points out that more and more are women and many have degrees in sociology and related subjects, alerting them to the dangers highlighted by the manipulative and hegemonic models. Even the Glasgow University Media Group have praise in this respect for investigative journalists like Jonathan Dimbleby. The Watergate scandal which saw the impeachment of US president Richard Nixon is just one example of the sort of work these reporters do. It was two newspaper journalists, Woodward and Bernstein (who worked for the *Washington Post*), smelling a 'scoop', who exposed the Nixon administration's misdeeds. In 1984, the report by *The Times* of Mrs Thatcher's banning of trade unions at GCHQ (the secret communications base at Cheltenham) showed the government in an unfavourable light. Duncan Campbell's making of a film about a secret project for a spy satellite is another example. He argued that the government had misled parliament over this issue. While it is true that the government and Director-General of the BBC tried to stop the film being shown, it nonetheless got very wide coverage in the press and its contents were published in the *New Statesman* before it was eventually allowed to be shown on TV (in censored form).

7.  While some or most of the press are owned by relatively few companies, there are important sections of the published media which are independent of them. For example, the *Guardian* is owned by the Scott Trust set up after the paper's owner, C P Scott, died. The trustees take no profit: eight of them take no income or dividends whatever; only three draw a salary and rarely discuss editorial policy and when they do it is usually at the request of the editor. Any profits are reinvested in the paper.

8.  In countries where there undeniably is manipulation of the content of the mass media (e.g. the former Soviet Union), their subject-matter is quite different. News stories are almost exclusively about good news, not bad. Stories of crime and deviance do not appear. Stories critical of the powers-that-be or which put them in a bad light do not appear. This is the reverse of the British press.

*Buy a copy of the English translation of* Pravda *(now available at most large newsagents). Identify the differences between it and the British national press. Do these differences lend support to the idea of the 'freedom of the press' in Britain?*

9.  The fight between the TV companies for ever higher audience ratings and between the newspapers for higher circulations mean that both types of media have got to pander to popular tastes. They cannot afford to push a point of view on an unreceptive audience. Where vendettas against personalities are carried on by media proprietors, this is only to attract readers. Characters are chosen for vilification who are *already* unpopular with the public. Journalists have a keen sense of 'news values', that is, what the public will find interesting. These determine editorial content, nothing else. News Corporation found this out to its cost when it took over *TV Guide* and moved its editorial content downmarket. It lost sales of half a million copies in the first year of ownership. There had been a place in the market for serious journalism in a listings magazine.

*The Royal Commission on the Press 1947–9 (the Ross Commission) asked newspapers proprietors, managers and journalists what constitutes news –*

*i.e. what interested the British public. Their answer, in descending order of importance, was:*

- *sport*
- *news about people*
- *strange or amusing adventures*
- *tragedies, accidents*
- *crime*
- *(last) public affairs.*

*A. Hetherington provides us with the following list based on his experience as former editor of the* Guardian:
- *Significance: social, economic, political, human*
- *Drama: the excitement, action and entertainment of the event*
- *Surprise: freshness, newness and unpredictability*
- *Personalities: royal, political, 'showbiz', others*
- *Sex: scandal, crime, popular ingredients*
- *Numbers: the scale of the event, numbers of people affected*
- *Proximity: on our doorsteps, or 10,000 miles away?*

*Are your priorities the same? Rearrange these in your preferred order and add any that are missing. Also, try noting the items that appear on tonight's news and how long is given to them. Later, rearrange and re-time them according to your news values.*

10. If the content of the media were really only propaganda or the embodiment of the dominant ideology, it would not appeal to people for whom it would be either boring or alien or both. In fact the mass media do appeal to the audience in their millions.

11. Against the neo-Marxist hegemonic model in particular, pluralists argue that the media cannot reflect the views of the dominant class in Britain because that class is itself highly critical of much of the political and other reporting of the broadcast media. Those on the right of the political spectrum argue that there is a left-wing 'bias' in the BBC and some of the other media. In 1986 the Conservative Party's Chairman Norman Tebbit complained bitterly about the BBC's reporting, by Kate Adie, of the American bombing raid on Libya. Other examples include a *Panorama* programme during the Falklands dispute (April 1982) which seemed anti-British, and another about right-wing infiltration into the Conservative Party (called *Maggie's Militant Tendency* and broadcast in January 1984) caused extreme anger in the government. It resulted in a court case being brought by two Conservative MPs. This was settled out of court and an apology was made by the BBC.

Another instance of supposed left-wing 'bias' in the media is the following: In September 1986, playwright Ian Curteis claimed he was asked by the BBC to make changes to his play about the Falklands because it showed Mrs Thatcher in too sympathetic a light. The broadcast media, then, are accused of being pro right-wing by the left and pro left-wing by the right. One of them must be wrong, and the truth is that they probably *both* are.

*In the right-wing journal the* Salisbury Review *(December 1987) there is an article by Ian Curteis called 'Bias and the BBC' (pp. 10–13) which*

elaborates on these points. Use the library to get a copy of it. What is your response to the points he makes?

12. Also against the hegemonic model it is easy to find evidence of very different cultures among journalists and others involved in the media rather than the monolithic culture the hegemonic model implies.

We have looked at the pluralist model's case against the other two views of the media, now let us examine the case against the pluralist model.

## The case against the pluralist model

1. Far from increasing the range of opinions expressed in the media, the effect of market forces is to reduce them. This is at present apparent in the press and will become increasingly so as broadcasting is opened up to competition. The pressures of competition too often mean less space; fewer resources for journalists (especially correspondents); less scope for gathering background material on a story and increased reliance on a handful of newsagency sources. Also the tone of papers is likely to become very bland, designed to offend the fewest people and to cater to the lowest common denominator. Advertisers in the market-place do not care about the depth of enjoyment of a programme, only that people do not switch off. This means that programme makers reliant on advertising will create content least likely to be objectionable rather than most likely to please.

2. Monopolization of ownership means that media diversity is an illusion. Even the new satellite and cable TV channels are owned by the old companies or consortia of them. In metropolitan areas there is usually a monopoly over local evening newspapers. In London the *Evening Standard* has a monopoly and real competition in the regions does not exist due to monopolization there.

In radio the story is the same:

> Travel from London to Bristol or Bournemouth, and whichever commercial radio station you tune to, you will hear the same format, the same records and even the same voice saying 'We promise not to talk over your favourite records'. The only difference between 'The All New 2-Ten FM', 'The All New 2CR' and 'The All New GWR' is the name. Ident engineering has ensured a series of clones that offer some of the least challenging radio in the UK.
>
> (NUJ Evidence to the Cross Media Ownership Review, February 1994, quoted in Williams (1994), p. 44)

*News items come from a variety of sources. Those identified in Table 4.1 on p. 67 include: casual sources, 'stringers', other media, aggrieved citizens, the fire brigade, the courts, the police, the services, press conferences, press releases, companies, unions, pressure groups with an interest in the publicity, local councils, the government, 'diary' events and investigative reporting.*

*Watch or listen to tonight's broadcast news and try to identify what the likely source of each story was.*

3. Journalists generally come from a very limited section of the population and hence articulate only a very limited view of the world. Applications for jobs are carefully sifted to exclude those who will not fit in. Even if not done deliberately, those doing the interviewing will tend to prefer those candidates who share their own background, views, manner of expression and so on. The same applies to promotion once the lucky candidate has got into the media institution. No-one is promoted unless they have acceptable views – which they will then put forward sincerely.

4. Working-class newspapers close down despite large circulations because of lack of attractiveness to advertisers. The different ratios of advertising revenue are illustrated in Table 7.4 on p. 144: this shows how dependent the popular Sundays and dailies are on sales compared to other parts of the press. So despite having a larger readership, newspapers in this section of the market are fewer in number and less secure financially.

5. The pluralist model is an inaccurate representation of news production in particular. Published news is monopolized by a few news agencies, predominantly AFP, UPI and Reuters. Broadcast news on all channels of radio and TV is totally controlled by only three institutions: IRN, ITN and BBC News. Thus the sources of news are not as diverse as the pluralist model would have us believe.

6. The media do not respond to people's tastes, they create them. People may feel that the media are giving them what they want, but this is only because they have been 'trained' to enjoy that sort of product.

### Examination questions

'Newspapers may appear to be run by professional managers and journalists but, in reality, it is the owners who wield ultimate power.' Discuss this statement with reference to sociological evidence and argument.

(AEB Sociology (with coursework), June 1993, question 7)

'Assess the extent to which it is possible to argue that the mass media reflect the culture of the ruling class.'

(AEB Sociology (with coursework), June 1994, paper 2, question 8)

'Examine the relationship between ownership of the mass media and control over the media's output.'

(AEB AS Sociology, June 1993, paper 2, question 7)

*There is an outline answer to this question in the skeleton answers section at the end of the book.*

'Do you agree that it is increasingly more relevant to talk about international rather than national media organisations?'

(AEB Media Studies 1997, examination specimen questions, paper 2, question 7)

# Further reading

Belfield, R. and Hird, C. (1991) *Murdoch: the Great Escape*, London: Time Warner.

*Benn's Media Directory*, London: Benn's Business Information Services Ltd (annually).

Cockerell, M., Hennessy, P. and Walker, D. (1984) *Sources Close to the Prime Minister*, London: Macmillan.

Congdon, T. *et al.* (1995) *The Cross Media Revolution*, London: John Libbey.

Curran, J. and Seaton, J. (1991) *Power Without Responsibility*, 4th edn, London: Methuen.

Evans, H. (1994) *Good Times, Bad Times*, London: Phoenix.

Greenslade, R. (1992) *Maxwell's Fall*, Simon & Schuster.

Killick, M. (1991) *The Sultan of Sleaze: The Story of David Sullivan's Sex and Media Empire*, Harmondsworth: Penguin.

McQuail, D. (1987) *Mass Communication Theory*, 2nd edn, London: Sage (useful for a more detailed discussion of the sociological theories and the mass media, pp. 62–78).

Williams, G. (1994) *Britain's Media – How They Are Related: Media Ownership and Democracy*, London: CPBF (a very good overview of media ownership and issues associated with it).

*Willings Press Guide*, London: British Media Publications (annually).

# 5 Mass media, mass culture, mass society

Figure 5.1 Pavarotti bringing 'culture' to the 'masses'.

This chapter concerns the more general effects of the mass media on society. Specifically it asks two questions:

● are the mass media creating a mass culture?

● if so, is mass culture creating a mass society?

The chapter will examine two perspectives which answer 'yes' to both questions, looking at the evidence and argument presented in each case. It will then turn to a further two perspectives that answer 'no' to both and in their turn offer evidence and argument in support of that conclusion.

---

*Culture*

'Culture' is usually defined sociologically as that part of human action and its products which is learned through the process of socialization (i.e. it is passed on between the generations). It refers to the attitudes, values and behaviour that are considered 'normal' in any society.

A formal definition is: 'culture concerns the conditions and the forms in which meaning and value are structured and articulated in society' (Corner 1991).

'Culture' has a second more common usage. Here it means the highest intellectual and artistic achievements of a society. Thus opera, art, literature and so on are considered to be 'culture' or 'high culture' and a person who is familiar with them is thought to be 'cultured'.

---

### Mass culture

If 'culture' in the art and literature sense has very positive connotations, mass culture has very definite negative ones. It refers to art and thought which is artificial, produced deliberately for consumption by the masses rather than representing the highest achievements of dedicated effort. Standardized products are manufactured solely for the mass market and there is associated mass behaviour in using them.

### Mass society

Mass society means a society which is homogenized, where the people are passive, unthinking and uncritical. People are alienated from each other, their work and their own authentic culture. It is a totalitarian society in which people are controlled, but do not realize the nature of their bondage. The effect of mass culture is thought by some writers to be mass society.

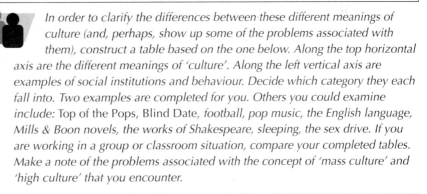

*In order to clarify the differences between these different meanings of culture (and, perhaps, show up some of the problems associated with them), construct a table based on the one below. Along the top horizontal axis are the different meanings of 'culture'. Along the left vertical axis are examples of social institutions and behaviour. Decide which category they each fall into. Two examples are completed for you. Others you could examine include: Top of the Pops, Blind Date, football, pop music, the English language, Mills & Boon novels, the works of Shakespeare, sleeping, the sex drive. If you are working in a group or classroom situation, compare your completed tables. Make a note of the problems associated with the concept of 'mass culture' and 'high culture' that you encounter.*

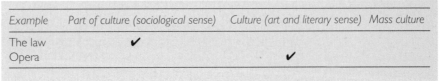

| Example | Part of culture (sociological sense) | Culture (art and literary sense) | Mass culture |
|---------|:---:|:---:|:---:|
| The law | ✔ | | |
| Opera | | ✔ | |

First we will examine the two perspectives which consider that the mass media are creating a mass culture and mass society in 'developed' societies.

## Media, culture and society: the view from the right

Both TV channels now run weekly programmes in which popular records are played to teenagers and judged. While the music is performed, the cameras linger savagely over the faces of the audience. What a bottomless chasm of vacuity they reveal. Huge faces bloated with cheap confectionery and smeared with chainstore make-up, the open, sagging mouths and glazed eyes, the hands mindlessly drumming in time to the music, ... the shoddy, stereotyped ... clothes:

here, apparently, is a collective portrait of a generation enslaved by a commercial machine.

(Paul Johnson, journalist, writing about the 'Menace of Beatleism' in 1964)

*The quote at the beginning of this section comes from, and refers to, 1964. Write an updated paragraph as if you were Paul Johnson. (You might refer to current TV programmes, magazines for young people, pop music or any other aspect of the contemporary mass media.)*

This perspective on mass culture has dominated most thought about it. Its supporters include Nietzsche and T S Eliot. Many others in literature and journalism as well as some sociologists subscribe to it. Basically society is seen as divided between an élite (who possessed and still possess a superior kind of culture) and the mass of the population. In pre-industrial times the latter had a genuine, if somewhat rough, sort of culture of their own (perhaps 'folk culture' would be a good term to describe it).

They could not appreciate Shakespeare or fine music, rich food or good wine. Nonetheless, folk culture had its particular qualities and character. It involved, for example, music, dancing styles (clog, morris etc.), medical remedies and restoratives, recipes, folk tales, nursery rhymes, events like carnivals, festivals and so on. These were passed down in a more-or-less unchanging way between the generations. Their precise characteristics differed somewhat around the country. Workers were happy with their lot, with family life and with their cultural milieu.

However, capitalism quickly polluted that culture and replaced it with a plastic commodity culture - mass culture. Big business and the state began to replace the family as the source of culture. The old traditions were quickly wiped out in most parts of the country. The working man and woman have become passive recipients of culture, not active participants in it. Today they sit in the cinema rather than take part in the folk dance. They buy fast food rather than make good food themselves with traditional recipes. Advertising has given them the constant desire for things which they can't have. Their world is filled with characters from the television who they don't really know, though they spend hours reading and talking about them as they once might have done about characters in the village. The mass media are particularly implicated in this as it has been their role to transmit and propagate mass culture.

All this has made the working class listless and alienated. They are no longer content with their condition in life. Many of the problems of capitalism (strikes, violence, riots, suicides, divorce etc.) are at least partly due to the inauthentic nature of the culture created for the masses by that economic system. All this is mainly the fault of the mass media. Their effect has been:

a diffusion among the audience of a sense of apathy. The intense involvement of the masses with their culture at the turn of the century has given way to passive acquiescence.

(Handlin 1964)

In short, mass culture has led to an alienated mass society.

*What is your reaction to this? Formulate a paragraph that you can agree on and if you are in a larger group compare your statements.*

A more recent exponent of this viewpoint is American film critic Michael Medved. For Medved the evidence of restlessness and turbulence is everywhere in society, largely a result of the entertainment industry's contemptuous attitude towards authority, the family and religion. He approvingly quotes a Hollywood insider who says that it is the

> failed family ... which has produced our present millions of prison inmates, rapists, drug addicts, burglars, muggers, sexual psychopaths, nonprofessional whores of both sexes and general goofolas.

Medved adds,

> The 'general goofolas' who shape much of the popular culture....make a significant contribution to the ongoing confusion. Their antifamily messages – promoting promiscuity, maligning marriage, encouraging illegitimacy, and undermining parental authority – may not make it impossible to maintain a solid marriage or to raise decent kids, but they certainly make it harder than it has to be.

A programme called *Studs* on the Fox network is particularly criticized by Medved in this context:

> Macho contestants go on steamy blind dates with each of three ... miniskirted young lovelies and then compete on the air for the title of 'King Stud'. Just how 'steamy' the blind dates were is established by interrogating the women in various ways in front of the cameras and a 'snickering and hooting studio audience'.

*What reaction do you have to this? What arguments/evidence can you put to support your view?*

Lacking a long history, the hindsight of the American right is slightly more restricted. They tend to romanticize the more recent past, harking back to the good old days of the '50s and '60s, even thinking that the mass media themselves were not harmful then. Medved quotes Peter Tortorici, senior vice president of programming for CBS quoting letters from parents saying they want programmes reflecting 'heartland values'. 'Shows from the past like *The Waltons* and *Highway to Heaven*, those shows haven't been around for a long time.' Medved himself cites the Andy Hardy movies of the '30s in which Mickey Rooney learned life lessons from his father, a kind but stern small town judge. The media are now out of step with what people want. Medved notes the following disparities between the people and the media:

- Our fellow citizens cherish the institution of marriage and consider religion an important priority in life; but the entertainment industry promotes every form of sexual adventurism and regularly ridicules religious believers as crooks or crazies.
- In our private lives, most of us deplore violence and feel little sympathy for the criminals who perpetrate it; but movies, TV, and

popular music all revel in graphic brutality, glorifying vicious and sadistic characters who treat killing as a joke.

- Americans are passionately patriotic, and consider themselves enormously lucky to live here; but Hollywood conveys a view of the nation's history, future, and major institutions that is dark, cynical, and often nightmarish.
- Nearly all parents want to convey to their children the importance of self-discipline, hard work, and decent manners; but the entertainment media celebrate vulgar behavior, contempt for all authority and obscene language – which is inserted even in 'family fare' where it is least expected (p. 10).

The slow but incessant drip of these media messages is changing the character of American society for the worse, according to Medved. Chapter titles in his book, *Hollywood vs America*, give a feel for his argument. They include the following:

| | |
|---|---|
| Comic Book Clergy | Kids Know Best |
| Forgetting the Faithful | The Urge to Offend |
| Promoting Promiscuity | The Infatuation with Foul Language |
| Maligning Marriage | The Addiction to Violence |
| Encouraging Illegitimacy | Bashing America |

*Medved's technique is to cite numerous examples of mass media output to convince the reader that the chapter headings are the overwhelming direction which the contents take. Do the same thing yourselves using examples from any of the mass media. Then think of counter-examples.*

**Essay**

The modern best-seller is concerned with supporting herd prejudices … the training of the reader who spends his leisure in cinemas, looking through magazines and newspapers, listening to jazz music, does not merely fail to help him, it prevents him from normal development.

(Q.D. Leavis, *Fiction and the Reading Public*, 1932)

[TV] … dulls human sensibility, dims awareness of the world, encourages separation–people from communities, people from each other, people from themselves.

(J. Mander, *Four Arguments for the Elimination of Television, 1980*)

*Explain and discuss the views expressed by these two authors.*

## Media culture and society: the view from the left

They're pointing out the enemy to keep you deaf and blind
They wanna sap your energy, incarcerate your mind
They give you Rule Britannia, gassy beer, page 3
Two weeks in Espana and Sunday Striptease.

(Dire Straits, 'Industrial Disease', 1982)

Pleasure always means not to think about anything, to forget suffering even where it is shown. Basically it is helplessness. It is flight; not … flight from a wretched reality, but from the last remaining thought of resistance. The liberation which amusement promises is freedom from thought and from negation.

(Adorno and Horkheimer, *The Culture Industry,* 1991)

Those who formulated this perspective on mass culture in an academic way are usually collectively referred to as the Frankfurt School, a group of neo-Marxists. They include such writers as T. Adorno, H. Marcuse and M. Horkheimer. Many of them were fugitives to America from Hitler's Germany. Most took up academic posts in America where the theory of mass society and mass culture was developed.

These writers, like the ones just discussed, are highly critical of capitalism, and for reasons which at first sight appear similar. They believe that the working class was once both dynamic and progressive. However, the capitalist system has made that class soulless and one-dimensional. Traditional centres of authority, like the family, have been replaced by the state and by big business. These provide a schooling system, lifestyle and entertainments which make the working class passive, uncritical, unthinking. Believing they are free, people are really manipulated. Believing they are happy, people are really in a 'euphoria of unhappiness'.

In a sense this theory is a more complex elaboration of the idea that the working class are pacified by 'bread and circuses'. The rulers believe of the working class that all they need do is keep their bellies full and their minds busy with entertainment and they won't give any trouble. The Frankfurt school sees the modern equivalent of bread as being all the consumer items that modern capitalism can provide. The circuses are the many elements which collectively comprise mass culture; Page Three girls, Royalty, TV stars, football, soap operas, and so on.

Those in authority within capitalism are able to propagate a myth of freedom and of choice. The masses are kept happy. They do not recognize the repressive nature of their 'freedom'. 'The hypnotic power of the mass media deprive us of the capacity for critical thought which is essential if we are to change the world,' says Marcuse. Again, mass culture is the route to a mass society.

Others on the left such as George Orwell and Richard Hoggart have also expressed concern about the nature and effects of mass culture. Hoggart, for example, thought that authentic working class life was being destroyed by 'hollow brightness', the 'shiny barbarism' and 'spiritual decay' of imported American culture so that traditional values were being broken down and replaced by a 'Candy Floss World' of 'easy thrills and cheap fiction'.

*What is your reaction to this? Formulate a paragraph that you can agree on and if you are in a larger group compare your statements.*
- *Add speech bubbles to figure 5.2 on p. 98.*
- *What speech bubbles might Herbert Marcuse add?*
- *What is your view on the reasons for the great media interest in the royal family?*

Figure 5.2    The Royal
Family: media favourites

*The radical left argue that the main function of the media is to titillate and entertain, so that the attention and interests of the working class are diverted from serious issues such as their exploited position in modern capitalism. The extensive coverage of 'the royals' does this particularly well. List other topics which appear regularly in the media (both printed and broadcast) which could be said to perform this function. What arguments could be used against the view that their purpose is to pacify the working class by keeping them 'happy'?*

We can illustrate these ideas by looking at the concept of 'the permissive society'. It is usually said about the 1960s that they were years which marked the beginning of new freedoms. People could, for the first time, explore their sexuality and other previously repressed desires. Fashion and other styles were liberated from the constraints under which they had operated in the past. However, the concept of 'permissiveness' contains all sorts of internal contradictions. It implies that someone is allowing ('permitting') freedom. But, freedom is not really freedom if it is merely sanctioned by some higher authority, perhaps temporarily.

For the Frankfurt school the sexual liberation of the '60s and later is an integral part of mass culture. Modern sexuality is not real sexuality, it is in a form which Marcuse refers to as 'repressive desublimation'. To sublimate something is to repress it. To de-sublimate it is, therefore, to give it expression. But repressive desublimation, an apparent contradiction in terms, means to give expression to, for example, sexuality, in a repressive way. An illustration would be the trivial sexiness and superficial eroticism expressed in the advertising world and in the *Sunday Sport*.

The aim of all this repression disguised as liberation is to keep the people passive and feeling content. The working class are potentially a revolutionary force, capable of overthrowing capitalism. The way to stop them doing so is to give them material well-being and the illusion of freedom. The mass media, the welfare state and the consumer society are all crucial in this effort.

Here, then, is the important difference between the postitions taken by the right and the left. The first sees the natural state of the working class as contented and static. The second sees it as discontented and dynamic. The first sees capitalism as disrupting this natural state by causing unease and discontent. The second sees it as repressing the natural state by creating a sense of ease and well-being.

While I do not know exactly what content was once carried in the smoke signals of American Indians, I can safely guess that it did not include philosophical argument. Puffs of smoke are insufficiently complex to express ideas on the nature of existence, and even if they were not, a Cherokee philosopher would run short of either wood or blankets long before he reached his second axiom. You cannot use smoke to do philosophy. … [Similarly you] cannot do philosophy on television. Its form works against the content.

(Postman 1984, p. 7)

 *Do you agree? What arguments would you use to support your point of view?*

Figure 5.3

Neil Postman, while not a Marxist, agrees with many of the arguments of the Frankfurt school. While printed materials demand a lot from the reader and helped create a 'serious and rational public conversation', television in particular has meant that 'much of our public discourse has become dangerous nonsense'. The average length of a shot on network television is only 3.5 seconds so that there is always something new to see. Television requires minimal skills to understand it and is aimed at the emotions rather than the intellect. Thinking and television don't mix. The action begins to look unpolished if people start saying 'let me think about that' or 'What do you mean by that?' Television is best at entertaining, but the problem for Postman is that all subject matter is presented as entertaining.

We are urged by the newscasters to 'join them tomorrow'. What for? One would think that several minutes of murder and mayhem would suffice as material for a month of sleepless nights. We accept the newscasters' invitation because we know that the 'news' is not be taken seriously, that it is all in fun … Everything about a news show tells us this – the good looks and amiability of the cast, their pleasant banter, the exciting music that opens and closes the show …

While the pluralists (see below) may argue that more people are more informed by the news, Postman argues that this is an illusion of information. He invites us to consider events in Iran, reported in the media. Most people hear about it, most have an opinion. Yet how many people know what language Iranians speak what 'Ayatollah' means or implies, know any details about Iranian religious beliefs or their

Figure 5.4    OJ Simpson
on trial. Television blurs
the distinction between
reality and soap opera
according to Postman.

political history, who the Shah was, where he came from and what happened to him? People don't really have opinions, they have emotions.

## The mass culture/mass society thesis refuted: pluralism and postmodernism

Again there are two perspectives which counter the arguments put above. Though they do not view the mass media as necessarily beneficial, neither sees the media as giving rise to mass culture or mass society. The first dates back to the 1960s but can still be identified in current writing. The second, postmodernism, is linked to it but is a perspective of the 1980s and '90s.

### Pluralism

> A fairly uniform pattern of mass media use is now common to all social strata in industrial societies, and judgements of what is 'good' and 'bad' have become blurred ... it seems now possible to conclude that ... industrial society does have something like a common culture which is that provided by the entertainment media.

> (Bell 1976)

Academic supporters of this view include D. Bell and E. Shils. Many of those working in the media would also subscribe to it. Pluralists reject the view that there is a 'mass culture' at all, at least in the negative sense that that term is used by the other two perspectives. For the pluralists it is not true that the working class had a 'true' or pure culture that has now been subverted. This is pure romanticism, they argue. The reality is that for working men and women in pre-industrial society life was usually nasty, brutish and short. Modern society has made most people literate and this has enabled them to be discerning consumers of an ever-expanding cultural output. This includes not only literature in the conventional sense, but also TV and radio output, films, journalism and so on. People are also far more politically literate and aware of the world around them than was the case in the past. This allows them to appreciate, and choose from, a wide range of options.

Class distinctions have become less and less important in influencing the choices made by individuals in this respect. Members of the working class are as likely to be watching *Panorama* as anybody else, while soap operas are now appealing to the middle class as well as the working class.

 *The quote at the beginning of this section states that a fairly uniform pattern of mass media use now pervades the class structure. What method from those listed on p. 33 could you most successfully use to put this idea to the test? Write about 200 words on how you would use your chosen method to test this hypothesis about class structure and media use.*

In support of their arguments, pluralists point to the way in which even 'high culture' now reaches a mass audience. With the advent of TV and radio, drama, music and opera have become accessible to more of the population than was ever the case in the past. The use made of these media by the Open University has additionally brought higher education to thousands who were unable to gain access to it before. The provision of public libraries has expanded the reading public.

The greater affluence of the population in general has provided the spare money for buying books and newspapers. Music recording and reproduction technology has developed very quickly in this century so that modern hi-fi systems with CD players and discs, DAT players and cassettes, as well as less esoteric (and cheaper) equipment are available to almost everyone. The latest manifestions of the mass media perhaps challenge the notion of mass culture. From the pluralist perspective they will mean:

- abundant supply of culture and information to almost everyone;

- considerable choice and diversity;

- control passing from producer to consumer;

- distinction between producers and consumers becoming blurred;

- decentralization of media production and consumption;

- interactivity not one-way communication.

(See Chapter 1, pp. 17–18 for more on this)

As well as this, one should take into account the expansion in the range of cultural output. Tastes of all sorts are catered for in virtually every area of output. Taking music as an illustration, there is easy access to the music of many nations as well as forms of music from Brahms to The Beatles, from Metallica to Mendelssohn. An individual's collection is likely to contain a mixture of these.

There is nothing intrinsically 'plastic' or false about the music, literature, films and so on of today. To say that there is is merely a form of snobbery. There are no objective standards to say that one is better than another. The individual simply has the freedom to make his or her choice based on personal preference.

Pluralists concur with recent research findings based on audience reception analysis which stress that the audience do not receive media messages in a uniform way. The ideas implicit within the mass culture/mass society idea are based on a naive hypodermic model, seeing the media as narcotizing the population. Actually the audience 'read' the media in an active and critical way both in studying it formally and as 'ordinary' viewers, readers or listeners. The very fact that people like Medved and

Althusser can critically address the media shows this 'reading' process in operation. If they can do it, anyone can do it, yet it is strange that these writers never stop to ask why it is that they, alone, are 'immune' from the media's baleful influence.

| Table 5.1 | How culture can be ranked | |
| --- | --- | --- |
| | *Books* | *Music* |
| Good | Shakespeare | Beethoven |
| Mediocre | Jeffrey Archer | Beatles |
| Bad | Mills & Boon | Sex Pistols |

- *Is it possible to rank art, literature and music in this way?*
- *If it is, what makes Shakespeare 'better' than Archer?*
- *If it isn't, is beauty simply in the eye of the beholder, with all of equal worth?*

### Postmodernism

> There is no human nature or true self..the goal of life [is] an endless pursuit of new experiences, values and vocabularies.
>
> (Featherstone 1991, p. 126)

---

#### *Postmodernism*

Postmodernism has two meanings. The first is a type of society – that which comes after the modern. It is information-rich, global and composed of a great many sub-groups and sub-cultures.

The second is a way of knowing the world, one which questions the nature of 'truth', 'reason' and even 'reality'. It says that there are no standards by which to judge cultures, works of art, literature fashions, religions, and other norms, beliefs or values. It adopts a relativist position: that is one which rejects the idea of universal standards of judgement. These ideas are associated with the names of Lyotard, Foucault, Baudrillard and others. The school is centred on the Ecole Normale in Paris.

To distinguish the two meanings of postmodernism some authors refer to postmodernity to mean the first and postmodernism to mean the second.

---

Postmodernist J. Baudrillard says that media technology has created a postmodern era. The characteristics of this are networks, connections and feedback, not hierarchical (élite and mass) production and consumption. It is a flat society, not a vertical one. However the effect of the enormous information flow which is going on is to blur the distinctions between the spectacle and reality.

People are given the same information in an increasingly diverse number of forms – for example about the media 'stars'. Viewers hop from channel to channel taking in the most remarkably diverse images in seconds. There is more and more information and less and less meaning. Individuals living in postmodern society suffer from information overload. Increasingly they do not search for meaning, they only accept the surface images. This is why we find it difficult to remember last night's television news: it becomes just a collage of fragmentary images.

However, postmodern culture is definitely not mass culture and postmodern society is not mass society. Cultural reproduction is not taking place, nor is narcotization. The masses engage in consumer culture where variety, not uniformity, is the rule. Mass culture is uniform, postmodern consumerism is based on difference and diversity, even chaos. Mass culture implies a distinctive 'élite' as well. In postmodernism the culture of the élite is indistinguishable from that of the 'mass' (in fact the notion of 'mass' is no longer appropriate): politicians and philosophers appear on game shows; musical styles merge; artefacts are consumed right across the class system.

Postmodern society is not a totalitarian mass society because people's refusal to search for meaning in media images is, according to Baudrillard, a sort of resistance – people are undermining any attempt to get them to see the world in a particular way by refusing to see the images they view as meaningful. Where they do choose to see meaning in images they are empowered, not narcotized by them.

With so much information available to them through the media, for the first time in history people are able to evaluate the way they live and to make real choices about changing it, selecting from a huge number of options they have access to via the mass media. Marie Gillespie's study, summarized on pp. 226–227, illustrates this kind of argument

---

### Relativism

The postmodernist view on knowledge is a relativist one. This means that it believes that there are no universal standards of 'truth' or 'value'. Judgements of works of art, science, cultures or anything else can only be made in terms of the standards set up by the artist, scientist or members of the culture concerned.

---

J. Lyotard also thinks that technological developments in information processing and communication are having important effects on society, making it 'postmodern'. Postmodern society is an individualistic fragmented society. There are no great trends or historical movements, for example 'Progress' or Marxism's historical materialism. These 'grand narratives' are meaningless in such a fragmented form of society. The notion of mass culture and mass society are themselves grand narratives and do not apply.

The universal access to huge amounts of different types of information leads to a general incredulity towards science and accepted knowledge, for example academic knowledge. However, knowledge is increasingly ceasing to be an end in itself, it is increasingly being produced only to be sold, usually in computer-readable form. The computer is becoming the real decision-maker. The important question is who controls the computer, and Lyotard thinks it will probably be a technical élite rather than the population as a whole.

Postmodernism has many critics. They argue that its account of 'postmodernity' is not grounded in empirical evidence, that it misrepresents the facts about technology, information and society in general and ignores the importance of structures and power in society. In addition the critics say that it is a male preserve (at least in the way it is reported and discussed), though this may be changing as women writers like Angela McRobbie join the ranks of postmodernists. On a more humorous note Ernest Gellner, who is actually a serious critic of the postmodernist perspective, criticizes it for being associated with authors whose names sound like stops on the Paris metro!

*Specific criticisms from these general points are listed below. Bring sociological evidence to bear in order to evaluate them:*

● *Some people in society are 'media rich' others are 'media poor' with very limited access to information. Postmodernist theory is only talking about the media-rich group.*

● *There is evidence of consistent 'bias' in the media, not information chaos with virtually random messages.*

● *There is evidence that people are affected in important ways by the media. They are not the empowered, knowledgeable consumers that postmodernism portrays them as.*

● *As well as there being important differences between social classes in access to mass media, there are important differences in their use of these media.*

*Construct an enlarged version of Table 5.2 with a short summary in each box:*

| Table 5.2      Table summarizing two negative perspectives on mass culture | | | | |
|---|---|---|---|---|
| | The Right | The Left | Pluralism | Postmodernism |
| What has been lost? | | | | |
| Why? | | | | |
| What is modern mass culture like? | | | | |
| What effect does mass culture have? | | | | |

### Examination question

'Evaluate the sociological arguments surrounding the claim that the mass media have created a mass culture in society.'

(AEB Sociology, A level (with coursework), June 1992, paper 2, question 7)

*See the skeleton answers section at the end of the book for an outline answer to this question.*

### Essay

'Film is probably the most powerful propaganda medium yet devised. As a consequence its potential for aiding or injuring civilization is enormous.'

(Agee, Ault and Emery 1982)

*How far would you agree with this view of film compared with, for example, the broadcast and published media?*

## Further reading

McRobbie, A. (1994) *Postmodernism and Popular Culture*, London: Routledge.

Medved, M. (1992) *Hollywood Vs. America*, London: HarperCollins.

Gillespie, M. (1995) *Television, Ethnicity and Cultural Change*, London: Routledge.

# *Deviance and the media*

Figure 6.1

This chapter addresses two issues. The first is whether the mass media produce deviant behaviour among their audiences. The second is the way in which the media portray deviance and deviants, the effects this portrayal has and the causes of it.

> ### *Deviance*
>
> Deviance has been defined as 'behaviour which is not consonant with those expectations and norms for individual conduct which are shared and recognized within a social system' (Mitchell 1968). How far there are 'shared and recognized' norms and expectations is debatable, however. What is deviance to one person may seem normal or just eccentric to another.

## The media as a cause of deviant behaviour

Over 2000 years ago the Greek philosopher Plato wanted to ban the dramatic poets from his ideal Republic. He feared that their stories about sex and violence among the gods would harm impressionable young minds. Since then new forms of mass entertainment have often attracted concerns about their harmful effects. Pearson's careful study of newspaper reports of deviance over several decades shows that this has happened in the cases of 'penny dreadfuls', music hall, film, rock music, horror comics and television. In 1908 New York Mayor George McLellan arbitrarily shut all 550 New York cinemas because he thought watching films was immoral and led to idleness.

Video games and computer networks are the most recent media forms to be fretted about. Martin Barker (1994) points out that with every new medium the claim is that 'this time it is different, this time there are special dangers' and Pearson shows that the media have always portrayed a Golden Age (usually around 20 years previously) where such dangers did not exist. Research by Barrie Gunter and Jackie Harrison at the University of Sheffield has shown that the amount of violence on British television has declined. They monitored over 4,500 hours of TV output and showed that the amount of violence in terrestrial broadcasts declined from 1.1% of the output in 1986 to 0.61% in 1994/5. Yet the moral panics about the effects of TV violence have not abated. The Chair of the Viewers and Listeners Association said of this research, 'It sounds like a whitewash.'

In contemporary Britain, Mary Whitehouse is a name associated with the 'moral majority' who are concerned about deviance in society and the influence of the media in increasing, even encouraging it. Mrs Whitehouse has come to symbolize conservative middle-class Britain, defending old values from the pernicious influence of liberals and deviants in the media and elsewhere. She, and others like her, are quick to point to the similarities between the showing of such films as *Rambo* and events like the killing of 16 people by the heavily armed Michael Ryan in Hungerford in August 1987 and the alleged viewing of *Child's Play 3* by two children who subsequently murdered two-year-old James Bulger. Graphic portrayals of mindless violence and of sex without love are themes which crop up quite frequently in this debate. Mrs Whitehouse believes that:

> It is a short step from the do-able to the done; and from the done to the done thing; for if a thing is done often enough it has a strong tendency to become acceptable and accepted ... the public should be free from this assault on their sensibilities.

> (Whitehouse 1974)

Similarly in America right-wing film critic Michael Medved believes that:

> Nearly all the available research suggests that the media sell violence and other forms of socially destructive behaviour in much the same way as they sell cars ... [with] ... hundreds of thousands of regularly repeated messages. The sheer weight of this material as it piles up over months and years of daily consumption ... assaults the average citizen more than 30 hours each week.

> (Medved 1992)

The conclusion of people like Whitehouse and Medved is that the media need to be carefully monitored and that actions such as censorship, the imposition of a 'production code' or boycotting, be taken where necessary.

---

### Production code

This is a list of rules which governs the making of films or other media output. Perhaps the most famous was developed by the American Production Code Administration (known as the Hays Office). The Hays code operated from 1930 to 1966. Its first General Principle was that 'No picture shall be produced which will lower the moral standards of those who see it. Hence the sympathy of the audience shall never be thrown to

---

the side of crime, wrongdoing, evil or sin.' The Hays Code did not, as is popularly believed, stipulate that when a man and a woman were shown in bed together the man always had to have at least one foot on the ground. However most other things were subject to the code.

An American child may be watching as many as 19,500 violent acts every year on television. *Average number of acts of violence depicted per hour per channel on a day's television in the US in 1994 = 15. In 1992 = 10.*

(*Guardian*, 22.4.95, p. 8)

*In what ways is this kind of information misleading?*

*Tables 6.1 and 6.2 summarize the results of the* Broadcasting Standards Council Monitoring Report 3. *The methodology of the study is summarized on p. 35.*

| Table 6.1 | The effect of language/sex/violence incidents upon programme evaluation | | | | | |
|---|---|---|---|---|---|---|
| | Bad Language | Bad Language | Explicit Sex | Explicit Sex | Violence | Violence |
| Pre 9pm programmes | Justified | Not justified | Justified | Not justified | Justified | Not Justified |
| Personal enjoyment | 96 | 80 | 105 | 85 | 100 | 80 |
| Suitability for children | 45 | 54 | 61 | 64 | 63 | 54 |
| Appropriate for TV | 80 | 71 | 92 | 80 | 92 | 71 |
| Suitable at the time | 69 | 59 | 84 | 65 | 83 | 61 |
| No personal offence | 68 | 78 | 86 | 80 | 92 | 73 |
| No warning necessary | – | 79 | 74 | 75 | 77 | 69 |
| | Bad Language | | Explicit Sex | | Violence | |
| Post 9pm programmes | Justified | Not justified | Justified | Not justified | Justified | Not justified |
| Personal enjoyment | 102 | 72 | 101 | 72 | 98 | 70 |
| Suitability for children | 39 | 28 | 33 | 26 | 45 | 33 |
| Appropriate for TV | 94 | 61 | 94 | 62 | 95 | 59 |
| Suitable at the time | 97 | 74 | 99 | 71 | 99 | 76 |
| No personal offence | 90 | 61 | 89 | 58 | 92 | 60 |
| No warning necessary | 67 | 49 | 61 | 52 | 70 | 48 |

An index of 100 means a programme that scored the same as the average enjoyment rating across all programmes.
More than 100 means greater than average enjoyment.
Justified or not justified is defined by the respondent themselves.

*Source*: adapted from Broadcasting Standards Council Monitoring Report 3, p. 24, Table 14.

● *What does this tell us? (Write 5 or 6 sentences.)*
● *What additional information would be useful and why?*
● *Why do you think Michael Grade (controller of Channel 4) described this research as 'risible'? ('Channel 4 Chief Ridicules Sex and Violence Survey',* Guardian, *March 1995, p. 10.)*

Table 6.2     Incidence of concerns by demographic groups (people encountering programmes in a two-week period with bad language, explicit sex or violence not editorially justified)

| | (a)<br>% reporting at least one such incident | (b)<br>Among (a) average number of incidents reported |
| --- | --- | --- |
| All respondents | 53 | 3.0 |
| Men | 52 | 3.1 |
| Women | 54 | 3.0 |
| 16-35 | 46 | 2.6 |
| 35-54 | 54 | 2.6 |
| 55 and over | 60 | 3.7 |
| AB | 49 | 2.4 |
| CI | 53 | 2.8 |
| C2 DE | 55 | 3.3 |
| Child(ren) in the family | 59 | 2.9 |
| Religious believers | 57 | 3.0 |

Source: BSC (1994) Monitoring Report 3, p. 25, table 15.

- *Summarize in a paragraph what these data tell us.*
- *What is the significance of this for the study of the media?*
- *What problems can you see with these data?*

Let us now examine the arguments which have been used to support the view that the media cause an increase in the level of deviant behaviour in society.

### Through prophesying trouble they create it and, additionally, amplify any deviance which may already exist

News and other factual programmes, by giving publicity to trouble spots and potential violence, actually cause that violence and trouble to occur. When this happens there has been a self-fulfilling prophecy. The apartheid South African government argued that this was occurring in its country and as a result introduced legislation which censored domestic and foreign media coverage of popular unrest there. It also placed restrictions on the movement of journalists around the country. The presence of the media encouraged the rioting because dissidents knew they would have an audience, the argument ran.

It was in recognition of this effect that British news editors some years ago decided to stop reporting a spate of bomb hoaxes which were plaguing airline companies. It was felt that the hoaxers were gaining satisfaction from the reports of their actions (planes delayed, searches of aircraft etc.). The number of hoaxes was dramatically reduced following this decision. There are tales of camera crews, in search of good pictures, deliberately inciting violence so that they could get them. In Northern Ireland too there are said to have been occasions when foreign camera crews have encouraged young Catholic boys to throw stones at the army in front of the cameras.

The process of self-fulfilling prophecy occurs like this:

Media reinforce and magnify threat of trouble

↓

consequent rumours and images solidify social groups

↓

cultural symbols become firm and understood by all

↓

participants learn how they are expected to behave

↓

hostility and preparedness for trouble spread among social groups

↓

groups cast as opponents become increasingly hostile

↓

trouble breaks out

↓

order is restored by police, courts and (sometimes) new legislation

Thus the mass media, almost single-handed, have created deviance out of little or nothing and, by predicting that something is going to happen, have made it happen. Academic studies of this process occurring include Stan Cohen's *Folk Devils and Moral Panics* (see p. 237) and Jock Young's *The Drugtakers*, though these both deal with events of some years ago. The former showed how Mods and Rockers were virtually created by the media through largely fictional accounts of violent incidents at South Coast resorts. The latter demonstrated how Notting Hill marijuana users were criminalized and forced into greater deviance by media exaggeration of their behaviour and lifestyle and subsequent police action against them.

More recently media coverage of 'hippie convoys' travelling to Stonehenge to celebrate the summer solstice, travellers moving in convoys around the country and 'raves' in countryside locations led to increased public concern and subsequently police action. These events had previously been peaceful, though drugs were usually involved. However the police intervention led to violent confrontation and conflict. In effect a problem was created where there had not been one before, and of course this too was reported by the media, further fuelling public concerns.

---

### Folk devil/moral panic

Folk devil: A group or an individual popularly represented as evil and a threat to society.

Hall *et al.* define a moral panic as happening when 'the official reaction to a person, groups of persons or series of events is out of all proportion to the actual threat offered'.

---

> ### Deviancy amplification
>
> The process by which the amount or seriousness of deviancy is increased through the reporting of it and the subsequent actions which are taken by the police or other agencies and response by 'deviants'. What is amplified is the reported deviance, the social reaction and the actual deviance that results from this.

> ### Self-fulfilling prophecy
>
> The process by which an event is caused to occur by the fact that a prediction is made that it will occur.

*Are there any similar examples of the self-fulfilling prophecy and deviancy amplification by the media that have occurred more recently? In thinking about this you should look for:*

- *detailed descriptions in the media of some deviant person or group;*
- *description of some trouble that they have caused in the past;*
- *a prediction of when and where they are likely to cause trouble.*

### By encouraging imitation of what is seen on the screen

*Child's Play III*:

> It has now achieved notoriety far beyond its power to frighten or distress. Its symbolic power is immense; on this single video rests the entire future of classification and censorship in Britain.
>
> (Margaret Ford, BBFC, *Sight and Sound*, September 1994, BFI)

She was referring to the murder of James Bulger by two boys who reportedly had seen and were imitating *Child's Play III* and another case in which a schoolgirl was tortured using direct quotations from the same film.

Here the argument is that individuals, especially children, are likely to copy what they see on the screen. To continue the theme of rioting and 'trouble-spots' discussed above, after the riots in Liverpool and Brixton in the early 1980s, heavily reported in the media, there were a considerable number of other (so-called 'copycat') riots in towns around the country.

Another example is newspaper stories of young killers or violent children who are addicted to video nasties like *Driller Killer*, *The Evil Dead*, *I Spit on Your Grave* etc. They became criminalized as a result of viewing these films, the theory goes. American Nathan Martinez was arrested in October 1994 for murdering his ten-year-old half-sister and stepmother, boasting to friends that it was 'just like the movie' *Natural Born Killers*. After the killing he bought the sound track of the film, apparently to reinforce the fantasy of enacting its plot. The film's director, Oliver Stone, said in its defence that 'lunatics' will do mad things anyway, but the form of their behaviour may be shaped by films like his.

A number of academic studies have been conducted and claim to show that imitation occurs, especially among children. Many of these have been conducted in laboratory conditions so that 'proof' of an imitative effect can be established. The most famous of these is the study by Bandura, Ross and Ross described on pp. 55–56. Others have been field studies, both correlational and experimental, one strand of which has been the effect of suicides in the media on real suicide rates; the so-called Werther Effect (from a novel by Goethe).

Phillips and Carstensen (1986), for example, claimed to show a correlation between 38 nationally televised news or feature stories about suicide in the US between 1973 and 1979 and a fluctuation in the rate of suicide among teenagers there. Neale and Davidson in *The Early Window* cite many popular accounts of 'waves of violence' such as bomb hoaxes and riots which are supposed to result from 'copycat' behaviour. The problem is that this has as much to do with news values as anything else: something becomes more newsworthy if it is believed there is a 'trend' or 'epidemic', particularly one that the media is supposed to have started. Similarly coroners' judgements about causes of death will be influenced by reporting of suicides, thus affecting apparent suicide rates.

Recently many people have become concerned about the influence of the new breed of cartoons being screened in Britain. Examples include *He-Man*, *Go-Bots*, and *Thunder Cats*. Imitation of these is seen as particularly undesirable because they:

- portray the goodies using violence to defeat baddies;

- do not show the unpleasant effects of that violence (the baddies never die);

- give status to characters merely on the basis of strength and fighting ability;

- encourage imitation of the hero characters through the sale of associated merchandise (swords, clothing etc.); violence is, therefore, being positively promoted;

- portray women in a very stereotyped way while the white male heroes are ridiculously macho; sexist attitudes and behaviour are, therefore, reinforced;

- associate evil with blackness and a sense of 'foreign-ness'; violence towards minority ethnic groups is thus condoned.

In addition, they are not primarily designed as entertainment at all. They have poor characterization, bad artwork and almost non-existent storylines. They are, in effect, merely advertising. *He-Man*, for example, was a toy produced by Mattel who then approached Filmation of California to make a cartoon about the character which would then be syndicated to the American TV networks. Mattel and Filmation are in constant touch about storylines, new characters etc. An attempt is always made to include in each episode every character currently on sale in order to maintain awareness of and desire for each of them. Thus, two profit-motivated corporations are cynically manipulating children with no regard for the effects of their products on the children themselves or the future of society as a whole, the argument goes.

> 'Some of the games show you violent moves you can later practise on your friends. I don't find myself becoming aggressive but some of my friends do. They start fighting and think they are in a video game.' (*Guardian*, 13.4.94)

Most recently there has been similar concern about Power Rangers. Heavily merchandised and very violent, this has much the same characteristics as the cartoons mentioned above but uses live actors and action. In 1995 it was shown twice a day on Sky and on Saturday mornings on terrestrial TV. A *Power Rangers* film was also released in that year. However *Power Rangers* was dropped by a Scandinavian TV network after a five year old was beaten to death by playmates and evidence suggested that they were influenced by Power Rangers action sequences.

*View an episode of* Power Rangers *in order to prepare a report on it. If possible talk to regular viewers of* Power Rangers. *Prepare a joint report and present it to the group you are studying with. The report should contain:*

- *a description of the plot and characterization;*
- *a short paragraph describing each episode of violence which occurred;*
- *your evaluation of the level of violence and any possible effects on the audience;*
- *an account of the views/reactions of any viewers you interviewed;*
- *an overall evaluation of the programme and any likely influences on the audience or sections of it.*

A considerable amount of concern has also been expressed about video games, which are often violent and sexist in content. In the USA one game in particular focused these concerns: *Mortal Kombat II*. This game is released with a health warning: 'This product features graphic sequences of arcade violence.' After a review of the research literature on video games Eugene Provenzo concluded that:

> there does seem to be a significant relationship between aggressive behaviour on the part of the subjects and the playing of video games. What the long-term impact of the games is on aggressive behaviour is not known. (p. 69)

However Provenzo does note that several studies have found that 'any activity … when played in aggressive modes increased subjects' subsequent tendencies towards aggressive behaviour.' (p. 69)

*Provenzo's book provides a useful summary of the recent literature in this area. Choose one of the studies he describes and critically analyse it.*

*Compare your reviews.*

*Video Violence and the Protection of Children*, the report by Elizabeth Newson, Prof. of Developmental Psychology at Nottingham University, blamed imitation as a major cause of the media's pernicious effects. Though not based on any original research, the report seemed in tune with the professional opinion of many child psychologists and psychiatrists and was signed by 25 of them. Dr Stephen Scott, a child and adolescent psychologist at the Maudsley Hospital, London, claimed to see 'a number of children who have seen horror videos and say they go out on the streets and are violent. Their hero types go around karate-chopping people. Given a certain family background this can tip them over the edge.'

### By desensitizing the audience to violence and other forms of deviance

This theory says that watching violence on television arouses children especially,

Figure 6.2 Anthony Hopkins as Hannibal Lecter in *Silence of the Lambs*. 'As an actor I have some responsibility. We have seen some terrible things in Britain recently. It's a terrifying world we live in and I don't want to encourage that through my films' (quoted in Medved 1992, p. xxvi).

making them excited. However, the more they watch, the more extreme must the violence be to arouse them. The result is that they become desensitized to it and are not shocked by real-life violence as they may once have been.

This argument applies particularly to 'video nasties'. In these films the level of violence is so great that more usual forms of violence seem mild by comparison. According to the authors of the British Parliamentary Group Video Enquiry, such films lose their power to shock. After repeated exposure, the viewer finds it necessary to search for greater and greater levels of violence. Of particular concern to them, as to others, is the violence against women which most of this genre of film contains. Violent rape, especially, is a constant theme in them, and the danger is that such events, either fictional or in real life, no longer shock or repel the individual. The ability to use the slow motion, freeze frame and replay buttons on a video recorder exacerbates this effect according to the critics.

*Martin Barker (in* Video Nasties*) argues that the idea of desensitization is 'vacuous'. The analogy is made with doctors and nurses who attend road traffic accidents. After some time the shock reaction goes. They have become desensitized. The problem with the argument is that their evaluative abilities are not affected. The desensitization argument 'makes a stupid equation between judgement and emotion'. We may react with less emotional shock to horror scenes, but we still retain our critical abilities. We probably become bored with such scenes.*
*Do you agree with Barker or the BPGVE?*

### Through eroding in-built inhibitions about acting in certain ways ('disinhibition')

If you turn violence into entertainment you take away the shock and the wrongness of it. We are supposed to have progressed since the days of Victoria, but looking at the increase in crime figures before the advent of television and after it, you will see the evidence that television does have a direct effect. (Mary Whitehouse)

This suggests that the inhibitions about sexual or violent behaviour are broken down if such behaviour is portrayed as 'normal' on the screen. This is particularly likely to happen if deviant behaviour goes unpunished in films. Feminists, in particular, are concerned about the media's treatment of women in this respect. The Women's Monitoring Network, based in London, reviews this and other aspects of media production. They argue that:

Society generally abhors violence and yet violence against women is both treated as commonplace and exploited for its news and entertainment value and marketability. This not only reflects current social attitudes but serves also to reinforce and encourage acceptance of them.

(Report no. 2, *Violence Against Women*)

These arguments are supported by both field studies and laboratory studies of the effects of violence on the screen. We saw in Chapter 3 that the laboratory study by Bandura *et al.* found an imitative effect after viewing violence on the screen. A field study which supports the case that media violence causes actual violence is

W. Belson's *Television Violence and the Adolescent Boy*, widely regarded as one of the best field studies conducted to date.

Belson carried out fieldwork with interviews of 1,565 London boys between the ages of 12 and 17. A central feature of the study was for the boys to sort cards which carried different statements about violence (e.g. 'I have thrown something at someone'; 'I have given someone a head butt'). Belson's study was unusual in that it tried to establish not just that boys who watched violent TV also committed violent acts themselves, but that the former caused the latter.

This was done by conducting a long-term study of both behaviour and viewing preferences, partly by asking the boys to think about their past behaviour and viewing so that it could be established which came first. He also tried to get round the problems of defining exactly what 'violence' was by delineating no less than 22 different kinds of behaviour, from swearing and abuse to very serious physical violence. The conclusion of the study was that children who tend to watch violent TV programmes do become more violent themselves to some extent, largely because violence comes to be seen as a legitimate problem-solving device for them.

Let us conclude the case against the media. The rapid growth of the mass media and, particularly, the spread of the use of VCRs in Britain (UK has a higher density of VCRs per head of the population than any other nation) gives great cause for concern. A NSPCC survey conducted in December 1983 and January 1984 showed that 36.7% of children had seen at least one film which could be roughly categorized as a 'video nasty'.

A National Viewers' Survey of a representative sample of 4,500 children between seven and 16 years published in 1984 yielded similar results: 45% of them had seen a 'video nasty' and the children's favourite viewing in the '18' rated category tended to be horror, occult or pornographic films. Unlike fiction in earlier eras, the video film is often sexually explicit, there is gratuitous violence and it is no longer the case that good triumphs over evil, rather the reverse.

Small wonder that in a survey of 404 consultants and senior registrars working in the field of child and adolescent psychiatry, 81.2% of those who responded considered that video was an important factor in their patients' lives prior to the survey. 50.5% of those who responded thought that there was an association between their patients' symptoms and viewing violent videos. Similar results were found in a survey of paediatricians and reports by teachers. One of the latter wrote:

> I (and my colleagues) are becoming increasingly alarmed at the way young children are given access to 'X' rated video films. We have noticed that children who watch such films become very nervous, excessively bite fingernails and become withdrawn. One *infant* child who was exposed to pornographic material became very disruptive and violent.

Mrs Whitehouse, herself a retired teacher, recounts a similar instance:

> We were talking [in class] one day about the effects of fear in horrific programmes and films. What actually did such programmes do to people? 'I know what happens to me, miss,' said one normally happy-go-lucky soul, 'I become so tired with fright that anyone could do anything with me.'

*A summary of the studies of media effects on violence can be found in Cumberbatch and Howitt (1989).*

- *Take one each and critically evaluate it.*
- *Summarize the study for the benefit of the others.*
- *Give your critique of it.*

Despite the passing of the Video Recordings Act in 1985 (which restricted what could be hired from video shops and imposed a categorization system on video films) children are still able to get access to 'video nasties'. Even video *games* such as Space Invaders and Roadrunner have been found to raise the level of aggressive play, and to lower the level of social play in five-year-old children.

As the capacity of computers increases and their graphics capability expands there are disturbing possibilities in the area of sex role stereotyping. One popular game at the moment is *Virtual Valerie* which allows the user to dress Valerie, a digitized woman, in different clothes or take them off her. More recently the internet has given uncensored access to sexually graphic images and even fragments of film. Development of this theme has so far only been hindered by the poor quality of computer graphics.

Censorship and other limits on the media need to be introduced so that children can grow up in a decent atmosphere, women be treated other than as sexual objects to be used and abused and violence not be seen as the norm. While this may be seen as an infringement of civil liberties by some, it is a small and necessary price to pay for the good of society as a whole.

*The Daily Mail's television critic Jeanette Kupfermann wrote:*

Young children can still buy videos that degrade, humiliate and desensitize, and while we don't know exactly why screened violence will trigger real-life violence in one person and not another, the indisputable fact remains that it creates a climate that not only acts as a catalyst for the disturbed but will raise our level of tolerance and even expectation of violence … common sense dictates that television violence seeps through and has an effect on people's behaviour.

*List the ways in which this quote sees the media as 'causing' violence. How would you respond to these ideas?*

## Do not adjust your set: in defence of the mass media

Those who reject the view that the media amplify the level of deviance in society argue that the case that they increase the amount of crime and deviance is not proven. This is so for the following reasons.

### 1. Methodological problems

Laboratory studies like Bandura, Ross and Ross', described in Chapter 3, are all unreliable. The reasons for this are elaborated on p. 56. Field studies examining the relationship between media violence and real violence are both ambivalent in their results and as unreliable as laboratory studies. This unreliability is due to the following problems:

- The methodology employed in field studies is never precise enough to establish a proven link between viewing violent programmes and films and subsequent deviant behaviour. The causes of a person's actions are many, various and difficult to identify, even by the person performing them. For an academic researcher to say that a particular behaviour was caused by exposure to the portrayal of deviance on the media is, at best, a guess. Even Belson's impressive research, which takes into account 227 possibly relevant variables which may affect violent behaviour, still may have overlooked other relevant variables such as subtle aspects of the personality.

- Those studies that do claim to establish a correlation between TV viewing and violent behaviour are really only showing that violent people enjoy violent programmes. It's not really worth spending a lot of time, money and effort to state such an obvious fact. Belson tried to get round this problem of cause and effect by asking the boys he interviewed to remember past behaviour and viewing habits. Unfortunately this procedure leaves plenty of room for forgetfulness, selective recall and plain lies.

- Most studies don't bother to define violence. Those that do adopt questionable definitions. Two examples are:

> the overt expression of physical force against self or other, compelling action against one's will on pain of being hurt or killed or actually hurting or killing.

> (Gerbner 1970, p.70)

> The overt expression of physical force (with or without a weapon) against self or other, compelling action against one's will on pain of being hurt or killed, or actually hurting or killing.

> (Gross 1992)

 *What problems can you see with these definitions?*

These positivist definitions assume that violence is an objectively identifiable phenomenon. However violence in the media actually needs to be treated in a phenomenological way. Whether an act, whether physical or spoken, is violent is very much context-dependent:

> All such studies presuppose that 'violence' is an element within films, or television, or video games, or comics … that can be separated from the form, narrative, genre and overall construction of the thing which contains it. More than 20 years of research into both media forms, and audience responses to those forms makes clear that this separation cannot be made.

> (Barker *et al.* 1994)

*Provenzo notes that there is a major difference between the violence in the video game* Space Invaders *and games such as* Bad Dudes *or* Mike Tyson's Punch Out!!
*Can you think of other examples of 'violence' in different genres or within the same to illustrate Barker's point?*

*You have been given a grant to conduct a large-scale content analysis of violence on television. Among other things you want to quantify the amount of violence, types of violence and its seriousness. You have employed 20 people to analyse videotape footage for these things. Devise a coding scheme or form of words which you can give them which will ensure that they all classify these things in the same way.*
*Can you take the point made by Barker et al. into account in devising this research?*

Moreover, there is disagreement as to whether violence in *fictional* programmes has more, or less, impact than *real* violence shown on the news. Perhaps violence in cartoons cannot be counted as violence at all because there is no attempt to make the characters 'real' in any sense. Also, it is not clear how far children are able to distinguish between what is and is not real in what they see on the TV screen.

Surveys of children are notoriously unreliable. Kids are inclined to say they have seen 'video nasties' they haven't. This was shown by Cumberbatch and Bates's study of five classes of eleven year olds who were given the National Viewers Survey questionnaire referred to on p. 114. The only difference was that bogus titles such as *Zombies From Beyond Space* and *Cannibal Fang* were added to the questionnaire. Sixty-eight per cent of the children claimed to have seen these films! Surveys of professionals, too, are really discovering no more than their personal view; they have no real idea about the influence the media may be having on people.

### Modality status

The modality of a media message refers to the extent to which it is perceived as 'realistic'. Viewers perceiving a message to have a high modality status will see it as portraying life 'as it really is' and will compare it to their own situation. Buckingham reports that children as young as seven are very aware of the modality status of a television programme.

Modality status is entirely subjective. Orson Welles's famous *War of the Worlds* radio broadcast in the US, parts of which included 'news bulletins', was mistaken by thousands of people as an actual news report of alien invasion and large-scale panic and evacuation was reportedly caused. In 1995 the BBC was censured by the Broadcasting Standards Council for broadcasting a programme called *Ghostwatch*, a spoof Halloween documentary, without giving adequate warnings that it was not a real documentary. Martin Denham, a Nottingham 18 year old, hanged himself five days after watching the programme. His parents said he had become afraid and obsessed by the programme, thinking it was real.

The truth is that the media can have a positive effect. They may sensitize children and others to violence and deviance, they may help to release violent emotions. In terms of intellectual skills, too, the influence can often be a beneficial one. This is true even of the much-criticized cartoon programmes. Bob Hodge and David Tripp in *Children and Television* suggest that TV viewing is not a passive, mindless activity, but one which develops a number of cognitive skills in children. In watching a programme even as apparently simple as the American cartoons, children are actively interpreting and constructing meanings. (Hodge and Tripp's work is also discussed on p. 45.)

> Television is not a time-out from thinking, as so many fear. It provides grist to the mills of thought, innumerable opportunities for cognitive growth.

> (Hodge and Tripp 1985, p. 92)

This conclusion is supported by C. Cullingford's analysis of the results of a survey of use of the media by over 5,000 children from many backgrounds in the US and the UK. He writes:

> Children are capable of intense appreciation and the closest critical scrutiny. They can be absorbed in a story and learn new information rapidly and efficiently. No account of children's responses should ignore this fact by being trapped into an over simple generalization … This proof of children's ability to attend to the intended message of the programme contrasts with some of the research evidence that gives an impression that children are being moulded into imitators of violence or into passive and inarticulate zombies.

Edgar's work too confirms these generally positive findings. He conducted a field study of 816 children in Australia and concluded that:

> the children in the sample made more sophisticated discriminations about mass media content than many people assume children are capable of … When talking about 13 year olds it can be said:
> 1. It is the context of violence, not the nature or extent of the violence that is important to children. As long as the rules of a western, crime film or war film are complied with, violence is acceptable and understood.
> 2. What disturbs children is something that relates to their own experience that they can identify with – and that something will differ for each child.
> 3. Children interpret film and television content differently from adults.
> 4. Children believe the news, and films which are simulated to look like news.

So the violence on TV is not only not harmful to children – it can be beneficial in that it helps them to develop these cognitive skills and to 'read' the plot of the programme. Violence acts as a signifier of conflict and difference, and as such it is essential to allow its portrayal in children's programmes and elsewhere.

## 2. Researchers' commitment to the subject

Chapters 2 and 3 pointed out that in research the aims of the research tend to structure the results that are obtained. Many researchers move into media research because they are passionately worried about the effects of the mass media. A clear example of this is Elizabeth Newson's study. Newson did no independent research, used American evidence (which is quite different from the British context) and did not take into account the other things that people do while watching TV; their use of the media etc.

The passion of such researchers means that they, not the audience, suffer from cognitive closure and selective exposure (to other research), selective perception (of the data and findings of other studies and their own) and selective retention. Medved falls into this category too. Like Newson he claims that: 'A wealth of scientific studies in recent years have removed most of the remaining doubts about the link between make believe brutality and real world aggression.' This is simply not true: not only is the jury still out on the media's influence on violence, the nature of the charges and admissible evidence as well as the law itself keep changing.

---

### *Flexipanic*

Flexipanic, used by Martin Barker in *Video Nasties,* refers to the flexible, but contradictory, use of argument by researchers and others who are motivated by worries about the media. For example, such people say that having fast forward, slow motion and freeze frame enables watchers to go straight to the gory bits and linger over them but at the same time feature-length films develop slowly and allow a degree of realism which makes horror scenes even more shocking.

---

Because of this commitment and concern the 'effects' of the media are thought about in a unidimensional way (see p. 61) and positive effects are ignored. In fact many studies of the media have identified positive effects.

Willis, for instance, concludes that video games 'involve a variety of capacities, ranging from hand-eye co-ordination to bargaining, empathy and complex reasoning. In this situation people are no longer viewing a screen. They are interacting with it so that the progress or outcome of the scenario they are faced with depends in large part on their actions' (Willis 1990, p. 40). So for Willis the mental work involved in game playing can have positive outcomes intellectually, morally and aesthetically.

Provenzo's review of the video game literature shows that in video arcades most youths spent more time talking to friends and doing other social activities than playing the games. In the home video games 'brought families together in common recreational interaction more than any other activity in recent memory' according to one study.

Davis (1989) says that television 'serves many useful purposes for children. It informs them and helps them structure their lives. It provides them with knowledge of the world apart from their own. [It gives them] ideas for play, work, education and self development at home and school.'

Taking the specific points made about programmes such as *He-Man* and the like, their defenders reject the claim that they are harmful in any way. Lou Sheimer, President of Filmation, argues that they have positive effects:

● the heroes act co-operatively in groups and this is a good model for children;

- that racism and sexism are avoided: there are female heroines behaving in a strong, self-reliant way; black villains are deliberately not introduced; He-Man's arch-rival, Skeletor, is purple.

- *He-Man* takes up only a small part of the child's day; other influences on behaviour are far more important;

- children know that He-Man is imaginary. Tom and Jerry were far more violent and had no storyline to speak of, yet the very people complaining about He-Man watched and enjoyed those cartoons with no ill-effects. The critique is merely a disguised form of conservatism. There is a large amount of self-mockery in the He-Man programme. It is tongue-in-cheek.

---

### *Prosocial effects*

'Prosocial' TV means television programming that has a positive social content. *Sesame Street*, for example, was developed with the help of psychologists to be educative and prosocial as well as entertaining (see Liebert and Sprafkin 1988). There have been relatively few studies of the prosocial effects of the mass media. Those that there have been have tended to concentrate on a content analysis of the number of altruistic acts and sympathetic responses in children's television programmes. See Cumberbatch and Howitt (1989) pp. 22–4 for a summary of these.

---

*Try a content analysis of one children's programme for prosocial content. Next, compare a programme which you think might be strongly prosocial with one you think might be weakly prosocial.*

### 3 Distortion of reality

Figure 6.3

Critics of the mass media grossly exaggerate the amount of sex and violence in the British media. American media researcher L. D. Eron was clearly exaggerating when he claimed on Granada television that children were having 'a diet of violence', watching four or five hours of cartoons a day. British television and video are probably the most regulated among the industrialized countries, yet one would not think so from descriptions of some commentators.

These critics also misrepresent and misunderstand the nature of serious violence and deviance in society generally, lacking any appreciation of the complexity of the motivations behind much serious violence. For example:

> Rape is motivated more by retaliatory and compensatory motives than sexual ones: it is a pseudo sexual act, complex and multidetermined, but addressing issues of hostility (anger) and control (power) more than desire (sexuality).

> (Burgess and Holmstrom 1979, p. 23)

Burgess and Holmstrom (1979, p. 23) give a graphic account of a rape victim's experience, which illustrates this point vividly and shockingly. These kinds of experience are a long way from Bandura's self-righting dolls.

> I was looking forward to having sex with him ... I was horny and was feeling neglected, and I love my sex. He took me outside and down an alley and threw me on the ground. I asked him what he was doing – told him he didn't have to do it there if all he wanted was a screw ... I told him that I wasn't a slut or whore that did it in an alley. It didn't matter ... First he tried natural sex; then he insisted on oral sex. I didn't want to but he forced me – it was choke or take it ... I said no. He started getting real mad ... Then he stood up and piddled all over me and said 'I feel better.'

> (Burgess and Holmstrom 1979, p. 23)

## 4. Contradictory results

There are at least as many studies of media violence which discover no effect on behaviour as do discover an effect, or at least conclude that the issues are so complex as to preclude clear results. Schramm *et al.* in a major series of studies conducted in the USA and Canada between 1958 and 1960 found similar results to those of Himmelweit summarized on p. 57. Eleven studies were carried out in all, involving interviews with a total of 6,000 students, 2,000 parents, several hundred teachers, officials and other knowledgeable people. In some cases, questionnaires and the completion of diaries by the subjects were also used. The conclusion was that delinquency and violence are complex phenomena with a number of roots and that TV is, at best, only a contributory cause.

Hagell and Newburn's recent study comes to a similar view. They compared the viewing habits and use of written media of 78 young offenders (12–18 years old) and a sample of 500 schoolchildren of mixed socio-economic background. There were few differences in viewing patterns. Contrary to expectations, 'offenders do not watch more television or select more violent programmes than schoolchildren generally. Indeed, offenders had less access to television, video and other equipment than [non-offending] children.' They conclude that 'The results of this research reinforce [our] view that those who blame the media for crime are on a doomed mission in search of a simple solution to a complex problem.'

No informed person can say simply that TV is bad or that it is good for children. For some children, under some conditions, or for the same children under other conditions, it may be beneficial. For most children, under most conditions, most TV is probably neither particularly harmful nor particularly beneficial.

This echoes University of Chicago professor Berelson's conclusion to his 1940s textbook:

some kinds of communication on some kinds of issues, brought to the attention of some kinds of people under some kinds of conditions, have some kinds of effects.

(quoted in Diamond and Bates, 1992)

W. H. Auden said of poetry that it can do 'a hundred and one things, delight, sadden, disturb, amuse, instruct'. It seems clear that the mass media can do the same and the research effort will be a difficult one. However, recent approaches have at least recognized this complexity, as the following section shows.

### 5. Differential audience reception means complex effects

Figure 6.4    Reactions to *The Camomile Lawn* (Channel 4)

'Too many rude shots with no meaning or impact.'

'I shall not watch any more episodes. Sex is only interesting to the participants.'

'I would rather watch on my own as parts of it were embarrasing to watch with my son.'

'My teenage daughter commented on the nudity but was more amused than embarrassed.'

'I didn't find anything that gave cause for concern.'

'I found it excellent.'
*Source:* Owen (1995), using data from the BFI audience tracking study in which a panel of 450 respondents report through diaries and other methods their experiences of and attitudes to television over a five-year period.

The reception analysis approach described in Chapter 2 indicates that the audience are skilled 'readers' of the media and that any understanding of 'effects' requires a phenomenological analysis. While thousands of people write letters to fictional soap opera characters and Dan Quayle was scandalized by and made speeches about an unmarried mother in a soap choosing to bring up a child alone and so 'mocking the importance of fathers', most evidence shows that viewers are sensible in making judgements about what they see on TV.

Gunter and Wober, for example, showed that most people see violence in drama as not a credible portrayal of reality. Angela McRobbie (1994) points out that the moral panic theorists like Cohen and Young did not take audiences into account. In moral panic theory audiences 'played a minor role and remained relatively untheorized', the assumption being that they would uncritically accept media messages. Recent studies have been much more sophisticated in this regard and taken audiences into account in their research design.

Peter Collet of Oxford University filmed people watching TV from equipment hidden in the cabinet. People have their eyes on the screen for only two thirds of the time they are in the room. They may be reading the newspaper, dozing and doing other things. They are not passive while watching either – they shout at the screen, make sarcastic comments, sing along with adverts, talk about the programmes while they are still on. They act collaboratively and create meanings as a group that are relevant to them.

It is just this sort of research that Hagell and Newburn have in mind when they suggest that 'research on what people are watching needs to be supplemented with further work on how they are watching'. Dr Susan Bailey from the Salford NHS Trust tried to do this by interviewing convicted murderers about their habits before the crime. She found that they tended to come from deprived backgrounds and to live mostly at night. They did mention violent videos but they watched them in a different way from most people; mostly at night and sometimes repetitively.

Paul Willis, too, stresses the importance of audience reception. He and his team conducted a 12-month ethnographic and interview research project in Wolverhampton. The methodology included taped discussions with different groups of young people plus 15 separate studies on a national basis covering a wide range of young people's cultural activities and involving further ethnographic work from Sunderland to London.

Willis concludes that 'TV is an omnipresent part of daily life' either in the foreground or the background. 'There is a widespread familiarity with and understanding of different conventions, stereotypes and TV genres.' Respondents said, for example:

'*EastEnders*, you know what to expect before it happens.'

'American soaps exaggerate the good points and ours exaggerate the bad points.'

'Comedy ain't meant to be realistic, it's meant to make you laugh'
(Willis 1990, pp. 30 and 33).

Willis usefully redefines what we should be talking about when we discuss media 'effects':

> The fact that young people have an active, creative, and symbolically productive relationship to what they see on television does not mean that what is provided has no 'effects'. But we need to find new ways of thinking about this familiar issue. 'Effects' are the result, not of TV programmes, but of the whole creative relation of viewers with what they see. More symbolic resources supplied through the TV screen would certainly enhance that relationship but not as a mechanical causation with measurable 'effects'. Instead of concentrating solely on the impact of particular programmes and of areas of content, such as violence, we should more properly consider what

is missing or disappearing from the current schedules. The scope for creative engagement with television depends in large part on the available range of programming and the diversity of youth experience reflected within it.

(Willis 1990, p. 37)

---

### Media effects/media effectivity

The simple notion of the effects of the media is founded upon the hypodermic model's stimulus-response assumptions. Stuart Hall has noted that this does not take into account the different ways in which the audience decode messages and the way this is structured by the preferred meanings within the text. He suggests that we talk about 'media effectivity' which takes these longer term processes of cultural reproduction and the structured interpretation of meaning into account.

---

Figure 6.5 To what extent are people influenced by what they see on television?

Generally, those who believe that the media provoke deviant behaviour have a naive and outdated view of how the media work. They tend to adopt the hypodermic model of media effects (see p. 21). Serious analysts of the media have moved beyond this model. They recognize that the audience consists not of a homogeneous mass but of individuals and groups. These watch, read or listen for different reasons, with different degrees of attentiveness and understanding and with different preconceptions. Any influence on them will not be constant, nor will it affect them all in the same way. Different people will be affected in different ways, or not at all. The simplistic use of the hypodermic model is illustrated in the following quote from the Women's Monitoring Network's report *Women as Sex Objects*:

> [The media] constantly present women as glamorous, alluring and available. This results in women being viewed as objects, to be used for the pleasure and profit of men. Inevitably, men's attitudes towards women are influenced by this voyeuristic approach.

There is nothing inevitable about it. Many men are able to dismiss for what it is the sort of fiction referred to in the quote. More sophisticated analyses, adopting a uses and gratifications approach (such as Schramm's), are far more equivocal in their results.

*Answer the following questions:*
- *What is the most violent programme or event that you have seen on TV?*
- *What was your reaction to it?*
- *Should it have been shown?*
- *What was the most sexually explicit episode you have seen on TV?*
- *Should it have been shown in that form, edited, or not shown at all?*
- *Do you feel that either had any influence on you?*

*Compare your answers.*

Some of those who wish to defend the media go beyond this critique of the available evidence and suggest that the amount of crime and deviance can be actually reduced thanks to the media. This can be achieved by catharsis, the subject of the next section.

### Releasing tension and desires through identification with fictional characters and events (catharsis)

> Catharsis is the release or dissipation of strong emotion.

The cathartic effect has long been recognized and was one of the prime functions of Greek tragedy. Psychiatrists have used it in the treatment of sex offenders by showing them blue movies to help them release their emotions. Films like *Rambo* and *Death Wish* could have a positive effect on those individuals with violent impulses by helping them to release them through identification with the hero of the film. Gunter and McAleer sum up this argument when they say:

> It seems that in the case of some youngsters, particularly those who have highly developed imaginations, the effect of these materials might even be beneficial. Violence … may provide a means through which some children can reduce their angry feelings.
>
> (Gunter and McAleer 1990)

However feminists in particular are critical of this view. Catharine MacKinnon, for example, dismisses the idea that pornography and rape fantasies are good for men. She says they are based on a ridiculous 'hydraulic model' of male sexuality (they let off steam).

*Thinking about violence you have seen on TV, do you feel that in your case it: (a) desensitized you to violence; (b) sensitized you to violence; (c) neither; (d) the effect depended on the extent of violence, how it was portrayed, whether the victim was portrayed and how, etc. (specify what)?*

### Sensitizing people to the effects of violence

Exposure to violence and other forms of deviance not normally encountered in everyday life is just as likely to make people more sensitive to it as the reverse. Bloody scenes of the consequences of violence and war (such as those in the film *Platoon*) often shock and revolt people so much that their attitudes are hardened against acting like this. As far as crime in general is concerned, sensitization to certain types of crime can make people more aware of it and more likely to report it. Child abuse cases, recently highlighted in the media, have heightened public consciousness of the problem and increased the rate of reporting of cases to the police and other agencies.

*Watch one episode of* He-Man *(or similar cartoon) and prepare a report on its content. Issues you may wish to consider are:*
- *How much violence is used?*
- *Are the effects of violence shown?*
- *Is violence used to solve problems in the programme and is its use applauded?*
- *Is there harmonious co-operation between the 'goodies'?*
- *Are there any reasons given for the heroes being seen as good, other than their superior force?*

*Imagine that you had been offered a grant of, say, £50,000 to research the question 'to what extent do video films make young people more likely to commit sexual or violent offences?'*
1. *What problems can you see with the project remit as it stands? (Make any amendments to the aim of the research project that you want, within reason.)*
2. *How would you go about researching this so that you would have some plausible empirical results for your sponsors?*

*Draw up a production code for TV drama writers on writing violent scenes on TV. You might consider whether they should be graphic and show the victim sympathetically (in order to sensitize people to the effects of violence); how much should be shown, where the limits are, and so on.*

*Below are some of the practical questions about the portrayal of violence on TV that broadcasters ask media researchers. How would you reply?*
- *Is it better if the aggression is shown explicitly or more implicitly?*
- *Does it matter whether a good person or a bad person is aggressive?*
- *Does it matter why characters aggress?*
- *Does it matter what happens to a character after he or she aggresses?*
- *Does it matter what happens to the victim?*
- *Does it matter whether a weapon is used or not? Should the weapon be realistic or not?*
- *Does it matter if the aggression occurs in some time other than the present? Does it matter if aggression is portrayed in a realistic or unrealistic past?*
- *What if the aggression is part of a comedy routine?*
- *Does it matter if the aggression is puppetry, animation or live action?*
- *Does it matter if the setting and story are presented as news, based on fact?*
- *How long should an aggressive encounter last?*
- *With what clarity and with what degree of connection should the motives for aggression, the aggression itself and the consequences of aggression be shown?*
- *Will it help if an advisory announcement is made at the beginning or end of a programme saying it is all true, or all fantasy, or whatever? Will it help if this suggests that children, aggressive persons or other sensitive people should not watch the programme?*

(Adapted from Dorr 1988, pp. 285–303)

# Images of deviance in the media

This section will examine three aspects of the media representation of deviance and deviants:

● how the media portrays deviance;

● the causes of this representation;

● the effects it has on the deviants and on society as a whole.

### The media portrayal of deviance

Social scientists have formulated the following hypotheses on this issue.

*Some sorts of deviance are highlighted and exaggerated in the media, others are ignored.*

The media are very selective in which aspects of deviance they portray. Table 6.3 gives the beginnings of the lists of types of deviance which are over- and under-reported respectively:

 *Continue the two lists in Table 6.3 by adding other types of deviance that are under- and over-reported.*

| Table 6.3 | Over- and under-reporting of types of deviance by the media |
|---|---|
| *Over-reported* | *Under-reported* |
| **Drugs** | **Drugs** |
| Cocaine abuse | Alcohol abuse |
| Marijuana abuse | Tobacco abuse |
| Glue sniffing | Food additives |
| **Crime** | **Crime** |
| Sex crime | Fraud and general white-collar crime |
| Violent crime | Theft and handling stolen goods |

On the question of the media's selectivity on drug reporting, Jock Young has developed what he calls his Law of Information on Drugs. This runs: 'The greater the health risk (as measured by the number of deaths) of a drug, the less the amount of information critical of its effects there will be in the media.'

He makes the point that alcohol and tobacco kill far more people than other, illegal, drugs. However, because they are used for relaxation and recuperation after work and don't disturb the individual's productivity, they are accepted. Nancy Reagan's heavily reported Just Say No campaign, designed to stop young people getting involved with cocaine, etc, made no mention of these. Only the drugs which threaten profitability are given media prominence.

*Deviants are seen as being on the fringe of society*

The media propagate the view that the vast bulk of the population are completely 'normal'. They are not trade unionists. They never go on strike. They hold no radical or militant political views. They are not feminists. They do not join movements like CND. They enjoy consumption for its own sake. They live in nuclear families and so on.

Figure 6.6 shows the general media view of society.

However, when there are mass disturbances, such as the miners' strike in 1984 or the Winter of Discontent in 1978–9, this model is no longer sufficient (it doesn't explain why there is so much support for the 'deviant' action) so a more sophisticated model has to be introduced (Figure 6.7).

Figure 6.6 The general media view of society

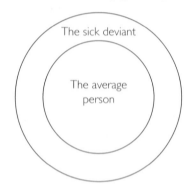

Figure 6.7 A more sophisticated model of the general media view of society

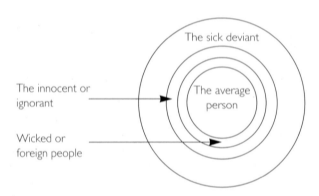

*A small number of deviants are blamed for social problems: they act as scapegoats*

For example, local government bodies which disagree with spending cuts by central government are seen as being in the hands of the Militant Tendency. This small and shadowy organization is blamed for what the media sees as crazy policies when in fact these councils have been elected by popular vote and there is widespread support for their policies. Individuals, too, are often identified as the prime troublemakers. Ken Livingstone, Tony Benn and Derek Hatton (ex-deputy leader of Liverpool Council) have all been cast in this role. They become folk devils: the subject of universal abuse and hatred whipped up by the media, particularly the tabloid press.

*Deviant movements and forces become personalized: their aims are forgotten by the media*

For example, militant unionism in Northern Ireland becomes personified by Ian Paisley who is then ridiculed as a ranting senseless bigot, effectively ridiculing the whole movement. This can be a very effective means of moulding the public's attitudes towards quite complex issues, whether deliberately or not.

*What other examples of the personification of deviant movements can you identify?*

*The 'Nemesis Effect': the media show us that those who deviate from the social norms always suffer for it in the long run*

Nemesis was the Greek goddess of retribution who ensured that evil-doers were punished. Thus the 'Nemesis Effect' in the media is the way the media show us that this happens to deviants of all sorts. This applies to drugs:

### LSD: THE FLY NOW, DIE LATER DRUG

(*Chicago American*)

It also applies to criminals (the cops always get their man/woman in fiction and usually on the news and *Crimewatch* too). Most recently it has applied to homosexuals. The AIDS scare and the media's concentration on its effects on the homosexual community and their sexual practices illustrate the Nemesis Effect in action. Indeed some have argued that AIDS is literally divine retribution for the 'unnatural' practices of gays.

*Have there been any recent examples of the Nemesis Effect in the broadcast news or the press?*

*Deviants are sometimes portrayed as being 'just normal people underneath'*

This occurs when deviants appear to threaten the status quo in society and is an alternative reaction to the moral panic one. The media respond by turning that deviance into a 'leisure-time only' activity. Punks, for example, are portrayed in the press as just normal kids underneath – they go to school and worry about exams like anyone else. Their parents are Mr and Mrs Average. Their clothes become high fashion and are soon to be found on the racks of the high-street stores. This can occur in the media itself. *Rolling Stone*, the American music paper founded in the 1960s, was once an alternative and radical publication. It adopted a questioning and threatening stance, rejecting the accepted values. Today it is much more sedate. It even carries recruitment advertisements for the armed services. Threatening deviance both outside and within the media, then, is neutralized and incorporated into the system.

## The effects of the media's distorted representation of deviants and deviance

### The amplification of deviance and social control

> **Social control**
>
> The ways in which conformity to 'accepted' norms and values is monitored and enforced. This may range from gossip and name calling (and the fear of it) to formal punishment.

The media act as an agency of social control through the use of the Nemesis Effect, the manipulation of the general public's attitudes towards deviance of all sorts and the other distortions of 'deviant behaviour'. The audience is dissuaded from following the deviants' example and, implicitly, threatened with the consequences of so doing. Social control is also achieved through the containment of deviant movements by incorporating them into the establishment. By treating deviant movements as 'just a fad' and their members as 'really just normal people going through a phase' and by commercializing the artefacts of deviant movements, the media effectively neutralize them as a threat to the established system.

Stuart Hall in *Policing the Crisis* and Martin Barker in *Video Nasties* have developed Stan Cohen's ideas about deviancy amplification (described above) to show how moral panics led by the media usually lead to increased social control. Both Hall and Barker show how moral panics are most frequent at times when society itself is in confusion or crisis and under threat of some sort of breakdown. By directing attention at one or another 'folk devil' through the media, the blame for this is shifted and the public's attention is redirected from the real crisis to, essentially, a scapegoat. More importantly the moral panic whipped up through the media usually leads to a call that 'something must be done' and so the climate is created for legislation or other action that generally increases the level of social control. A good recent example of this is the panic about 'hippie convoys', 'raves' and 'travellers' which was followed by the Criminal Justice Act, giving police very much wider powers than they previously had.

 ### Examination questions

'Explain and evaluate the role of the mass media in the social construction of "moral panics" in society. Illustrate your answer with reference to at least two examples of "moral panics".'

(AEB A, Sociology, Winter 1994, paper 2, question 8)

*There is an outline answer to this question in the skeleton answers section at the end of the book.*

'Examine sociological explanations of the contribution of the mass media to the process of deviance amplification.'

(AEB AS, Sociology, Summer 1994, paper 2, question 7)

### The anxious viewer

Gerbner and Gross thought that the cultivation effect of violence on TV was to make us draw parallels with the television world and the real world and so create an image of a 'scary world'. However Sparks takes an 'active viewer' approach like those discussed above and so reaches different conclusions. Sparks does not think it is plausible to think that TV shows cause fear 'in any important degree'. However crime shows and other relevant media output can 'address fears, play upon them, exploit or reassure them' (p. 155), in other words they work on and change anxieties that were already present.

> ### *Cultivation theory*
>
> The mass media and TV in particular present a 'pseudo-reality' quite different from everyday life. For those people who have limited social contact and high TV exposure, they adopt the pseudo-reality.
>
> A related concept is the idea of enculturation. This is associated with George Gerbner, who argued that the main influence of the media was to convey ideas about social behaviour, social norms and social structure. See p. 153.

## The causes of the media's distorted view of deviants and deviance

Manipulative theory argues that those in the media, who represent the political and economic establishment, deliberately distort deviance in the ways we have examined. This is done in order to strengthen the status quo, ensuring that 'normality' continues and those who threaten it are marginalized and ridiculed in the public mind.

Hegemonic theory, which is subscribed to by far more writers, argues that this process is an unconscious one. Those in the media unwittingly portray deviants and deviance in this way because their lives and behaviour are so foreign to the average journalist. Journalists unconsciously use concepts of newsworthiness and public interest which are derived from the viewpoint of the dominant class(es) in society. They genuinely see society as based on fundamental consensus, with only a few sick or evil people not adhering to the consensual view. They cannot recognize the frustrations and rejection of society that can lead to deviance; they have never felt such emotions. So, they genuinely believe that deviants must be sick, stupid, mindless, gullible or 'just normal really'.

Pluralist theory states that in the area of deviance, as with the others we have examined, the media are giving the public what they want. People *like* to see the good guy win and the bad guy lose. They are comforted by the belief that the police always, or at least usually, catch the criminal. The pluralists agree that the facts are that the police only rarely do so, especially with some types of crime such as burglary, particularly in inner city areas, but people don't want to know this. It would only make the public uneasy if the media insisted on telling them harsh facts such as these and the only noticeable effect would be a decline in sales and viewing figures.

Conservatives like Whitehouse and Medved, however, would disagree with the academics on many issues concerning the media and deviance. They believe, first, that the media often treat deviance approvingly. Second, and as a result, they believe that the media encourage deviance not only among certain social groups but the population as a whole. Conservatives consider that too often deviance is shown as going unpunished on TV and in video films. For conservatives, then, the effect of the media is to *promote* deviance, but not to operate social control.

 ### Exam/Essay questions

'Whilst some studies have claimed that the mass media have a direct and powerful effect on the attitudes and behaviour of audiences, others have argued that these effects are limited or indirect.'
*Outline and assess these arguments.*

(AEB AS, Sociology (with coursework), June 1992, paper 2, question 7)

'The history of mass communication research is conspicuously lacking in any clear evidence of the precise influence of the mass media. Theories abound, examples multiply, but convincing facts that specific mass media content is reliably associated with particular effects have proved quite elusive'. Discuss.

(Cumberbatch and Howitt 1989, p. 25)

## Further reading

Bryson, B. (1994) *Made in America*, London: Minerva (especially chapters 14 and 15 on advertising and the movies).

Cumberbatch, G. and Howitt, D. (1989) *A Measure of Uncertainty: The Effects of the Mass Media*, London: John Libbey (contains useful summaries of the outcomes of research projects on the effects of the media, concentrating on violence and pornography but also addressing gender, disablement, age and other issues).

Eysenck, H. J. and Nias, D. K. (1978) *Sex, Violence and the Media*, London: Maurice Temple Smith.

Gunter, B. (1987) *Television and the Fear of Crime*, London: John Libbey.

Gunter, B. and McAleer, J. L. (1990) *Children and Television: The One Eyed Monster*, London: Routledge.

Hagell, A. and Newburn, T. (1994) *Young Offenders and the Media*, London: Policy Studies Institute.

Hodge, B. and Tripp, D. (1985) *Children and Television*, Oxford: Basil Blackwell.

Lodziak, C. (1987) *The Power of Television: A Critical Appraisal*, London: Pinter.

Pearson, G. (1983) *Hooligan: A History of Respectable Fears*, London: Macmillan.

Phelps, G. (1991) *A Student's Guide to Film Classification and Censorship in Britain*, London: BBFC publications.

Provenzo, E. (1991) *Video Kids: Making Sense of Nintendo*, Cambridge, Mass.: Harvard UP.

Sparks, R. (1992) *TV and the Drama of Crime*, Milton Keynes: Open University Press.

## Useful addresses

The Women's Monitoring Network publications are available from:

**The Women's Monitoring Network**
c/o A Woman's Place
Hungerford House
Victoria Embankment
London WC2

# 7 / Advertising and the media

Figure 7.1 Product placement: In *Goldeneye*, James Bond drives a BMW Roadster, wears a Brioni suit and Church's shoes, sports an Omega watch, sips Smirnoff Black and crashes through a lorry delivering Perrier water!

ALBERT R. BROCCOLI PRESENTS PIERCE BROSNAN AS IAN FLEMING'S JAMES BOND 007 IN "GOLDENEYE"

Advertisements are often ignored in the sociological study of the media. This is strange given that an American 18-year-old, for example, will have seen around 350,000 commercials on TV (Bryson 1994) and a 40-year-old around 1.5 million (Cashmore 1994). One would think that curiosity about the effects of this exposure to a deliberate attempt to influence would have stimulated more of an academic research effort than it has. The lack of attention to advertisements is perhaps explained by the sociologist's desire not to be associated with market research, the kind of enquiry paid for by, and conducted in the interests of, manufacturers and suppliers of services.

There is a need to include the study of advertisements in any examination of the mass media, however. This is because, first, many commentators believe that they can be an important influence on the content of the media. Second, advertisements are clearly designed to influence our attitudes and behaviour where much other media output usually is not. Where better, then, to study whether the media have the power to affect us in these ways? Third, by ignoring the presence of advertisements, arguments become distorted.

For example, the manipulative model of the media (see chapter 4) gains considerable weight if one takes advertising content into account. Conversely, the pluralist's criticism (p. 87) that in socialist countries where the media are manipulated the printed and broadcast information is positive and happy, whereas ours is negative and full of trauma, carries less weight. As the *New York Evening Post* recognized as far back as 1909:

> In the magazine proper everything goes askew. The railroads cheat us and kill us. The food manufacturers poison us ... Workmen go without work ... The list is endless. But what a reconstructed world of heart's desire begins with the first-page advertisement. Here no breakfast food fails to build up a man's brain and muscle ... No razor cuts the face or leaves it sore ... Worry flies before the face of the model fountain pen ... Babies never cry ... A happy world indeed ...

In discussing the importance of advertising in the media there are two important areas for us to examine:

1. how advertisements affect the audience;

2. the impact on the mass media (i.e. structure, content etc.).

## 1.   How advertisements affect the audience

It is commonly stated in the textbooks that nobody really knows whether, or how far, advertisements change people's attitudes towards products and brands, or even how far they encourage people to buy an advertised product. It is certainly unclear whether advertising increases total sales of goods or simply encourages the consumer to buy one brand rather than another. However, in view of the fact that 40% of the price of toothpaste and 32% of the price of a bar of soap is spent on advertising and that it can cost up to half a million dollars to show a 30-second commercial once in the USA, it would seem that the companies which commission the advertisements have no doubt.

Details from companies about their sales figures before and after an advertising campaign are the most obvious way of judging the effectiveness of advertising, but we can assume that where figures are released they tend to be the success stories. For example Nestlé's Gold Blend advertisement featuring an on-going drama between a male and female character centring on coffee and mutual attraction, led to a 15% rise in sales after one year (two instalments) and 40% after 5 years (11 instalments) (Cashmore 1994).

By contrast British Telecom refused to divulge whether their 'It's for yoo-hoo' series of advertisements led to a rise in the number of telephone calls (a uniquely quick and easy test of success for the advertiser). This secrecy, plus the fact that they subsquently changed their advertising agency and changed to a different type of advertisement indicates that those advertisements were either ineffective or counter-productive.

For the purposes of academics, though, advertising campaign figures present some problems. First in most cases the figures are usually kept confidential by companies. Second, they would only reveal the effectiveness or otherwise of the particular campaign to which they relate, not of advertising in general.

Advertising agencies have an obvious interest in persuading their clients of the effectiveness of advertising before a campaign is launched, and over the years they have developed quite sophisticated ideas about how advertisements work. We will look at some of these.

The earliest theory of advertising derived from the behaviourist school of psychology which assumed that people, like animals, respond in an automatic and predictable way to stimuli. Thus, it was believed that advertising worked in the following simple way:

ADVERTISING : CONSUMER : SALES

The use of simple catch phrases mark this sort of advertising.

'Good morning, have you used Pears' soap?'

was an early one (late nineteenth century) devised by Thomas Barratt to cash in on a phrase ('good morning') that would be used every day. This was so successful that it became impossible to hear the words 'good morning' without the phrase 'have you used Pears' soap' springing, unwelcome, into the mind. Such catchphrases are still used today ('It's Good To Talk' is a current BT one) and when set to music they can be unforgettable for the generation exposed to them ('you'll wonder where the yellow went when you wash your teeth with Pepsodent').

 *Identify more up-to date advertisements that use this sort of catch-phrase.*

However, this approach ignored the role of the emotions and the subjective perception of advertisements, so the second mode was developed that looked like this:

AWARENESS : INTEREST : DESIRE : SALES

This was the unfortunately-named AIDS model (so called because of the first letters of the steps involved). It assumed a rational action on the part of the consumer who took in the ad, remembered it and eventually bought the product. It led to a fashion in so-called 'reason why' advertising. An early example (1909) by H. Gordon Selfridge who was determined that his about-to-open store must have equal status with Harrods, etc. within seven days of opening ran:

> The Great Principles upon which we will build this Business are as everlasting as the Pyramids. These Principles are Integrity, Truthfulness, Value-giving, Progressiveness, Dignity, Liberality, Courtesy, Originality, a daily presentation of what is New, coupled with a determination to Satisfy.

However, research showed that recall of a particular ad isn't very important in influencing the decision to buy. So, in the 1960s advertising agencies tried to encourage positive attitudes towards particular aspects of the brand. Thus, the aim was now to *modify attitudes*. Recently, multinational companies have started to adopt this approach in TV advertising (for example British Petroleum), trying to improve their corporate image among the British public, especially if a takeover bid is imminent. Similarly Levi jeans advertisements centre more on image than direct message, with grainily lit handsome men and beautiful women engaging in enigmatic encounters to the backing of rock and blues music (which itself usually shoots up the charts as a result).

*Examine the current issue of three monthly magazines of different sorts. Find the relative numbers of ads using the AIDS approach and the attitude modification approach. Attempt to identify the reasons for the different sorts of advertisements in these magazines.*

Again, however, research evidence showed that advertising doesn't really work very well if the product fails to please. Making the purchase and using the product appear to be at least as important in influencing attitudes as the advertising itself. If the product doesn't give satisfaction it is unlikely that the advertisement will persuade us to like it or the company which makes it.

The most recent model of how advertising works is closely linked to the 'uses and gratifications' approach to media influence (see p. 24). It holds that people use advertisements rather than advertisements using people. Not everyone is interested in a particular product or service, thus, agencies need to *target* their audiences (i.e. make sure the ad reaches the sort of people who might buy the product). Also the advertising strategy should be appropriate to the needs and interests of the people it is aimed at and to the nature of the product. Thus, 'reason why' advertising should be used for some types of product (say a car), whereas advertising appealing to the emotions or the senses should be used for others (say perfume).

Table 7.1 Types of purchase and examples

| Type of purchase | Examples |
|---|---|
| 'Trivial' | |
| Day-to-day convenience | Tea, bread |
| Occasional convenience | Shoe polish |
| Minor luxury | After-shave |
| Small durable | Kettle, iron |
| 'Serious' | |
| Major durable | Car, washing machine |

This model requires agencies to conduct careful research into the potential market for the products they are working on. That market can be described in terms of a number of important characteristics. Social grade is one of the most crucial variables in this respect. To measure it agencies use a scale as shown in Table 7.2.

Table 7.2    Measurement of social grade

| Grade | Occupation | % in Popn 1986 |
|---|---|---|
| A | Higher managerial, administrative and professional | 3.1 |
| B | Intermediate managerial, administrative and professional | 13.4 |
| C1 | Supervisory or clerical and junior managerial, administrative and professional | 22.3 |
| C2 | Skilled manual | 31.2 |
| D | Semi-skilled and unskilled manual | 19.1 |
| E | Casual labourers, state pensioners, the unemployed | 10.9 |

Age is also important and agencies normally use the following groupings:

-15    15–24    24–35    35–55    55+

Some advertising agencies have adopted a psychometric approach to the market. Instead of simply using scales of social class, they also try to measure attitudes and classify according to this dimension. Interviewers ask people whether they agree or disagree with statements like:

● I always go to the same holiday resort because it is familiar.

● I think things used to be better than they are now.

● I think that people who do not have children are selfish.

Different sorts of people can be identified as a result of the analysis of answers, these being close to the commonly used categories of yuppie, preppie, and so on (though probably not 'lombard' – loads of money but a right d***!) with their associated attitudes. It is useful to be able to identify (for example) attitudinally experimental people so that the impact of advertising campaigns for a new type of product (like Super Noodles) can be tested on them.

*The advertising content of three magazines was sampled by Vestergaard and Schroder. The magazines were* Playboy, Cosmopolitan *and* Woman. *Study Table 7.3 and decide which is X, which Y and which Z. The answers are at the end of this chapter.*

| Table 7.3 | Percentage of advertising in three magazines (X, Y and Z) | | |
|---|---|---|---|
| | *Percentage of advertisements Magazine X* | *Percentage of advertisements Magazine Y* | *Percentage of advertisements Magazine Z* |
| Hygiene | 26 | 10 | 3 |
| Beauty | 39 | 18 | 1 |
| Clothes | 7 | 12 | 14 |
| Household implements | 2 | 18 | 0 |
| Food, detergents | 5 | 31 | 0 |
| Tobacco | 6 | 8 | 15 |
| Beer, spirits | 3 | 0 | 25 |
| Leisure | 3 | 0 | 5 |
| Technological toys | 2 | 0 | 38 |
| Employment | 3 | 0 | 0 |
| Investment, insurance | 3 | 2 | 0 |

*Source:* Vestergaard and Schroder (1985), p. 74.

*In what ways have the readership of these magazines been 'targeted' by advertisers?*

*List the sorts of advertisements which appear in* The Times *and the* Sun *in any one day. Construct a similar table. Identify the differences and comment on the different markets they are aimed at.*

Even direct-mail advertisers are now able to target potential consumers for the type of products they are selling. This is despite the fact that the only information they have to go on is a list of names and addresses which they have either bought (there are hundreds of different lists on sale) or got from the register of electors which is available to anyone in local libraries. A system called 'Monica' developed by the market analysis company CACI draws inferences about people's ages from their names. For example:

*Pre-family* (18–25): Lynn, Julie, Lorraine, Michelle, Sharon, Kevin, Gary, Steven, Hugh, Daniel

*Young family* (25–44): Pamela, Judith, Heather, Hazel, Janet, Keith, Christopher, Brian, Martin

*Mature family* (45–65): Joyce, Eileen, Kathleen, Sylvia, Brenda, Eric, Frank, Dennis, Kenneth, Raymond

*Retired*: Hilda, Florence, Annie, Violet, Ethel, Ernest, Percy, Herbert, Arthur, Cyril

*If you are working in a group, test whether these ideas are correct. Establish whether their names give a clue to age, as suggested here. Consider older and younger relatives in addition to those present. Identify any addresses locally which give a clear indication of the socio-economic status of the inhabitants.*

Socio-economic status can be determined from the address. Britain's postcodes have been divided into 11 groups. These include, for example, group B: modern family housing/higher income (e.g. Tamworth, Andover) and group G: poorest council estates (e.g. inner Liverpool and Glasgow). An advertiser wishing to sell, say long winter holidays in Spain, would be well-advised to direct this mailshot at Violet and Arthur in Prestatyn (group K: better-off retirement areas). If it's nappies, then Pam and Phil in Telford or Basildon (group E: better-off council estates) are a good bet. For these people the adverts dropping through the door may not just be 'junk-mail' but actually of interest to them.

Cinema advertising has also become specialized, its target group being the unmarried young. Attendance is dominated by the 15–24 group, those between 25 and 34 do still go but the over 35s rarely attend. It has renewed its usefulness for advertisers by redefining its audience.

An additional attraction for advertisers is the possibility of creating attractive and inventive advertisements for the big screen. A screen sometimes 47 feet wide with amplified and high-quality sound and an attentive young audience sitting in the dark is an advertising agency's dream. Furthermore, while TV advertisements are laden with restrictions, about the only thing a cinema advert can't do is incite unrest, depravity or violence among the audience.

Cinema has been helped in this by the new targeting strategy of many advertising agencies. Guinness, for example, used to use 'buckshot' advertising (including women's press, national and local papers etc.), but now defines its target groups as home drinkers and regular pubgoers. Gordon's gin have deliberately used cinema advertising in order to change the age profile of its drinkers. Barry Smith, creative director of Foote, Cone and Belding, formerly Gordon's ad agency, says:

> We want young people to think about drinking gin rather than rele-
> gating it to something their parents would indulge in.

Additionally, the type of film being shown allows advertisers to have a fairly clear idea about the profile of the audience. Films for the younger age group will, of course, attract bigger audiences. *A Passage to India* attained a total audience of about 2 million people in 1985, but *Ghostbusters* achieved 82 million. For those companies wishing to advertise gin, jeans, a new make of car or the services that their bank can offer young people, cinema is the ideal medium. Increasingly pressure groups are becoming aware of the attractions of targeting. The TUC commissioned a film encouraging a boycott of South African goods to be shown on cinema screens, while Index on Censorship, a group against restrictions on expression, also commissioned Saatchi & Saatchi to produce a three-minute film about them and their cause.

### Reception analysis and advertising

Figure 7.2 'We are not as empty-headed and manipulable as many, including advertisers, seem to think' (Cashmore 1994)

Vance Packard's *Hidden Persuaders* suggested that advertisers see the audience as:

> bundles of day-dreams, misty hidden yearnings, guilt complexes,
> irrational emotional blockages ... image lovers given to compulsive
> acts ... increasingly docil[e] ... in responding to their manipulation
> of symbols that stir us to action.

Many popular and academic views of advertising have adopted a similar view of the audience. David Buckingham in *Children Talking Television* is, however, an exception. He suggests that, as in the study of the effects of media violence, previous research on the effects of advertising has been loaded with researchers' preconceptions about the power of adverts. For example, if you ask a child 'would you like to have most of the things they show on TV commercials?', as Atkin did (1980), the answer is fairly obvious. Similarly simply demonstrating that heavy viewers eat more chocolate bars than light viewers does not 'prove' that advertising stimulated a desire to eat more of them. Buckingham shows that adopting a careful reception analysis approach gives very different conclusions.

Buckingham rejects the behaviourist hypodermic model of looking for the effects of advertising. This argues that children are particularly susceptible to the hypodermic injection of TV advertising messages because they are empty slates, ready to be filled with outside influences. Adults by contrast may be more resistant because they have already developed a set of preferences and views which (to some extent at least) 'inoculate' them against the advertisers' messages. Buckingham agrees with many recent studies of child socialization such as those of Debbie Epstein and Prout and James that children should not be seen as 'deficient adults' in this way. They are in fact active constructors of their own culture and are just as able to interpret, and reject, media messages as adults are.

The general methodology which Buckingham employed is described on p. 38. In the study of advertising the children in particular were shown a video tape of four commercials. The results, in summary, are as follows:

- Children are clearly aware of the functions of advertising and sceptical about it (although 7 and 8 year olds also have some imaginative ideas about the function of advertising):

    Ben (8) 'They're trying to persuade people to buy things or do things.'

    Nancy (8) 'that's why they advertise it, cause they can't get anyone to buy it, so they just try and … make it look really good.'

    Some of the more imaginative reasons for advertising were:
    - to allow the actors to change their clothes;
    - to change the clip of film;
    - to get the scenery ready;
    - to allow people to go to the toilet.

    But all the children except one who gave this sort of reason *also* gave answers like Ben and Nancy's.

- That while children did say they pestered their parents to buy things they had seen, this was done with the realization that they probably would not get them (they were 'trying it on'). They did not ask for things they knew they would not get. They substituted these with requests they knew were more realistic.

- That at Christmas time children consciously used advertisements to help them because they knew they would be asked 'what do you want for Christmas?' and so they needed to generate a list. This finding confirms the 'uses and gratifications' model rather than the 'hypodermic model' of media effects (see pp. 21 and 24).

- Children saw 'other people' as being influenced by advertisements, but they hardly ever saw themselves as influenced in this way. These 'other people' were usually children younger than themselves.

- Children were critical, even cynical about free gifts and the quality of merchandise being advertised generally:

    Sally (10) 'We got this spinning wheel out of the packet (of Honey Nut Loops), spin it round and it breaks.'

- Children apply their own interpretations of the content of advertisements. People appearing in adverts were described as 'ugly', 'stupid', 'prattish', 'wallies' and 'boring old has-beens'. Ten-year-old Anne complained that adverts showing women doing the washing and ironing were sexist and Donna, also 10, was unhappy about the fact that boys' sporting events got most prominence.

- Children apply their well-developed TV literacy (see p. 27) to advertisements. They were able to 'read' the intentions of the advertisers (at whom the ad was aimed) and discuss technical aspects of its production. For example, in an advert for Lucozade, footballer John Barnes kicks an empty can into a waste bin. A number of children said that he did not have enough time to drink the whole can and that the kick into the bin was edited from a number of shots. And in an advert for Radion washing powder there was wobbly camerawork because the ad was supposed to be shot by the family appearing in it. Vanessa (8) said: 'It looks like someone not professional has done it, but really someone professional has done it.'

- Children are 'wise consumers'. Some reported that before buying a toy they had seen on TV they tested those their friends had bought. Others reported comparing prices of similar goods in different shops.

- Children often remembered an advert very well, but could not associate it with any particular product.

Although these results do suggest that children are very active in interpreting, modifying and even rejecting advertising messages, Buckingham qualifies this conclusion in the following ways.

- Although these sorts of responses to advertisements do give children 'cognitive defences' against the hypodermic injection of the message, there is no guarantee about when, or if, they will be used while watching television or buying goods. Children have them, but they may not use them.

- The methodology used in this study made it more likely that these defences would be articulated. Buckingham said that the children interviewed seemed to be competing with each other to see who could be the most cynical and clever about adverts.

- While children were generally sceptical about advertising, they displayed a great enthusiasm for watching adverts. Nancy (12) said: 'I just watch the adverts all the time. (The).. first thing I watch is the adverts, then I watch the programmes.' Buckingham suggests that children derive a great deal of pleasure from adverts. They enjoy using catch phrases, parodying adverts (for example the Prudential's 'I want to be' campaign) and singing the songs in adverts together – though often inventing new words! Buckingham partly agrees with the conclusion reached by Nava and Nava that 'young people consume commercials independently of the product which is being marketed'.

*Look back to Chapter 2 and try applying the different models of media 'effects' to Buckingham's findings.*
*How do Buckingham's findings compare with your experience?*

## 2.   The impact of advertising on the mass media

Views on this can be summarized under three headings.

### The no-impact model

This suggests that advertising has no impact on the other sorts of content of the mass media. Those in official or establishment positions in the media tend to argue that advertising has no effect on its nature or content. For example, Stephen Murphy, a TV officer at the IBA with long experience as a BBC producer, categorically stated in an interview with media sociologist James Curran that advertising pressure is not transferred to programme content. Similarly, Royal Commissions on the Press (1949, 1962 and 1977) have each said that it is difficult to find evidence of any such effect.

### The manipulative model

This suggests that advertisers use their position of influence to manipulate the editorial content of the mass media. The page proofs of the Glasgow Media Group's *Bad News* contained allegations of subtle and crude financial pressure, but this was retracted for fear of libel action. Where a medium is largely funded through advertising revenue,

> there is a pervading fear that valuable advertising will drain away in the face of persistent criticism that names and condemns specific products.
>
> (Ian Breach, the former motoring correspondent of the *Guardian*).

Perhaps the best example of manipulation by advertisers of media content comes from an examination of the rise of the 'soap opera'. Soap operas are so called because they began from an advertising campaign for soap powder. They started on American radio through sponsorship by soap-powder manufacturers, Procter & Gamble, who made Oxydol washing powder. Procter & Gamble were under serious competition from Unilever, the makers of Rinso, but Procter & Gamble managed to recover their market position through subsidizing the radio serial *Ma Perkins*. The plugs they got in both the script and the advertisements which interspersed the story gave rise to a dramatic increase in sales of Oxydol which finally triumphed over Rinso.

A modern equivalent is the manipulation of the content of TV programmes by advertisers in programme-length commercials. At the moment these are confined to children's animated adventure programmes. Examples include Tonka's *Go-Bots*, Hasbro Bradley's *Transformers*, *My Little Pony* (and others), Mattel's *He-Man and Masters of the Universe* and *She-Ra Princess of Power*, and LJN's *Thunder Cats*. In total there are 65 series designed to sell children the characters and their apparatus. In each case the toy companies retain control over the content of the programme. The companies have found that this increases sales dramatically. Hasbro's sales literature says to retailers:

> Every GI Joe figure, every vehicle, every accessory will star in this historic television first! Think of the enormous excitement this series will generate among kids for all GI Joe toys. Get ready for the sales impact!

This sort of programme, being popular with children, is displacing other forms of broadcast children's entertainment and in virtually every case contains doubtful sex role models, attitudes towards violence, and so on.

An example from the press involves the *Observer* newspaper. Its city correspondent advised shareholders of Harrods on the best way to beat off an unwelcome bid from Tiny Rowland's Lonrho. This was in the context of a general campaign by that paper against his aggressive bid for Harrods and a more longstanding series of articles which were critical of Lonrho's dealings in Africa, particularly sanctions-busting deals with Rhodesia. Lonrho responded by cancelling its advertising in the *Observer*. Soon afterwards Rowland bought the paper. This has meant that certain areas of business and foreign reporting were subsequently not covered by the paper (e.g. the paper's diarist Peter Hillmore was dissuaded from writing about Tiny Rowland's friend Conservative MP Edward Du Cann (now Managing Director of Lonrho).

*Examine the 'feature' pages (i.e. ones about holidays, motoring, cooking, etc.) of local and national newspapers over the next week. Pay particular attention to the advertisements on the page.*

*Comment on the relationship between the feature and the advertisements. Identify which of the two above models are verified, if either of them are, by your research.*

Another example of manipulation is the giving or withholding of co-operation by the military when films needing such co-operation are made. These films are beneficial because they attract recruits and improve the image of the armed forces. In a sense they are 'advertising' the armed services. The US Navy has a Hollywood liaison office which has worked with Hollywood on such films as *PT109* (about the life of John F. Kennedy), many John Wayne movies, *Operation Petticoat* and, more recently *Top Gun*. The military are the only people who own the hardware needed in such films (jets, helicopters and so on) and they loan them to 'appropriate' films.

Co-producer of *Top Gun*, Don Simpson, says that the military top brass at the Pentagon were 'very positive' about his film and admits that 'we did them well'. On the other hand, Oliver Stone's *Platoon* did not get such co-operation. The military judged this film (about Vietnam) to be 'wholly unrealistic', especially in its portrayal of drug use, black–white relations and the treatment of the Vietnamese. While no-one says that the military have editorial control, they clearly only support films which they consider portray them 'accurately' (e.g. *Top Gun*) and their project officer on site can withdraw co-operation at any time if anything deviates from what has been agreed.

*In September 1995 the film* Apollo 13 *was launched in the UK, starring Tom Hanks. At the time NASA was threatened by severe cuts in its budget and serious questions in government about the whole future of the space programme. If you can, watch the film (again) with that context in mind and consider:*

● *the likely amount of co-operation the film-makers received in order to make the film;*

● *the likely impact of the film on the attitudes of the audience towards NASA and the space programme.*

A final example of the manipulative model here is subtle inclusion of advertising in films where there are no formal adverts. This is termed 'product placement':

> Arranging the appearance or mention of specific brand names in motion pictures has become a multi-million dollar business. Firms charge clients fees ranging from $5000 to $250,000 for guaranteed placement in a contracted number of films with escalation clauses for particularly extensive or prominent appearances. Some companies (for example Coca-Cola, Pepsi, Anheuser-Busch) have formed

their own in-house divisions dedicated specifically to product placement and/or Hollywood advertising activities.

(Wasco 1993)

In 1992 the Radio 4 soap opera *The Archers* began mentioning the names of actual
beers rather than the fictitious ones they had previously used. When the BBC buys a
programme from the USA its price reflects the amount of 'hidden' advertising it
contains.

However, arguments against the manipulative view are that:

● commercial TV companies have a monopoly over televised advertising, hence
they can resist pressure;

● the ITC is vigilant about influence such as this; loss of licence to broadcast may
result;

● radio advertising time is bought in chunks; times of transmission are set by the
stations themselves on a rotation basis, which helps avoid pressure from
advertisers;

● the *Sunday Times* continued to get adverts from Distillers even when it was
campaigning against that company's heartless treatment of the victims of its drug
Thalidomide. This shows that a good cause, especially one with news value, will
hold sway over financial pressure.

### The revenue allocation model

This is more sophisticated than the last. Its main proponent is J. Curran. His argument
essentially says that where advertisers place revenue in the media will affect those
media in important ways, including which survive and which do not. Let's examine his
argument point by point.

1. Changes in where advertisers have placed their business have tended to favour the
development of some forms of mass media over others.

Table 7.4    Distribution of advertising revenue between the media (%)

|  | 1938 | 1948 | 1954 | 1960 | 1965 | 1970 | 1975 | 1979 | 1985 |
|---|---|---|---|---|---|---|---|---|---|
| National newspapers | 25 | 14 | 17 | 20 | 20 | 20 | 17 | 16 | 17 |
| Regional newspapers | 27 | 31 | 31 | 21 | 24 | 26 | 29 | 28 | 23 |
| Magazines and periodicals | 15 | 13 | 19 | 12 | 11 | 9 | 8 | 9 | 6 |
| Trade and technical journals | 12 | 16 | 13 | 10 | 9 | 10 | 9 | 10 | 8 |
| Other publications | 2 | 1 | 1 | 1 | 1 | 2 | 2 | 3 | 5 |
| Press production costs | 5 | 8 | 6 | 7 | 4 | 6 | 5 | 6 | 6 |
| Total press | 85 | 83 | 88 | 71 | 70 | 72 | 70 | 70 | 65 |
| Television | 0 | 0 | 0 | 22 | 24 | 23 | 24 | 22 | 31 |
| Poster and transport | 8 | 14 | 9 | 5 | 4 | 4 | 4 | 4 | 4 |
| Cinema | 3 | 4 | 3 | 2 | 1 | 1 | 1 | 1 | 1 |
| Radio | 3 | 0 | 1 | 0 | 1 | 0 | 1 | 2 | 2 |

*What does Table 7.4 tell us about the changes in the distribution of advertisers' revenue over time?*
*What other information would we need to be able to predict likely consequences for the mass media of these trends?*

2. As we have already seen, some sections of the media have had to specialize in terms of their audience in order to deliver a particular type of person to advertisers. This has allowed them to continue to attract revenue in the face of competition from TV.

Money for *television* advertising comes from particular types of product manufacturer – household cleansing products, toothpaste, food and drink and the like. This is because TV cannot deliver a targeted audience to advertisers. Some limited selectivity is possible; the audience changes a little according to time of day and day of the week, but hardly at all by type of programme, according to Curran. However, he may be wrong about this. In 1992 NBC dropped three successful shows from its schedules because they appealed to older viewers who were comparatively unattractive to NBC's advertisers. The shows were *In the Heat of the Night, Matlock* and *Golden Girls*: all very successful in the ratings.

 *Illustrate this last point by giving examples of how the TV audience might differ at different times of the day and week.*

The press has managed to defend itself from competition from other media partially through its ability to deliver to advertisers a particular type of readership target group. Additionally, government limitations on broadcasting have increased the attractiveness of the press for advertisers (though this may change if the BBC is allowed to advertise). Target marketing has led to the launch of many new periodicals, many of which check first with advertising agencies to ensure that they will reach a suitable audience (this occurred before the launch of *Over 21*, for example).

3. Where advertising money is being spent has had a number of consequences for different media.

Advertising revenue allocations have reinforced the conservative bias of national newspapers. Those which can attract an affluent, middle-class (and, therefore, conservative) readership can easily attract advertising revenue. Some areas of the press have disappeared altogether as a result of this. Examples include the *Daily Sketch, Reynolds News, Picture Post, Illustrated* and *Everybody's*. These all closed down because they could not attract advertising income, appealing as they did to old and poor people – not an attractive proposition for most advertisers. Also their circulations tended to decline as they lost readers, in particular, to the new TV medium (that group of people read less and watch more TV than others).

Conservative papers which include 'serious' news coverage can reach readers who have money to spend, have influence over corporate spending and watch comparatively little TV. Advertisers find it worth paying to get the attention of such people. For these reasons the quality papers are able to survive even with remarkably low circulations. Popular papers cannot because of their lower advertising revenue. The *Daily Herald* closed in 1964 with a larger circulation than *The Times* and the *FT*. *Women's Weekly* (read by a working-class readership) derived 5p per copy from advertising revenue in 1976, *Harper's and Queen* got 92p.

| Table 7.5 Sources of revenue of newspapers | | |
|---|---|---|
| Type of publication | % From advertising 1986 | % From sales 1986 |
| Popular dailies (the *Sun*) | 27 | 73 |
| Popular Sundays (*Sunday Mirror*) | 31 | 69 |
| Quality dailies (*Guardian*) | 58 | 42 |
| Quality Sundays (*Observer*) | 66 | 34 |
| Regional dailies (*Yorkshire Post*) | 61 | 39 |
| Regional weeklies | 84 | 16 |
| Consumer magazines | 41.5 | 58.5 |

 *Identify the types of magazines which will find it easiest to attract advertising revenue, giving examples.*

Political papers, in particular radical ones, do not suit advertisers. They don't have a suitable editorial environment, they don't cover a consumer market (i.e. the politically committed tend not to be concerned with consumer goods) and they don't reach a specialized group. Hence, there are few of them.

In addition the direction of advertising revenue allocations has caused women's magazines to be oriented to young middle-class women because such women have spare cash. Magazines for the middle class also appeal to advertisers because they use coated paper, have an editorial style that suits glossy adverts, have a high readership per copy and have a readership with a low exposure to the TV. There are 5.5 million young middle-class people in the population (young = under 35), 16 million older working-class people, yet there are far more magazines for the former category than for the latter. General women's weeklies have suffered in particular. In 1958 there were seven with a circulation of over one and half million each, by 1967 there were only four. They have largely been replaced by magazines for young middle-class working women. Between 1965 and 1975 there were 34 new beauty/fashion/home interest/young woman magazines launched (compared to only seven general women's magazines launched).

Finally advertising money has added weight to private rather than public broadcasting, giving it a better financial base. Advertisers are willing to pay for a stable, reliable and predictable audience. This pushes TV programming into such populist areas as soap operas, situation comedies and variety programmes. These have universal appeal and they tend to displace more serious documentaries, current affairs programmes and the like. The BBC has been forced to adopt a populist approach, too, by the competition from the ITV stations. In 1958 the BBC's audience share dropped below 30% and from that point it began consciously to imitate its rival. This policy has proved successful. In 1987 the audience share of the BBC channels overall was 48%, while 52% went to the commercial channels, including Channel 4. Increases in the licence fee are difficult to justify if the BBC is not providing what the audience wants.

4. The content of the media has been adapted to suit the requirements of the advertisers, Curran argues. This has had several results.

The popular and quality press have polarized, so the journalism is now very different in each. The quality press have not provided material to cater to popular tastes for fear of diluting the quality of their audience (and, hence, their attractiveness to advertisers). The popular press, though, want quantity rather than quality and, hence, they are happy to provide whatever will attract the largest number of readers; Page Three girls, scandals about soap opera stars and so on. Some advertisers will clearly be unhappy about their company name being associated with such an environment. The Co-op and Tesco withdrew their advertisements from the *Star* in 1987 because they felt that it had gone too far down-market under the editorship of Michael Gabbert (Gabbert was sacked soon afterwards).

Programming on TV has been affected as channels seek to deliver a large and predictable audience to advertisers. Scheduling strategies are used to manipulate audience numbers. One is to transmit light entertainment programmes early in the evening, following them with a sequence of programmes that expand and consolidate the mass audience. Another is 'hammocking' programmes of low audience appeal between two 'bankers' (programmes which can be relied on to attract a large audience). A third is to schedule a programme of limited appeal at the same time as an equally unpopular programme on the other main channel. These are all adopted to get and keep as big an audience as possible. In commercial radio the attempt to deliver a target audience to advertisers has led to programmes for the specialist market such as *Hullabaloo*, a programme for teenagers on Capital Radio which generates appropriate advertisements (and, hence, revenue). In this way radio is trying to fight back against the loss of audience to TV.

*Examine the shelves of a local newsagent. Count the number of magazines directed to each special interest (or estimate the space). Identify which types of interests predominate and which are not represented. On the basis of the evidence you collect, comment on Curran's view that the press and other media have been shaped by the need to deliver target audiences to advertisers.*

Lastly consumer magazines have subordinated themselves to the needs of advertisers so that editorials become merely extensions of the advertisements ('aditorials'). Service features on investment, travel, motoring, property and fashion have grown in terms of editorial space in national newspapers since the war. This has been done in order to attract associated advertising revenue. Fear of loss of advertising revenue serves as a check to criticism of particular products or brands. However, the influence of advertisers is much more pervasive on women's magazines than on national newspapers. In these and other consumer magazines there is less commitment to journalistic integrity. Providing a conducive editorial environment for adverts in these magazines is much more important than it is in the national press.

In some cases advertisers are invited to share the cost of editorial features (the magazine *Honey* did this on several occasions in 1973). Aditorials such as this are appearing on the deregulated commercial Italian TV though the audience is not informed that the company whose products are receiving such flattering attention is paying for the privilege.

*This is an interview study on the effectiveness of advertising.*
*1. Choose sample size and method of sampling.*
*2. Choose a current advertising campaign in the broadcast or printed media.*

3. Conduct the interview around the following questions:
   - Have you seen the advertisement for X?
   - Can you describe the advertisement?
   - Do you know what sort of product X is?
   - What did the advertisement tell you about X?
   - Have you bought X since you saw the advertisement?
   - If not, do you intend to buy any?
   - Had you bought X before seeing the advertisement?

   You should, of course, elaborate on these questions.

4. Devise a way of collating the material you have gathered so that you can summarize the findings about the effectiveness of the campaign you have chosen.

5. Conduct the study.

Semiological analysis can be applied to advertising as to any other form of media message.

Figure 7.3

Study this reading ('deconstruction') of an advertisement for Johnson's Baby Lotion. What's your view of this reading?

Underneath it all you're still a Johnson's baby.

Life is hard on a grown-up skin. That's why you need a gentle, effective cleanser to wipe away what the day's put on.

Johnson & Johnson

The photograph shows a clear, fresh face with an open and trusting expression. She has what could be a nappy around her neck, but apart from that there is no sign of any clothes, makeup or jewellery. She is in a state of nature, of innocence before The Fall. The copy runs *Underneath it all you are still a Johnson's baby*. The first three words are ambiguous. They could refer to underneath makeup, underneath clothes or underneath the image that is presented to the world, partly with the aid of accessories, clothes and makeup. You are still a Johnson's baby makes the link between the past (baby) and present (adult) use of Johnson's and puts the reader/model in the role of a child who can rely on Johnson's as their 'parent', a source of permanence in a changing, demanding world. The copy around the bottle suggests that the working woman suffers pollution of her natural state as a result of her entry into the world of work. Women need Johnson's to return them to their natural baby-like state of nature by removing the detritus of life.

*Choose an advertisement from any magazine and attempt a similar reading of it. This can be done in an unstructured way (as above) or using Table 7.6 (one example has been given for guidance).*

Table 7.6    Sample decoding of an advertisement

| Denotive codes | Connotive codes | Promises | Problems |
|---|---|---|---|
| Young woman with towel around neck, preparing to apply *Johnson's Baby Lotion* with cotton wool | Cotton wool and white towelling = babies. Fresh skin, open expression and no makeup = innocence, happiness and naturalness | Return to babyhood. Youth, happiness, and authenticity | Stresses in the adult world, especially for women. Ageing, especially for women. Responsibilities. |

The Peacock Committee, (of 1986) ... argued that the BBC should have the option of privatising Radio One, Radio Two and local radio ... But Peacock went on recommend that the BBC should not take advertisements at the present time ...

(Wagg 1987)

*Discuss the possible consequences of permitting BBC television and radio to carry advertisements.*

## Further reading

Nava, M. and Nava, O. (1990) *Discriminating or Duped? Young people as consumers of advertising/art Cultural Studies*, 1, 15–21.

Buckingham, D. (1993a) *Children Talking Television*, Lewes: Falmer, chap. 10.

Buckingham, D. (1993b) *Reading Audiences: Young People and the Media*, Manchester UP.

Cashmore, E. (1994) *... And There Was Television*, London: Routledge, chap. 6.

Williamson, J. (1992) *Decoding Advertisements*, London: Marion Boyars.

Young, B. M. (1990) *Television Advertising and Children*, Oxford: Clarendon.

## Answer

The answer to Table 7.3 on p. 137 is
X = *Cosmopolitan*, Y = *Woman* and Z = *Playboy*.

## Useful addresses

**Advertising Standards Authority**
2 Torrington Place
London WC1E 7HN
0171 580 5555

# Mass media, politics and policy-making

Figure 8.1   The media
infatuation with royalty
extends into politics and
policy-making.

This chapter begins by reviewing some of the important developments in the
relationship between politics and the mass media. It then goes on to give an account
of four perspectives on the relationship between the mass media, politics and policy
making. These are, in turn:

- the hegemonic model

- the pluralist model

- the manipulative model

- the postmodernist account

The first three of these are outlined in Chapter 4 and it would be advisable to review
that chapter quickly before reading this one. In each case an account is given both of
the arguments and evidence in favour of the perspective concerned and the
arguments against the others which arise from it. The chapter concludes by applying
the four perspectives to questions about the relationship between the mass media
and 'reality' that are often brought up in examination questions.

*For many of the exercises in this chapter you will need to study as many
TV news broadcasts on all four channels as possible. Try to record them
for later detailed analysis. If recording facilities are not available then
make detailed notes while watching.*

# The mass media, politics and policy-making: the background

In the early days of broadcasting and film, politicians were very unskilled in using the new media. In the first newsreels politicians such as Lloyd George were filmed as if they were addressing an audience from the platform. The tone of voice used and the gestures were the same as those made at a political rally. The camera shot was from the side and the speech was addressed to the make-believe audience, not to camera. Even Churchill, brought up in a world without TV and film, was uneasy in the presence of cameras, appearing wooden and relying on cue-cards. He learned, though, to make effective use of the radio, as did his contemporary President Roosevelt whose 'fireside chats to the nation' on radio were expertly designed to enhance his image.

Today politicians are more adept at using the media, in fact they are schooled in its use and in presenting themselves well. The Conservative Party has employed Saatchi & Saatchi, Labour used the film director Hugh Hudson to make the famous *Kinnock* broadcast. Mrs Thatcher had her teeth altered and changed the timbre of her voice in order to improve the way she looked and sounded on television. The Labour Party employed consultants who advised them on how to dress in public.

As a result of such developments many fear that the media tail has begun to wag the political dog and that image management has become more important than policies. From this viewpoint it is no surprise that an actor was chosen as President of the United States, that political leaders are becoming increasingly photogenic and skilled at using the media or that political events on both sides of the Atlantic are increasingly stage-managed media events, attended only by the party faithful.

More positively, the media explosion and globalization that has occured in the past two decades may mean that there are innumerable alternative sources of information and many more 'voices' being heard than in the past. If so, then our society at least has the potential to be more democratic than it was, and the mass media have a large role to play in this.

# The hegemonic model

Perhaps the best known studies which adopted the hegemonic approach to political issues and the mass media are those conducted by the Glasgow University Media Group (GMG). A group of publications in the 1970s and '80s will be used to illustrate their perspective (the methodology these used is outlined on p. 42). These are:

*Bad News* (1976)

*More Bad News* (1980)

*Really Bad News* (1982)

*War and Peace News* (1985)

The conclusions of these studies are as follows:

1. 'Biased' use is made of the words in the broadcast news: 'trouble', 'radical', 'pointless strike' etc. all structure the listeners' perspective on stories.

2. Stories are reported in a selective way. For example, Prime Minister Harold Wilson said that a strike at British Leyland was 'manifestly avoidable' and that this was the fault of workers and management. The evening news reported him as saying that only the workers were to blame.

3. The effects of strikes are far more likely to be reported than their causes.

4. Visual effects are also used in a 'biased' way, for example, film of piles of rubbish and rats may be used to reinforce the verbal message of the voice-over, both concentrating on the effects of a strike rather than its causes. Similarly film of a group of pickets round a fire outside some factory gates shouting over each other to get access to the microphone reinforces the message of anarchic and dangerous strikers.

5. The tactics of protesters are more likely to be reported than their views.

6. There is a hierarchy of access to the media, so that 'experts' and establishment figures are more likely to get their views aired than workers and ordinary people.

7. There is a unitary frame of reference given in the news, that of the dominant ideology. News is reported in a simplified and one-sided way.

8. The media set the agenda for public debate, that is, they determine which are the most important issues of the day. This is done on the basis of the frame of reference of the reporters, which is predominantly anti-union, pro-establishment and middle of the road politically. For example, at the top of the media's agenda during the miners' strike was picket-line violence (caused by miners). Police violence and intimidation were very much on the miners' agenda, but these were consistently absent in news coverage. Such structured absences are a consistent part of news reporting.

9. In setting the agenda the media act as gatekeepers, excluding some stories from the news and including others. Some themes will often recur in the news, for example stories about strikes at British Leyland are more likely to be included than more important and longer strikes elsewhere and they are likely to be constructed in terms of the problems of a radical, irresponsible and greedy workforce in that company.

10. News coverage of the party politics is sympathetic towards the right wing of the Labour Party and the left wing of the Conservative Party (what Mrs Thatcher used to call the 'wets'). The research was completed before the rise (and demise) of the Social Democrats, but the argument is that the sorts of values they stood for, and which are represented today by the Liberal Democrats, are those espoused by most people working in the media. Extremism, either on the right or on the left, is given the same sort of treatment that striking or immoderate unions get.

 *Make a note of any examples you find in the news broadcasts you study to illustrate these findings.*

In *More Bad News* the GMG say that the fundamental reason for these biases is the particular world view that journalists have. This echoes the interests and attitudes of the dominant class in society very largely. The effects of this world view are twofold:

1. It defines what counts as 'news' and whose opinions are important enough to be sought, who should be interviewed and so on when telling us about it.

2. It provides journalists with a way of interpreting events and 'explaining' them.

These points are central features of the hegemonic model of media bias we discussed in Chapter 4. In their more recent *War and Peace News* and in *Getting the Message* the GMG seem to have added some elements of the manipulative theory to their analysis of media bias. For example, they stress the pressures on broadcasting journalists to put the establishment line, even if it does not accord with their own view. Sometimes, however, journalists can 'escape' these pressures and present a critical point of view or even an anti-establishment line. Jonathan Dimbleby is named specifically as a TV journalist whose views are out of the ordinary for a journalist and who has been able to use the media to express them. Powerful forces within and outside the media have an important influence on journalists, but they don't totally control them.

---

### Enculturation

This concept, developed in Gerbner and Gross's 1976 publication, is close to the hegemonic approach. These authors argue that the broadcast media adopt an unconscious view of the world which they transmit to the public at large, effectively acting as an agency of socialization:

> television is the central arm of American society. It is an agency of the established order and as such serves primarily to extend and maintain rather than to alter, threaten or weaken conventional conceptions, beliefs and behaviors. Its chief function is to spread and stabilize social patterns, to cultivate not change our resistance to change. Television is the medium of the socialization of most people into standardized roles and behaviours. Its function is, in a word, enculturation
>
> *( Gerbner and Gross 1976 )*

---

*An interesting assignment to test the statements made by the GMG and others about the world view of journalists is to interview a journalist or journalists. It will be most convenient, probably, to approach a journalist on a local paper near to you. Journalists often begin their career on local papers and progress to nationals or to the broadcast media anyway. In advance of the meeting prepare a detailed list of questions. These should be designed to assess such issues as whether s/he feels s/he has total freedom in the way reports are written, particularly reports of strikes etc., what the main constraints on news reporting are, what makes a 'good story' and so on. Delicate areas such as the journalist's political views and attitude towards unions will have to be approached with some caution.*

*The aim of this exercise is to look for a dominant perspective in the press. If you are studying the media in a group, buy copies of all the daily newspapers on one particular day and allocate them among the different members of the group. In half an hour or so each member should:*
- *identify particular examples of a viewpoint operating in one direction or*

another with regard to politics and policy-making (attention should be given to editorials and cartoons, as well as news stories);

- *roughly quantify the amount of attention given to stories about political issues compared to other types of news (foreign, crime etc.);*
- *prepare a summary of what the main news values of that particular paper are, perhaps in order of priority, for example sport, foreign news, domestic political news, sudsology (stories about soap operas and their stars) etc.*

*Individual reports can then be given to the group as a whole and comparisons made.*

A variant of the hegemonic theory argues that the media frequently initiate a moral panic about 'the state of society today' (because of minority groups, the unions, youth or whatever) and in so doing establish the basis for the legitimate installation of repressive measures by the authorities. This is the basic argument of *Policing the Crisis*. The authors of the book, Hall *et al.*, maintain that the capitalist economy goes through periods of crisis from time to time. The profitability of companies declines, many go out of business. There is unemployment and hence increased poverty. Inflation rises and there are currency crises. Levels of discontent increase.

At such times the capitalist establishment needs to keep a tight grip on society. The powers of the forces of law and order need to be strengthened and trade unions and political dissidents are intimidated into quiescence. However, this cannot be done by using the brute force of the police and army in a simple and direct way. To do so would unmask the basic brutality and oppressiveness of capitalism. First the approval of the public for such measures must be obtained. This is achieved by the media's whipping up of concern about 'the collapse of law and order'. A hegemonic definition of the situation has been achieved. The climate is soon right for increasing police powers, political arrests, harsh sentences and so on.

An example of this process in action is the year-long moral panic about 'mugging' in 1972. This was followed by a tightening of what they call the 'control culture', that is, the police and courts began to act with increasing vigour against deviants. Similar moral panics can be identified prior to this, for example, the 'cosh boy menace' (1951), teddy boys (1954), soccer hooligans (periodically from 1961), mods and rockers (1964), skinheads and Hell's Angels (1969).

*The passing of the Criminal Justice Act followed a wave of concern about 'travellers' moving around the country and squatting (see p. 130). This can be seen as an example of a move by the control culture against folk devils. Are there any more recent examples you can find?*

In a similar vein, Steve Chibnall's *Law and Order News* argues that crime reporting is used to reinforce consent for the dominant ideology in capitalism. He suggests that law and order news during the period 1965–75 was organized around the dominant theme of 'The Violent Society'. There was a single over-riding image; that of a law and order crisis. This arose as a result of:

1. the pro-capitalist ideology of most of the media (concerned about any erosion of the stable social base for the profitable exploitation of the working class);

2. the news values of journalists which are highly compatible with this ideology (looking for stories which arouse the emotions, which involve goodies and baddies

etc.) and the fact that the dominant source of news stories was the forces of law and order themselves, particularly the police. Their interpretations of events were accepted uncritically and, if they needed to, they could manipulate the media to their own ends.

The same theme is found in Liz Curtis' *Ireland: The Propaganda War* (1984), written during the period of the Troubles in Northern Ireland. She argues that the army in Northern Ireland is the most trusted supplier of news to the media institutions. The media allow them regularly to lie and use their privileged access for their own propaganda ends, and to cover up torture, brutality and mistakes. Moreover, programmes are routinely censored by broadcasting and publishing media so that the views of the Catholic republicans are not allowed expression. A blind eye is turned to Protestant loyalists' violence while that of the IRA is graphically described and portrayed as motiveless.

People killed by soldiers 'die in an incident involving the army'; those killed by the IRA are 'gunned down by terrorists'. In this way the consent of the bulk of the British people is built up and maintained for the Government's policy in Northern Ireland. From a republican point of view, of course, that policy involves the maintenance of an army of occupation by a colonial power.

Figure 8.2

## The pluralist model

These critics of the media simply assume that if the media are 'biased', then this will inevitably influence the audience. This assumption is based on a simplistic model of media influence which comes from the hypodermic model of effects (see p. 21). The problem with this kind of approach is that it ignores the fact that the audience have a barrier of prior attitudes and emotions through which they filter the message received. To avoid cognitive dissonance individuals will practise selective exposure, selective perception and selective retention.

> ### Cognitive dissonance
>
> Cognitive dissonance refers to a state of disharmony between our atti-
> tudes, beliefs and values and information we receive from the outside
> world (as experienced, for example, by the person who enjoys smoking but

reads a medical report about its ill-effects). Dissonance theory says that people who experience this will strive to achieve equilibrium, or consonance, again. They can use a number of strategies to do this, for example by 'explaining away' or denying unwanted messages, by seeking alternative information, by saying 'it's not that important'. Only sometimes is consonance achieved through reconsidering their own attitudes, beliefs or values and effectively undergoing attitude change. These ideas come from Festinger's work.

Pluralists stress the active role of the audience in interpreting media messages. They stress the use people make of the media and their active interpretation of media messages. The audience are not simply passive receivers of media influence, nor do they uncritically accept that they are receiving an objective view of reality through the media. This is illustrated by the fact that people are aware that newspapers do not take an impartial view, as terrestrial television is required to do (see Figure 8.3).

Figure 8.3    Perceptions of sources of news concerning events of national and international significance (%)

*Source*: adapted from Gunter *et al.* (1994)

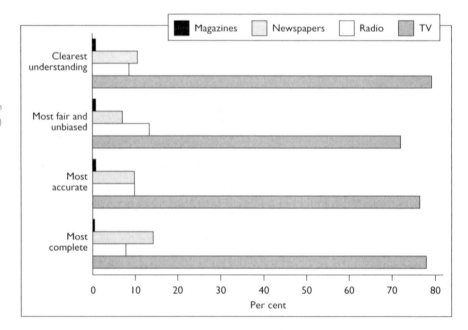

A study by Gunter *et al.* (1994) showed that most people do not believe that TV channels are 'biased' towards any political party. Sixty-six per cent of TV viewers thought that ITV was neutral, next came Channel 4 at 65% followed by BBC2 and BBC1 at 63% and 56% respectively. Those who thought there was a 'bias' were evenly split between a perceived 'bias' in favour of Labour and Conservative, though more people than in the past tended to think there was a pro-Conservative 'bias' on BBC channels (which is quite different from what many Conservative politicians say). This disagreement between the public at large and between the public and the political élite about the nature of 'bias' on television shows that there *is* no important or consistent 'bias': if there was there would not be so much disagreement about its nature.

So the pluralist position rejects the arguments about consistent political 'bias' in the media put forward by the modified left (hegemonic) and the manipulative models. It maintains that the media respond to the demands of the public and are subject to numerous pressures from competing quarters, both élite and non-élite.

An example is the leaked memo from inside the Labour shadow cabinet in September 1995. Someone (probably on the left of the party) gave a copy of a memo to the *Guardian* seven months after it was written. The memo, titled *The Unfinished Revolution,* was from party adviser Philip Gould to the shadow cabinet and stated that more power needed to be concentrated on the Labour leader (Tony Blair) and that links with unions should be further severed in various ways. The leak took place just as the Trades Union Congress was having its annual conference and Blair was due to speak to it. This put Blair in a very uncomfortable position and set the agenda for the reporting of his speech and media reporting generally of the relationship between New Labour and the unions. This was, presumably, exactly what the person who leaked the memo wanted. Clearly there was manipulation of the media going on, but in this case from someone on the left of the Labour Party.

Journalists and editors have well-formed ideas of what the public are interested in, what is 'hot news' and what are the important issues. These will also shape the content of political reporting. This is summed up in the phrase 'news values'. A visit by the Prime Minister to South Africa is newsworthy, a Labour MP's visit to the former Soviet Union (CIS) isn't (unless something unusual or scandalous happens there). The very concept of 'biased reporting' used by other models is erroneous – it assumes that it would be possible to report events objectively. Of course, this is impossible. There must be selection from all the events which occur in the world, and those which are reported must be approached from a particular angle. This angle is shaped by news values, and by the practical constraints on the medium. The latter include:

● Is there a reporter there?

● Have we got/can we get pictures (for television)?

● How much will it cost to get these things?

● Can we get access?

Rather than articulating just one point of view and acting to maintain the political status quo, the media are a central arm of democracy. Not only do they expose political wrong-doing but perhaps more importantly they are used as a kind of 'sounding board' by politicians. Potential policy ideas are 'floated' through the media and government is able to gauge reaction to them. Thus the media are used in the early stages of policy formation. The mass media are also an important route of information to the government about public opinion and current issues of concern. An example is the passing of the Dangerous Dogs Act after there had been a spate of reports in the press and television about children being mauled by dogs, particularly pit bull terriers and their use by criminals to terrorize others and as protection from the police.

 *How strong are these kinds of arguments, in your view?*

Pluralism, with its view that there are a variety of 'voices' heard in the media, is clearly at odds with the findings and perspective of the GMG. A well-researched and cogent critique of their work, based on a pluralist point of view, was made by Professor

Martin Harrison of Keele University (Harrison 1985). Harrison was allowed access to the transcripts of the ITN broadcasts and most of his comments relate to their news coverage, not that of the BBC (though he believes that they are probably true of the BBC as well). Using this and other information he makes the following criticisms of the GMG's findings:

1. The five months which the *Bad News* study covered was not representative in terms of the pattern of industrial relations in the country (there were an abnormally large number of days lost in strikes) or of news behaviour (which at different times of the year would have adopted other stories, for example, during the conference season).

2. The GMG were selective in what they looked for (e.g. they claimed that there was no news reporting of employers' lock-outs, withholding pay or refusing overtime money; in fact there were several instances of such reporting).

3. The GMG are mistaken in believing that undue attention is given to strikes in some industries (e.g. car manufacture, especially at British Leyland), while other industries are ignored (e.g. shipbuilding). In fact, news values are determined at least as much by the 'knock-on' effects of strikes beyond the plants actually involved as by the measure of the number of days lost. Also, the official statistics by which the GMG measure the 'real' severity of strikes are crude and inaccurate at best.

4. The GMG argue that the media are too concerned to illustrate the effects of strikes on consumers of goods and services. However, it is legitimate to give priority to the effects rather than the causes of strikes when those affected outnumber strikers by more than one thousand to one in some cases.

5. The GMG have a naïve view of news values; priority is often given to stories which have a historical background (for example years of strikes at British Leyland). This background is lost by the short-term nature of content analysis studies and is not appreciated by the GMG. Novelty, too, is important in news values, as are stories which involve broader issues (e.g. a strike over the introduction of containers at London docks involves the question of new technology versus jobs). Strikes with a political dimension and those which for some other reason are controversial are also likely to be reported. How many competing stories there are on a particular day will also be an important determinant of whether a strike story is, or is not, included. To sum up, news values neither work consistently for the trade unions nor against them. Film may be chosen because it is good visual material, not for any anti-union message it may contain.

6. A number of the allegations made by the GMG about TV news are simply not true. Harrison demonstrates this by reference to statistical material from the ITN transcripts. These unfounded allegations are:

   ● that the news does not normally name the trade union involved in a dispute;
   ● that the news does not normally state whether a dispute is official or not;
   ● that the news does not normally state the cause of an industrial dispute;
   ● that access is not normally given to shop-floor workers in unofficial disputes.

For example, the ITN report of a strike by Glasgow's dustcart drivers stated who was on strike, mentioned the TGWU, the application for the strike to be made official and the essence of the men's demands.

7. The GMG's approach, while claiming to be objective and scientific, is actually slanted in favour of the unions and searches for only one sort of bias. While there is a chapter entitled 'The Trade Unions and the Media' in *Bad News* there is no chapter on Management and the Media. This needs to be studied too, as management also argues that the media are 'biased' against them (the management organization Aims of Industry claims that most managers believe this). It is harder to persuade management to appear on TV than unions, argues Harrison. Consequently, broadcasters have to put management's side of a dispute for them. Indeed, in a sample of television news coverage of the first eight months of the coal dispute it was found that the time given to pro-strike miners, their families and NUM officials outstripped that given to the NCB (89 minutes compared to 35 minutes and 30 seconds). It was only when the NCB realized that their low profile was having this effect that this imbalance was corrected.

8. The GMG make sweeping generalizations on the basis of very sparse examples and evidence. For example, they found two cases (out of 216 studied) where a worker had his/her occupation or position captioned in lower case letters, for example, 'shop steward' rather than 'SHOP STEWARD'. On this evidence they include a ten-page section headed 'Lower Case is Lower Class'.

9. On the specific point about Wilson's speech, the main thrust of the speech was against the workforce at British Leyland in general and the Cowley plant in particular (which had been strike-prone for some years). Though the management's deficiencies were also mentioned, this was a side issue.

Harrison's basic argument is that there are numerous pressures on the media, many of which are in competition with each other:

> Television is more productively considered not as essentially one dimensional but as conveying a range of contradictory contentions and explanations – the site of ideological conflict, rather than simply fostering 'a climate of conformity'. (p. 127)

This is a clear statement of the pluralist approach. The GMG, blinkered by their own preconceptions, have picked up on one of the elements in television and presented this as the only one, usually on the basis of limited and selective evidence.

 *On the basis of your analysis of TV news, which side appears to be correct – Harrison or the GMG?*

Greg Philo, speaking for the GMG, replies that Harrison undertook the book on the suggestion of, and partly financed by, ITN. This has undermined his academic impartiality. More importantly, the transcripts used by Harrison and supplied by ITN are inaccurate.

> sections of the text broadcast by ITN are missing. Some are very long … Most are smaller … There are dozens of transcription errors … plus, astonishingly, the inclusion of passages which ITN did not in fact broadcast.

Philo implies that Harrison has been duped by ITN, who supplied him with poor evidence in order to sustain their case. He concludes that Harrison 'has produced a study of television content without having either the pictures that were shown or the actual words that were spoken' and as such his book cannot be regarded as a serious critique.

However, Harrison's is not the only research to question the findings and conclusions of the GMG. Though the GMG's finding that TV news is biased in favour of the political middle ground is supported by a much earlier study conducted by Blumler and McQuail called *Television in Politics: Its Uses and Influence*, Blumler and McQuail's explanation for this is quite a different (and essentially a pluralist) one.

Interviewing a panel of respondents on three occasions before, during and after the election campaign of 1964, they found that the effect of party political broadcasts was mainly to shift opinion in favour of the Liberal Party, occupying the middleground of party politics. More interesting though, was the finding that television news coverage was even more influential than the party political broadcasts in shifting opinion in this direction. The reason for this is that TV can reach uncommitted voters (who would not bother to attend party rallies etc.) and that such voters will naturally tend to support middle-of-the-road policies. The pro-Liberal influence of the media is therefore a result of the nature of the audience, and not any 'bias' in the media institutions themselves, as the GMG believe.

*Here are two studies with complementary results (though different explanations of them). The GMG's focuses on media output, Blumler and McQuail's on the effect the media have on the audience. If you wanted to study some aspect of the mass media and politics and policy-making:*
- *What would be your research question/s?*
- *What would be your methodology?*

Most practising journalists would agree with Harrison's point that the broadcast news is the site of a battle between conflicting views and interests. In general they also subscribe to the pluralist viewpoint. They see themselves simply as acting as the conduit for a variety of views. For example, Nicholas Jones, a correspondent on BBC radio news, argues that radio news is itself neutral. Any 'bias' in industrial reporting is due to the differing ability to communicate which workers and management have. Industrial disputes are increasingly about getting publicity, with each side trying to gain approval for their stand in the hope that this will help them to win their case.

*Construct a questionnaire designed to establish how far the respondents' political view influences their choice of newspaper, their perception of the political standpoint of particular papers, and of the influence of the press on their own views.*

Jones quotes the use of *The Jimmy Young Programme* as a kind of tennis ball in a rail dispute, with Sir Peter Parker (then chairman of BR) and Ray Buckton (of ASLEF) appearing on alternate programmes to reply to each other. In the coal dispute of 1984–5 the NUM eventually lost the propaganda battle for and through the media, not because of any bias in the media but because they relied too heavily on the presentational skills of Arthur Scargill. This led to a disjointed portrayal of their side of the dispute rather than one based on a proper communications strategy. While successful in the short-term, reliance on Scargill alone could not be sustained throughout a long-running dispute. The NCB won the advantage in using the media to present its case in the final few weeks.

In this they were building on the techniques of news manipulation developed by British Rail, British Steel and particularly by Sir Michael Edwardes when he was chairman of British Leyland. One of his techniques was to give press statements from behind the steering wheel of his car so that he could simply drive away from any embarrassing questioning. His management team carefully monitored news reports so that any 'inaccuracies' could be 'corrected' by phone. Jones admits that BL's methods led journalists occasionally to feel themselves under pressure to reflect management's interpretation of 'the facts'.

Unions, on the other hand, have only recently become adept at media manipulation. They suffer the disadvantage that there are often a number of them involved in one dispute, so it is difficult to ensure that 'the union view' is presented clearly and consistently to the media. Many unionists have an inbuilt suspicion of journalists and so refuse to talk to them. Despite this there have been attempts, especially by the TUC, to use the media as effectively as management do. The Labour Party, too, has become media-conscious, following the trail blazed by the Tories in this respect.

 *Listen each day this week to the* Today *programme on Radio 4 (transmission times usually 6.30 am to 8.40 am weekdays). In-depth coverage of the sort referred to by Jones is provided here. Does the evidence from the programmes tend to confirm or refute Jones's view?*

There are, however, a number of problems with Jones's answer to criticisms of studies like that of the GMG, which he states is one of the reasons why he wrote the book. Perhaps the main one is that he is only referring to radio news. It is true that on radio there is more time to hear a variety of views on an issue. Both unions and management are often given the opportunity to air their views on the news and, more especially, on the numerous programmes given over to current affairs by Radio 4. Moreover, the medium lends itself to giving a fuller background to a dispute than television news does. So, while there might be a case for the idea that the radio presentation of industrial disputes is impartial. This may not apply to television.

Constraints of time, the nature of the medium (being primarily visual rather than oral) and the quite different nature of programming all mean that the charges levelled by the GMG still stand. Furthermore, one can sense in Jones's book an antipathy towards Arthur Scargill and what he stands for. Meanwhile, moderate trade union leaders like Scargill's predecessor Joe (later Lord) Gormley get approval. There is even a sneaking admiration for management, despite their clever ploys for manipulating journalists like him. This, if true, confirms the GMG (*et al.*) view about the unitary and essentially conservative world view of middle-class, male, white journalists like Nicholas Jones.

## The manipulative model

This approach agrees, in a sense, with the pluralists that the media act largely as a 'conduit' for the views of others. However, from this perspective only a limited number of views gain access to the media, primarily those of élite groups in government, business and the military (particularly the government), while others are excluded. Thus the mass media transmit a one-sided viewpoint, but it is one which originates from outside the media not inside (as the hegemonic model claims). The following paragraphs examine some of the ways in which the media is manipulated.

In the broadsheet press there is a particular form of bias in political reporting which is subtly introduced. It results from the lobby correspondent system. Lobby correspondents are privileged journalists who are allowed to watch and record debates in Parliament and have access to parts of the building where others are not allowed to go. MPs give them privileged information and they get special press briefings from the Prime Minister's press secretary and from Government departments. They get advance copies of documents and they can usually get answers to questions they wish to put to members of the Government. The *quid pro quo* for all this, though, is that they must work according to the Lobby Rules: 'The cardinal rule of the Lobby is never to identify its informant without specific permission' and '*don't talk about lobby meetings before or after they are held*'.

Professor Peter Hennessy (formerly the *Financial Times* lobby correspondent) argues that this secrecy and privilege means that lobby correspondents are used by the Government to manipulate the news. Unofficial 'leaks' with no attributable source can be given by ministers to the lobby correspondents in order to shape public attitudes. Lobby correspondents know that they must not give offence to the authorities or they will lose their privileges and the easy access they have to news stories. This system means that the lobby correspondents give up any independence they once had as journalists and become, in effect, the mouthpiece of the Government. They take their line from the official view and allow the timing of the release of news to be dictated by the Government and the civil service.

Since Mrs Thatcher's fall quite a lot of detail has been learned about the normally secretive lobby system she used, all of which seems to confirm Hennessy's view. When Bernard Ingham was Mrs Thatcher's press secretary he was described as 'the most powerful man in Britain' (the title of a Radio 4 programme about him). This is not because he headed the Government Information Service (with its 1,200 information officers) – which he did – nor even because he had developed a close personal relationship with Mrs Thatcher, which he had. It was rather due to the fact that each weekday at 11am in Number 10 he held an unattributable briefing session for the lobby correspondents of the press and broadcasting media (with the exception of *Guardian*, *Independent* and *Scotsman* who did not attend what they considered a corrupt system).

A second briefing took place at 4pm in the House of Commons. Twice a day he had the undivided attention of the nation's media and he used it to tell them of the PM's views, changes in policy, cabinet decisions, new initiatives and so on. None of this was attributed to him or to Mrs Thatcher but, usually, to 'sources close to the Prime Minister'. It was said that he never lied, rather that the briefings were 'partial', that he was 'economical with the truth'. In the words of Sir Frank Cooper (ex MOD Permanent Under Secretary)

> The work of the Number 10 press office…is very much to swing and sway the media to report information in a way which is calculated to do one thing, namely enhance the standing of the government of the day. (Radio 4)

Those newspapers sympathetic to the government's view are believed to get (in addition to the twice daily news transfusion) an extra dose of selective briefings. These give them exclusive news which helps to sell papers and gives the government the opportunity further to soften up public opinion.

Press conferences are another technique used by élite groups to manipulate media content. For example in 1988 the government held a press conference to announce an increase in expenditure on the inner city initiative from £2,000 to £3,000 million. Eight cabinet ministers and Mrs Thatcher herself attended the conference which was carefully stage-managed. Each minister was well briefed, Mrs Thatcher so much so that she thanked one journalist for asking a question which allowed her to display her command of the facts.

Several senior civil servants have expressed concern that such media events are little short of party propaganda and that political bias had entered government publicity in a major way. The same concern has been expressed about government advertising. Between 1985 and 1989 there was a fourfold increase in government expenditure on advertising and by 1989 it reached £120 million per year, much of it being used to soften public opinion concerning controversial policies. Critics have suggested, again, that the morality of these campaigns is questionable.

On 9 May 1989 a High Court judge stopped the delivery of 23 million leaflets concerning the poll tax on the grounds that they were potentially misleading. The Opposition complained that the government was spending tax payers' money (roughly £1 million in this instance) to finance a party political advertising campaign. The court action had been brought by the London Borough of Greenwich against the then environment secretary Nicholas Ridley. The case concerning the leaflet *How it Will Work for You* related to the omission of the fact that partners of a cohabiting couple are each responsible for the payments of the other. The total 'information campaign' about the poll tax was budgeted at £1.75 million.

Generally the government's 'spin doctors' are able to use a whole range of techniques to put the government's preferred 'spin' or angle on the news. These include:

1. The provision of photo opportunities: setting up a newsworthy photogenic situation and ensuring that media cameras are there in large numbers. The intention is usually to portray a government member or government policy in a good light.

2. The inclusion of sound bites into speeches. These are short, sometimes humorous, phrases which encapsulate a view. They are intended to be picked up by the media in headlines, captions and news reports. They are usually written by speech writers and other wordsmiths. For example Mrs Thatcher's famous 'You turn if you want to, the lady's not for turning' was written by Ronald Millar, playwright and comic scriptwriter.

 *Listen for similar sound bites.*

3. The manipulation, timing and presentation of statistics. Statistics which reflect poorly on government policy are often released on a busy news day (so that they do not grab the headlines) or when Parliament is out of session. The 'silly season'

during the summer when there is little news is a good time to release good news, but not bad, to the media.

*In an excellent and readable small book called* Our Masters' Voices: The Language and Body Language of Politics, *Max Atkinson shows how politicians use a variety of techniques to manipulate their audience and their media images. These include a variety of 'claptraps' (designed to manipulate applause), tricks with body language and the use of particular sorts of discourse.*
*If you can, get a copy and read one of two chapters (especially 1, 2 or 3). Then watch politicians' televised speeches on television and try identifying the use of the techniques Atkinson talks about.*

Journalists and politicians both know that this sort of manipulation is going on, but journalists need the co-operation and participation of ministers and other members of the élite and so have little power to stop it. This collusion was demonstrated in an interview on Radio 4's *Today* programme in June 1995. Government minister Michael Heseltine suggested that the line of questioning should switch from an imminent leadership contest to European issues. Attacking Labour's divisions over membership of the European Community, Heseltine said: 'Can you imagine Dennis Skinner swilling ale in a German beer cellar'? and then joked with the interviewer that finally he 'managed to get the quote in'.

David Miller, a member of the GMG, shows (in Eldridge 1993) how the Northern Ireland Information Service (NIIS), the public relations division of the government's Northern Ireland Office (NIO) worked to paint a particular picture of the conflict there. Themes that the NIIS works at include the following:

● that Britain is 'above' the conflict, not a participant in it;

● that there is good news in Northern Ireland despite the violence and other problems;

● that Northern Ireland is 'getting back to normal';

● that civil rights grievances have been met;

● that the RUC are essentially 'friendly bobbies';

● that containing the IRA is the best policy. Of course, manipulation can be achieved through explicit or implicit threats. The government can put pressure on the BBC by threatening to reduce its licence fee. Ministers can launch a campaign of criticism of bias against broadcasters in order to intimidate them (and have done so). Horrie and Clarke give a number of examples to illustrate the effects of this. During the 1992 Gulf War the BBC had become so paranoid by criticisms of bias that it took *'Allo 'Allo* off the air and feature films with a military or morbid theme like *The Naked and the Dead* were also taken off. BBC disc jockeys found that a list of 67 songs were also vetoed for the duration. These ranged from Elton John's 'Saturday Night's Alright for Fighting' to Lulu's 'Boom Banga Bang' and even Desmond Dekker's 'The Israelites'.

Perhaps more importantly the effects of government pressure were felt in serious programming too. Glenwyn Benson, who became *Panorama*'s editor under John Birt's

Directorship of the BBC, was a confirmed, even hard-line, Birtist and was thus unpopular with the 'old guard' on the *Panorama* team. She did not want to rock the political boat after so many conflicts with the government (some of which had proved expensive: *Maggie's Militant Tendency* had cost nearly £600,000 on court defence costs and damages and collectively they had nearly brought about the privatization of the BBC and the introduction of advertisements).

How far *Panorama* has moved since *Maggie's Militant Tendency* is illustrated by a *Panorama* programme called *Babies on Benefit* about welfare dependency among single mothers. This took up a theme of the Conservative Party Conference that single mothers got pregnant in order to claim welfare benefits. Benson announced to her staff that she did not care if only five people were watching, so long as the BBC could not be accused of bias or sensationalism. *Panorama*'s staff now talk about 'The Drive For Five', a kind of shorthand for submitting to government repression.

Senior figures within the media are concerned about the use of these sorts of pressures by the government. The controller of Channel 4 and ex- BBC 1 and 2 controller Michael Grade said in a speech in Edinburgh in 1992 that under DG Birt and Marmaduke Hussey, Chair of Board of Governors, the BBC had 'all-too-frequent and debilitating negotiations with Downing Street', accusing them of carrying out the government's policy for them which would lead to a much reduced BBC and leaving the mass audience to commercial TV and satellite stations.

## A case study: the manipulation of the mass media during the Falklands conflict

The manipulation of the media during the Falklands war is now well documented and below a case study about it is presented. One could argue, of course, that governments have to manipulate the media during wars. However, for Robert Harris (the author of *Gotcha! The Media, the Government and the Falklands Crisis*), while this may be true of a global war it is not true of a relatively limited operation like the Falklands. Paul Scott Mowrer, the editor of the *Chicago Daily News* goes further, arguing that:

> The final political decision rests with the people. And the people, so that they may make up their minds, must be given the facts, even in war time, or, perhaps, especially in war time.

Harris worked in press and broadcasting, including the BBC's *Newsnight* programme, and gives a detailed account of the government's manipulation of the media during the crisis. The Falkland Islands were invaded on 2 April 1982. Immediately that it was decided a Task Force would be sent, the world's media clamoured for places aboard the ships (hundreds of journalists' names were put forward by over 160 organizations, 20 from the BBC alone). Fleet HQ at Northwood said, initially, that none could go, then (under pressure from Minister of Defence Nott and Bernard Ingham) it said six could, then ten and finally 15. In the event 28 were allowed to go, accompanied by five MOD press officers (or 'minders' as they were universally known). This was a victory by Whitehall over Northwood. Whitehall wanted them to go because the Government saw them as a means of conveying propaganda. As one of the minders said to Michael Nicholson of ITN with the Task Force:

You must have been told you couldn't report bad news before you left. You knew when you came you were expected to do a 1940 propaganda job.

Correspondents were obliged to submit material for censorship, theoretically of a purely military kind. This was done first by the minders, then by an officer on board ship. During the Falklands conflict the MOD had control over the flow of military information, the justification being that it had responsibility for making sure that lives were not lost.

The journalists with the Task Force tended to identify with the troops. During the campaign the *Sun* carried a banner on every edition which read:

### THE PAPER THAT SUPPORTS OUR BOYS

Even the serious newspapers had no doubts – *The Times* ran a massive leader headed:

### WE ARE ALL FALKLANDERS NOW ...

The broadcast journalists aboard the Task Force became rather exasperated, though, as film was delayed (taking an average of 17 days to get to London – the first 54 of the 74 days of the dispute saw no pictures of any action in this country). The Navy had the capability of getting pictures back, but would not give the journalists access to the satellite communications required. Journalists also suspected that there was selective delay going on – items carrying bad news or written in a pessimistic tone took longer than good news or upbeat items. Censorship soon began to stray beyond the merely military into broader areas. Peter Archer of the Press Association, with the Task Force, sent a telex to his London boss saying that his reports were being censored in this way. The word censored was censored.

It was clear to the journalists that the Navy resented their presence and did as much as possible to hamper their work. Perhaps the worst thing that the Navy did to get them out of the way was putting the representatives of the *Guardian*, *The Times*, *Telegraph*, *Star* and *Sun* aboard an ammunition ship at the height of the fighting and then transferring them to an Exocet missile decoy ship. When Argentine air attacks began while they were on the ammunition ship one of the journalists innocently enquired why no one aboard was wearing anti-flash gear. 'Because if we get hit, what you'll need is a f***ing parachute' was the reply.

In London too there was clear manipulation going on. Cooper, the Permanent Under Secretary at the MOD, held a press conference on 20 May just before troops landed in force saying that there would be no D-Day style operation, but a large number of attacks by small numbers of British troops all around the islands. This is the story the papers and other media carried the following day. In the event there was a single mass landing at San Carlos Bay. Ian MacDonald, the MOD's spokesman, ensured that the TV carried only the news that the MOD wanted by reading out a statement and then ordering the camera lights to be switched off. Only then would he answer questions, unrecorded by the cameras.

Perhaps as a result of the feeling of being manipulated and frustrated at the lack of pictures, two programmes were shown on BBC which, it was later claimed, committed 'treason' or, at least, the lesser sin of being 'unacceptably even-handed'. These were *Newsnight* of 2 May (in which Peter Snow referred to 'the British version of events' and 'the British' (not our) 'troops'. The other was the *Panorama* programme which highlighted the arguments opposing the sending of the Task Force. These (and a few other instances) led to the BBC's receiving calls complaining about the 'disgusting' even-handedness and 'undue reverence' for Argentine casualties. After the showing of the *Panorama* programme there were hundreds of calls to the BBC to complain.

The press reacted critically too. The *Sun* called the programme 'a bloody disgrace' and the *Mail* suggested the BBC was run by 'lightweight liberal intellectuals' and politically biased as a result. Director General designate Milne was unrepentant. He put unbiased reporting of all sides above what he regarded as an appeal to popular taste by appealing to jingoistic nationalism. Milne and Howard were supported by the political centre – Steel and Rodgers notably. Audience research showed that 81% of the public thought that the BBC had been reasonable in its coverage of the Falklands crisis and the same proportion thought it should continue giving coverage to the full range of opinions.

So, people telephoned in to complain. But those who telephone are always atypical, as the polls show. Most people generally thought the broadcast media were unbiased. The press were more obviously pro-Task Force and therefore pro-government policy. The tabloids (especially the *Sun* with its rabid anti-Argentinianism) were clearly right behind the government and doing a '1940 propaganda job' as required. Yet jingoism may not have been what the public wanted. The *Sun*'s daily readership declined by 40,000 between March and June 1982 while the *Mirror* gained 95,000. Such headlines as the *Sun*'s on 20 April STICK IT UP YOUR JUNTA and its antics of sponsoring a *Sun* missile for Galtieri's gauchos were clearly not to the taste of at least some of its readership. Its wildly inaccurate reporting probably didn't help:

## NAVY STORMS SOUTH GEORGIA

(days before it did)

## IN WE GO!

(three weeks before the landings).

 *A similar case study of government manipulation of the media is found in Media Hits the Pits by David Jones et al. This is available for £1.50 from the CPBF (address at the end of the chapter). Obtain a copy of this booklet and discuss your view of the argument it is presenting.*

 *Following the Falklands campaign the government set up an internal inquiry on information policy. Called the Study Group on Censorship and chaired by General Sir Hugh Beach, it had members from the media, the MOD and the Foreign Office. Its brief was:*

To consider, not least in the light of experience during the Falkland Islands operations, whether any new measures, including the introduction of a system of censorship, are necessary in order to protect military information immediately prior to or during the conduct of operations.

*Distribute the following roles among the group:*
- *civil servants from the MOD (including the 'minders' who were with the Task Force);*

- *Bernard Ingham – the Prime Minister's press secretary;*
- *senior military officers;*
- *representatives of tabloid and broadsheet press, radio and television news.*

*Your task is to hold a meeting to draw up notes for a report on the subject above. The meeting should also try to achieve a written set of statements on both the rights and responsibilities of the media in these circumstances. Before the full meeting, however, the various parties should get together to decide what their positions are on this – what they would ideally like and what they would be willing to agree to.*

*(For a summary of the actual conclusions of the Beach Report, see Adams 1986)*

Figure 8.4 Allied bombardment of Bagdad, 1991. The Gulf War was televised live. What effect would such coverage have had on the Falklands War?

## Postmodernism

Postmodernism has much in common with the pluralist perspective. It sees society as fragmented into innumerable sections and as being in a state of constant change. It also does not see a fixed relationship between any one social group and the mass media. These relationships too are in flux. Unlike pluralism, postmodernism is quite heavily theorized, initially by the founders of the school in the Ecole Normale in Paris and subsequently by their followers. We can highlight the main points of postmodernism which are of relevance for this chapter under the following headings:

1. The globalization of the media and society

2. The fluid nature of the identity and the self

3. The social construction of meaning

4. The variety of sources of power and advantage

5. The critique of 'grand narratives'

We will examine these in turn:

## 1. The globalization of the media and society

We saw in Chapter 5 how, for postmodernists like Baudrillard, we are living in an information age. Pyschologically the world is getting smaller and world cultures are becoming increasingly homogenized. Pictures in the living room and in newspapers give individuals a view of other places and other political systems. Meanwhile the authority and legitimacy of politicians and the political system are undermined by the mixing of genres and styles that occurs within postmodernity. A flood of images of all sorts hits the individual: politicians appear on game shows and chat shows; newspapers give us the intimate details of their sexual lives; political systems around the world are compared and criticized; authority figures from around the world are put on a pedestal and then knocked down.

One effect of this, as Baudrillard says, is to blur the distinction between image and reality. Another is to free us, in a sense, from concepts like 'duty', 'authority', 'hierarchy' and so on. Within postmodernity we are at the same time cast adrift and empowered. The old certainties are undermined and we are empowered to create our own set of values and understandings from the global information flood around us.

## 2. The fluid nature of the identity and the self

Traditional sociological concepts like 'socialization' carry with them the image of the individual who is born, empty, into a society and is quickly filled with that society's norms and values. This is a model rejected by postmodernist theory (though it had been criticized much earlier, for example by Dahrendorf, 1968, and Wrong ,1961).

The account of Gillespie's study (Chapter 10, pp. 226–227) shows how London Punjabis step outside their cultural environment and use the media to create their own version of what being a 'London Punjabi' actually means. These young people are, effectively, creating their own identities and stepping outside the narrow confines of their 'socialization'. Similarly Prout and James mount a determined critique of the idea of 'child socialization' and argue that even young children create their own cultures and identities. From seeing children as defecting miniature adults who are not yet properly socialized we should see them as, effectively, a minority ethnic group.

This viewpoint, then, has important implications for our understanding of the political influence of the media. In postmodernity people are no longer likely to see themselves as long-term identifiers with a particular party. Similarly class-based affiliations to parties are also on the decline (a situation Ivor Crewe calls 'class dealignment') as the importance of class itself declines. This is likely to mean that:

- people are more open to media messages about politics, but

- the number and range of messages they receive is huge and much greater than before the rise of postmodernity.

Thus it is very difficult to identify a single overall direction of media influence. Media content and potential influence, like postmodernity itself, is diverse and highly fractured.

## 3. The social construction of meaning

Sociology is sometimes said to have undergone what is called a 'linguistic turn' during the 1980s. By this is meant a move towards examining the importance of discourse in society, the ways in which patterns of communication shapes our view of reality. In many ways this can be seen as a re-visiting of earlier perspectives such as the phenomenological view of Peter Berger and Thomas Luckmann in their book *The Social Construction of Reality* (first published in 1966). Recent theory on this is associated with postmodernism and with the method called discourse analysis, itself close to semiology. Potter and Wetherell provide an example from a newspaper article:

> ### Islamic Terrorists Blow Up Plane
>
> In Beirut last night the hijackers of the British Airways 727 finally released the passengers and crew. As the gunmen left they detonated a large quantity of explosive and the plane was quickly gutted by fire. This followed a period of intense negotiation in which the authorities made it clear that they were not going to meet the hijackers' main demands.

Potter and Wetherell ask us to note the following about this article.

- That a newspaper reader would be very familiar with this type of story. It fits into a stereotypical pattern which we categorize as 'hijackings' that we hold in our heads.

- That some of the terms in the story come ready evaluated: 'the gunmen', 'hijackers' and 'terrorists' all have negative associations (other words could have been used which do not).

- The effect of the above is to place this story firmly into a cognitive structure and set of understandings of the world. A very different structure would be addressed and confirmed if the story were written from the perspective of, say, a militant Palestinian group.

 *Try rewriting the story from the perspective of a militant Palestinian group.*

Norman Fairclough, in *Language and Power*, makes a similar set of points about the discourse of Thatcherism. Unconsciously the media propagated this discourse and set up new ways of thinking about the world in the process. Some examples are:

- free market;

- state interference;

- nanny state;

- parental choice;

- community care;

- community charge (though this was contested, in the media and elsewhere, and often replaced by the equally loaded 'poll tax');

- Mrs Thatcher's use of the word 'we' of herself both to include the listener and to exclude certain other groups.

The key point is that discourse does not just represent reality, it *creates* reality.

### 4. The variety of sources of power and advantage

While critics of postmodernism would attack this concentration on discourse as ignoring the realities of power and advantage, its defenders would say that, through the media, control of discourse can have important effects on the distribution of power and advantage. For example through influencing how housing need is articulated in the media, pressure groups like Shelter can have an important influence on housing policy. The government finds that housing policy begins to be discussed in terms of homelessness, negative equity and decline of the housing stock. Ministers find that they have to defend policy on this ground in the media and policy-making begins to be thought of in terms of the discursive agenda set by Shelter and other pressure groups. Again, discourse not only represents reality, it is *part of* reality. Postmodernists and discourse analysts would say of this example that both housing policy and the discourse about it are contested terrain. Power and advantage in such contests is divided among many players and is constantly shifting.

### 5. The critique of 'grand narratives'

This very dynamic, highly fractured, view of postmodernity means that what are sometimes called the 'grand narratives', like functionalism and Marxism, no longer apply. Any attempt to explain a large number of aspects of society in one all-encompassing theoretical framework is doomed to failure. The large organizing concepts on which such theories depend, such as 'class', 'the nation-state' or 'the family', are just out of date now. As Zigmund Bauman says, within post-modernity,

> there are *many* 'life-worlds', *many* 'traditions' and *many* 'language-games'.

---

#### Post-structuralism

This term, often used together with post-modernism, is used to refer to the declining significance of 'macro' characteristics in society like class and the increasing importance of micro processes such as discursive inter-action between individuals and groups. 'Declining significance' and 'increasing importance' here can mean in society itself or in theoretical terms – our understandings of the workings of society – or both.

---

The centrality of pressure groups in contemporary society and the relationship they and their members have with the mass media illustrate some of these points about postmodernism and postmodernity.

For example, in the early part of 1995 there was a public outcry, expressed through the media, about the British veal trade with the continent. Ports and airports were picketed and there were violent clashes with the police. One protester was killed under the wheels of a lorry exporting calves. The relevance of what happened for this discussion is as follows.

● Protesters were drawn from all social groups. Sociological tools such as class and age categories seemed almost irrelevant. When people decide to align themselves with such movements, and perhaps become activists, they are constructing their own identity unconstrained by categories like age and class.

● A bishop joined the protesters to bless the calves as they passed in the lorries and

Alan Clark (once a Conservative minister) expresed his support, thus highlighting the collapse of the élite/mass distinction.

● The media gave access to many of the 'voices' concerned: the protesters, the police, the owners of businesses concerned, the port authorities etc. This demonstrates the pluralistic nature of postmodernity and the role of the mass media within it.

● The protesters used their own cameras to record and publicize events, shaping the nature of 'veal-trade' discourse and demonstrating the empowerment that information-rich postmodernity can bring.

For writers adopting a postmodern perspective, examples like this are not just isolated incidents but mark a change in the nature of politics. For example Angela McRobbie (1994) says:

> The proliferation of these groups and the skill with which they engage with the media is an extremely important development in the political culture.

She suggests we need a 'new' political sociology which should fruitfully explore the sphere of influence and effectiveness of these organizations.

## Ontological dimension of political reporting: 'news' and 'reality'

A glance at the AEB's questions on reporting news shows that they often ask about the relationship between the 'reality' presented in the news (including political issues) and the 'real world'. Some of these questions can be found at the end of the chapter. It seems appropriate, therefore, to conclude this chapter with a summary of how one could apply some of the perspectives we have been examining to this sort of question. Table 8.1 applies each of the four perspectives we have been examining to this issue and terms that are often used are defined in the concept boxes.

---

*Ideology*

Ideology is difficult to define in a sentence or two. Rather than try to do this, the best way to explain it is to list its characteristics. Hartley (1983 ) says that the characteristics of an ideology are:
1. It consists of values and beliefs or ideas about the state of the world and what it should be like.
2. These values, beliefs and ideas form a framework, structured in a systematic way: they are not just a set of attitudes. The structuring can be psychological or logical or both.
3. Ideologies concern social groups and social arrangements - in other words, with *politics* in its widest sense of being concerned with the distribution and ordering or resources.
4. An ideology is developed and maintained by social groups, and it links the individual and the group.
5. Ideology provides a justification for behaviour.

---

> ### *Ontology*
>
> Ontology refers to the nature and status of being and reality. An ontological issue is one which questions the nature of reality, asking for example 'Is it really there?', 'Is it socially constructed?' 'Is your reality the same as my reality?' and so on. Giddens talks about 'ontological insecurity', by which he means the uncertainty that people may feel when their fundamental beliefs and behavioural routines are taken away from them: they begin not to be sure about who they are or the nature of the world in which they live.

> ### *Distortion*
>
> 'Distortion' as used in the exam question below ('distorted picture') is a metaphor. In it the news media are represented as a kind of cracked mirror which gives a distorted (twisted, broken) reflection of reality. The problem with this metaphor is that there is no simple, stable, uncontroversial 'reality' for the news media to reflect (or distort).
>
> There is a second sense of distortion, not used in the exam question, which is simply to misrepresent motives, facts or statements. This implies deliberate intent and in this sense the manipulative model would concur with the view that the news media give a 'distorted' presentation of events.

Table 8.1    Television viewing by age

| | *Hegemonic model (neo-Marxist)* | *Pluralist model (neo-Weberian)* | *Manipulative model (Marxist)* | *Postmodernism* |
|---|---|---|---|---|
| Can reality be 'objectively' portrayed? | No: any description of reality comes from a particular point of view (eg 'the cat sat on the mat'). | No: too many events mean it is impractical. | No: agrees with hegemonic and pluralist models about this. | No: 'reality' doesn't exist apart from the meanings we bring to it. These are culturally situated. Anyway, 'portraying' reality in the news actually changes it: news discourse is *part of* 'reality'. 'Reality' and discourse about reality are inseparable. |
| Do the news media produce an ideological view of reality? | Yes: news media articulate the dominant (hegemonic) point of view which is ideological in ways that meet all five of the criteria (see ideology concept box). | No: news values determine which parts of reality are shown but there is no ideology consistently in operation (for example there is no structured framework – point 2, and no one social group has monopoly of access to the media to propagate its ideology. | Yes: sees capitalist and other elite interests as operating to ensure that news content is manipulated in the desired direction. All five of the criteria for an ideology are met. | No: it is not ideological because a number of groups have access to the news media. Indeed, the very notion of fixed 'ideologies' is probably out of date in a postmodern world. |

| | Hegemonic model (neo-Marxist) | Pluralist model (neo-Weberian) | Manipulative model (Marxist) | Postmodernism |
|---|---|---|---|---|
| Is news 'created' by the news media? | Yes, in the sense that the dominant ideology shapes the selection of what is 'news' and how it should be understood. | No. News values are used in the selection and portrayal of political news, but these values merely reflect the public's attitudes. | Yes. As far as the tabloid press is concerned this is true even in the sense that stories are invented in order that some political effect can be made (stories about 'loony left councils' for example). | Yes, in the sense that news discourse, like other types of discourse is a central part of the social construction of reality. |
| Is reality being 'constructed' by the news media? | Yes. A particular image of reality is being constructed in news output. This is consistent and stable and reflects the dominant ideology. This has an influence on social reality in that it serves to maintain the status quo. Thus the news media work at social reproduction. | No. The news media represent reality in numerous different ways. The audience are selective and educated. Through selective exposure, perception and retention, the media have no other important effect on reality than confirming the audiences' preconceived views of them. | Yes. By manipulating the news media politicians and others can change the way the world is. | Yes. Reality is nothing more than our mental construction of it. The news media contribute to the process of development and change of our mental constructs and so they 'construct' reality in that sense. |
| Some examples? | News reporting of economic policy is structured in terms of the benefits of expansion and growth at the expense of alternative perspectives like that of environmentalists which stress reduction in non-renewable resource use and in pollution. | News reporting of government employment policies, especially on television, puts each side of the story: opposition parties' reactions, likely effects on the unemployed, business reactions and so on. | Through manipulating political news reporting the outcome of an election can be influenced. | The carefully constructed discourse of party political broadcasts is designed to 'shape' our understandings of reality and our perspectives on policy. These are, however, only one example of the many forms of 'text' we are exposed to through the media. |

### Examination questions

'Assess the view that the mass media produce a distorted and ideological picture of the world'

(AEB AS, Sociology, Summer 1994, paper 2, question 8)

'In presenting the "news", the mass media cannot give an objective account of the world around us because they must select from many events.'
To what extent do sociological evidence and argument support this statement?

(AEB Sociology (with coursework), June 1994, paper 2, question 7)

'To what extent does the concept of "the social construction of reality" aid our understanding of the production of news by the mass media?'

(AEB A, Sociology, November 1993, paper 2, question 7)

'"News" is not simply reported by the media; it is created by the media.'
Examine the evidence for this view.

(AEB AS, Sociology, June 1993, paper 2, question 8)

## Further reading

Atkinson, M. (1984) *Our Masters' Voices: The Language and Body Language of Politics*, London: Routledge.

Gunter, B. *et al.* (1994) *Television: The Public's View*, London: John Libbey.

Jones, D. *et al.* (nd) *Media Hits the Pits*, published by and available from the Campaign for Press and Broadcasting Freedom, 9 Poland Street, London, W1V 3DG.

## Useful addresses

The Television News Archive at Vanderbilt University systematically records, abstracts and indexes the most widely viewed national television newscasts so that they are readily available for study by individuals, schools, colleges and universities. Currently there are around 23,000 news broadcasts in the collection. Tapes are loaned from the Archive for an agreed use period (typically 45 days). The Archive produces a monthly publication, *Television News Index and Abstracts*, that is a guide to the collection.

The archive can be contacted by email at: tvnews@tvnews.Vanderbilt.Edu

# 9 Gender and the mass media

Figure 9.1

This chapter is divided into the following sections:

1. Gender, technology and society, which examines the ways in which media technology and content are 'gendered' and the ways in which gender issues affect their use.

2. Representations of gender in media content, which explores the regularities that have been found in the way gender is represented in the output of different media and genres.

3. Gender, media and feminisms looks at the different feminist perspectives and the approach they take to explaining gender issues in the study of the media.

4. Finally gender and media effects considers how far it is possible to make general statements about the effects that the media may have on male and female roles in society.

## 1. Gender, technology and society

For many authors the technologies of the mass media are highly gendered, with clear gender identities.

> ### *Gender identity*
>
> This refers to the beliefs, values and feelings people have about both their own selves and about media technology and content in terms of how they relate to generally accepted notions of gender roles.
>
> Skirrow uses the related concept of 'gender valence', which is a measure of the degree to which media technology or content involves male or female gender identities.

According to Skirrow, for example, video games:

> are particularly unattractive [to women] since they are part of a technology which ... is identified with male power, and they are about mastering a specifically male anxiety in a specifically male way.

Similarly Sherry Turkle argues about computers that women:

> use their rejection of computers ... to assert something about themselves as women ... It is a way to say that it is not appropriate to have a close relationship with a machine.

The computer is a cultural symbol of what a woman is *not*. In rejecting computers women are rejecting something they see as gender-coded. Ann Gray notes that people say women generally avoid computers and video games because they are simply too complex. This is clearly not the case because women routinely use other complex equipment (which men often claim not to be able to operate) like sewing machines, microwave ovens and washing machines. For Gray an important factor in all this is men's domination over the domain of domestic leisure, which alienates women from the technology associated with it, and women's confinement in the domain of domestic work. By contrast the telephone is the key technology that many women would hate to lose because it is a way of 'saving the sanity' of those that have a sense of isolation in their homes. Similarly Dorothy Hobson suggests that radio has a female gender valence, being particularly important for working-class women with young children in terms of timetabling their day and as a link with the outside world.

Gender identities and gender valence can change over time. Lisa Lewis's discussion of videos gives an interesting example of this happening. She notes that the streets are usually no-go areas for young women and so girls are usually pushed into 'bedroom culture'. Yet here too they find male dominance. For example most videos on MTV are designed around the discourse of male adolescence including:

> ideologies of rebelliousness, independence ... sexual promiscuity ... street culture ... and female conquest.

As a result music videos have had a male gender identity. Lately some female musicians have begun to challenge this, for example Cyndi Lauper and Madonna. They have invaded men's spaces and began to celebrate female modes of expression and experience. In 'Borderline' Madonna portrays a teenager

> immersed in male street-corner culture. She is shown street dancing, spraying graffiti on urban walls, and loitering on a street corner with female peers. She blows kisses and initiates flirtation with street boys, and takes her female companions into the male turf of the

pool hall. In short, she appropriates activities and spaces typically associated with male adolescence.

This challenging, subversive style can be interpreted by women watching as a strategy of opposition. Girls often imitate these stars in their image, demeanour and argot (vocabulary and delivery style). They could be dismissed as 'wanna-bes' but actually develop female friendships and solidarity through this means; a 'gendered support system for girls'. Of course, this imitation is promoted by the fashion and other industries who target this group's expendable income but it is nonetheless important for female symbolic expression.

Gender identities influence media use, of course. But so do the social contexts of use and the gendered relationships of power in the household more broadly. Ann Gray in *Video Playtime* shows the importance of class, gender and viewing context for the use of television and videos. Her in-depth research into the video use of 30 women of different social classes shows clear differences between social classes I and II compared to IIIn and IIIm. Unfortunately the sample size of the women in social classes IV and V was not big enough (5) and their domestic circumstances were so diverse as to not allow Gray to come to any firm conclusions

Social class IIIn, IIIm (15 women) had a far heavier reported use of TV and video than social classes I and II (10 women). The differences between the viewing habits of men and women were much clearer in IIIn and IIIm than in I and II. The higher the social classes the more concern there was about children using the TV and video 'too much' and the more effort to control it there was. The lower the social class, the more TV and video were an accepted (and dominant) part of life and of conversation. The higher the social class, the more preference there is for 'classics' and British productions (a perceived sign of quality).

In all classes, however, the context was important and affected how the women used the video. By context is meant whether viewing was:

- family together,
- children only,
- male and female together,
- male only or
- female only.

In all classes, too, women tended to give control to men, citing their employment as justification. Men enjoyed documentaries and current affairs and, especially in classes IIIn and IIIm, sport. Politics, space, science, science fiction, action adventure were also 'men's domains' in the men only context. Men tended to archive tapes and to organize their viewing more. Soap operas, weepies, romance and costume drama were enjoyed by the women watching alone in all groups.

However, women with higher education had more similar tastes to their partners, so for classes I and II men and women agreed with this polarity:

| Positive | Negative |
| --- | --- |
| classics | popular |
| quality | trash |
| important | trivial |
| British | American |

While for IIIn to V the following gendered polarity was important:

| 'Male' genres | 'Female' genres |
| --- | --- |
| hard | soft |
| tough | soppy |
| real | fantasy |
| serious | silly |
| factual | fictional |

However all the women enjoyed programmes which stressed personal relationships, believable characters and a strong story. So across the classes there is this polarity:

| Male | Female |
| --- | --- |
| heroic | romantic |
| public | domestic |
| societal | familial |
| physical | emotional |

Table 9.1 Participation in selected home-based leisure activities by social class 1991-4

| Great Britain | | | | | Hours per week<br>All |
| --- | --- | --- | --- | --- | --- |
| | AB | C1 | C2 | DE | persons |
| Watching TV | 13.5 | 15.4 | 17.5 | 20.2 | 17.1 |
| Listening to the radio | 9.2 | 8.7 | 11.6 | 10.9 | 10.3 |
| Listening to CDs, tapes<br>  or records | 4.3 | 4.0 | 3.4 | 4.4 | 4.0 |
| Reading books | 5.1 | 4.3 | 3.2 | 3.4 | 3.8 |
| Reading newspapers | 3.6 | 3.3 | 3.4 | 3.2 | 3.3 |
| Caring for pets | 2.6 | 3.1 | 3.2 | 3.5 | 3.1 |
| Gardening | 2.4 | 2.0 | 2.2 | 1.8 | 2.1 |
| Cooking for pleasure | 1.8 | 1.8 | 1.8 | 2.0 | 1.9 |
| Watching videos of TV programmes | 1.6 | 1.4 | 1.7 | 1.9 | 1.7 |
| DIY or house repair | 1.6 | 1.6 | 1.7 | 1.4 | 1.6 |
| Sewing and knitting | 0.9 | 1.3 | 1.4 | 1.5 | 1.3 |
| Reading specialised magazines | 1.2 | 1.1 | 1.0 | 0.8 | 1.0 |
| Watching other videos | 0.7 | 0.9 | 0.8 | 1.3 | 1.0 |
| Reading other magazines | 0.6 | 0.8 | 0.7 | 0.8 | 0.7 |
| Exercising at home | 0.6 | 0.8 | 0.4 | 0.5 | 0.5 |
| Using games computer or console | 0.5 | 0.4 | 0.5 | 0.6 | 0.5 |
| Car maintenance | 0.4 | 0.4 | 0.9 | 0.3 | 0.5 |

Source: *Social Trends*, vol. 25, p. 216, table 13.2.

 *Develop a scheme for categorizing these home-based activities so that you can make some general statements about social class and the use of leisure time.*

David Morley (1986) studied 18 families' use of the television with a particular interest in gender differences. His methodology is summarized on pp. 37–38. The findings are summarized under eight headings:

1. Power and control over programme choice: 'Characteristically, the remote-control device is the symbolic possession of the father (or the son, in the father's absence), which sits "on the arm of Daddy's chair" and is used almost exclusively by him. It is a highly visible symbol of condensed power relations …'. This is confirmed by Hobson: 'Many … women have told me that they are restricted in what they are allowed to watch' though she says it's more than having control of the remote control – the man will come and turn off things and not allow the woman to watch them. 'I have to go and get his tea.'

Findings like these lead Morley to talk about 'the politics of the living room'.

2. Styles of viewing: 'Essentially, men state a clear preference for viewing attentively, in silence, without interruption … they display puzzlement at the way their wives and daughters watch television. The women describe viewing as a fundamentally social activity, involving ongoing conversation, and usually the performance of at least one other domestic activity (ironing etc.) at the same time …'

3. Planned and unplanned viewing: 'It is men … who speak of checking through the paper (or the teletext) to plan their evening's viewing. Very few women seem to do this … Many of the women have a much more take-it-or-leave-it attitude, not caring much if they miss things (except their favourite serials).'

4. Television-related talk: 'Women show much less reluctance to "admit" that they talk about television with their friends and workmates …'

5. Technology: use of video: 'None of the women I interviewed operate the video-recorder themselves to any great extent, relying on their husbands or children to work it for them …'

6. Solo viewing and guilty pleasures: 'A number of the women in the sample explain that their greatest pleasure is to be able to watch "a nice weepie" or their favourite serial when the rest of the family isn't there.'

7. Programme-type preferences: 'masculinity was primarily identified with a strong preference for "factual" programmes … and femininity identified with a preference for fictional programmes'. James Lull (1988, p. 248) agrees with this finding:

> Men everywhere prefer sports, action-oriented programmes, and information programming (especially news), while women prefer dramas (including serials, soap oeras and films) and music/dance/comedy-based programmes.

8. National versus local news programming: 'it is men and not women that tend to claim an interest in news programming. Interestingly, this pattern varies when we consider local news programming, which a number of women claim to like …'

- *Compare these findings with your experience.*
- *What critical points would you make about this piece of research? (Think about the methodology: Morley interviewed people in the context of their family group.)*

- *Morley recognizes that wider relations of power and inequality are at play here. In what ways might these affect media use in the household?*
- *Van Zoonen suggests that 'it is not the fact of being woman or man that explains programme preferences, but programme preferences that construct a particular and appropriate gendered identity'. What might she mean?*

*Devise a research project to investigate the use of the different mass media in different types of households. Decide which method you will choose (questionnaires or interviews are obvious choices), select your sample, plan the details of data collection, conduct and pilot and then do the research. Write up the results and compare them to the studies described above.*

## 2. Representations of gender in media content

For clarity this section deals with different types of media and the ways in which men and women are typically represented within them.

### Film and television fiction

According to many writers the media portray women in only a limited number of roles; the nagging wife, the difficult mother-in-law, the sex object, and so on. Women are rarely pictured as combining a marriage and successful career. Where women *are* seen as strong and dynamic, they are usually both single and sexy;

> Wonderwoman was incapable of doing her amazing tricks unless she shed all her clothes except a one-piece that exhibited starkly her full figure. The continuing message of *The Incredible Hulk* seemed to be that beneath the feyest male lurks massive power, even if *his* clothes-shedding somehow seemed to split his shirt but not his pants.
>
> (Downing 1980)

In the first season of the TV series *Superman* Lois Lane is (in the words of one of the villains) 'galactically stupid' because Clark Kent's disguise of a pair of glasses fools her into not recognizing that he is Superman.

The one-dimensional portrayal of women is most apparent in pornography, which treats them as flesh rather than human beings. While porn may be considered a minority taste, this is becoming less true with the spread of VCRs. It is estimated that altogether Americans watch between 16 and 20 million pornographic video films per week and that even the higher social classes are beginning to watch them.

In the cinema women are relatively well represented in terms of numbers and status. For the earlier generation there were numerous big female stars such as Marilyn Monroe, Bette Davis, Lauren Bacall, Mae West and Katharine Hepburn. While cinema became very male-dominated in the 1970s and '80s, today there are many strong female leads again, such as Sigourney Weaver, Jodie Foster, Holly Hunter and Whoopi Goldberg. However, as one of these women stars, Meryl Streep, points out, women such as her receive far less money than an equivalent big name male lead for a film role.

*Which films have been showing at your local cinemas in the last few weeks? Were the stars men or women and how were the genders represented in terms of the roles played?*

An interesting content analysis study of the presentation of women in soap operas comes from D. M. Meehan's, *Ladies of the Evening: Women Characters of Prime Time TV*. She suggests that there are essentially only ten female character types presented in the American drama serials she studied. These are:

1. *The Imp*: a rebellious tomboy character. She is adventurous, not really sexual, often finds herself in trouble. The imp is the opposite of what society expects a woman to be and the trouble she gets into is often a result of this (e.g. Elly Mae Clampett in *The Beverly Hillbillies* and Sabrina in *Charlie's Angels*).

2. *The Goodwife*: is domestic, attractive, home-centred and content. She does not wish to become involved with the world outside the home, leaving this to her lucky husband (e.g. Olivia Walton in *The Waltons*).

3. *The Harpy*: is an aggressive single woman. She is powerful, even overpowering, and not afraid to take on or chase after men (e.g. Hot Lips Houlihan in *MASH*).

4. *The Bitch*: is a sneak and a cheat. She is manipulative, dangerous and deceitful. She lacks the power to be a real villain (invariably male), but she causes real trouble for the forces of good (e.g. Sable Colby in *The Colbys*).

5. *The Victim*: is the passive female who suffers accident, disease or violence, depending on the type of show. Medical series, in particular, very often have female victims of disease, especially if the doctor is young and handsome (e.g. *Young Doctors*).

6. *The Decoy*: is a heroine disguised as a victim. Apparently helpless and dependent, she is actually strong and resourceful. She is quite likely to be mistreated, hurt or captured, but she is capable of overcoming her difficulties. Often she is the physical and intellectual superior of many of the men in the show (e.g. Purdy in *The New Avengers* and Jennifer Hart in *Hart to Hart*).

7. *The Siren*: the Siren of Greek mythology was a female creature who lured sailors to their deaths with her tantalizing voice. The TV siren is equally dangerous, using her sexuality to lure her victim to a sticky end. This female character often appeared in Western series such as *Maverick*, *Bonanza* etc.

8. *The Courtesan*: is close to being a prostitute, and perhaps is or has been one (this information is not for American television audiences, however). In Western series she appears as a saloon keeper or cabaret hostess.

9. *The Witch*: has extraordinary power deriving either from a supernatural source or from extreme wealth. Despite this the witch is invariably dominated by a man and is persuaded, often reluctantly, to suppress her power or use it for his aims. Samantha in *Bewitched* is perhaps the best example. She uses her limitless power mainly for domestic tasks and to help her rather stupid husband, Darrin, in his advertising career.

10. *The Matriarch*: has power, prestige and authority. She is seen in a positive light, despite the fact that she is too old to be sexually attractive. Her status is almost

that of a hero. As a result of all this she is a character rarely seen on American drama serials (e.g. Granny Moses in *The Beverly Hillbillies* and Ma in *Bonanza*).

*Watch an episode of any current American drama serial on television. Pay careful attention to the female characters in it. Do they conform to one or more of the ten character types described above? Are there any character types in the episode which fall outside these? If so how would you describe that type? If you are working in a group, take one serial each for analysis.*

*Try illustrating these characters by reference to more modern serials you are familiar with.*

*Present your findings to the group as a whole for discussion.*
*In your view, does the characterization of women in British serials differ significantly from the types outlined in Meehan's study of American serials?*

*Figure 9.2 Attempt a semiological reading of this Pirelli tyre advertisement featuring Carl Lewis. See p. 148 for an example to help you.*

**POWER IS NOTHING WITHOUT CONTROL**

*Studies of women in the media very often discuss the sorts of roles they are portrayed. There is rarely any analysis of male roles.*
*Make a list of the soap operas currently on BBC and commercial television. Then note down the important male characters in them. Finally classify them into 'role types' in the same way as has been done above for women.*

Other findings of this study are:

- that women are portrayed as either good or evil, never a combination;
- that 'good' women are portrayed as submissive, sensitive and domesticated;
- that 'bad' women are portrayed as rebellious, independent and selfish;

- that male evil characters are always counterbalanced by good ones; this is not so with female evil characters.

- that the number of occupations which women are portrayed as holding is limited to a few, primarily housewife, receptionist and whore; male roles are also few in number compared to reality but are more exciting: doctor, spy, detective, astronaut etc.

- that women are portrayed as lacking any sexual appetite.

While studies such as Meehan's could be criticized for being dated and referring to series of the 1960s and '70s, the constant recycling of such series on satellite and cable channels means that they are still relevant. Moreover, many of the points she makes are relevant even in more recent television. The *number* of women portrayed in the media depends very much on the medium concerned and the genre type. Soap operas have a relatively high proportion of women, though they are still outnumbered by as much as seven men to three women in some types of soap opera. Cartoons have a particularly low number of women (often stylized as cats etc.). In advertisements there are three all-male ads to every one all-female ad. Some types of comedy programme (such as *Bottom*) have almost no women while others (like *Absolutely Fabulous*) have very few men.

There is evidence that the content of TV is becoming more 'feminized' with the increased programming of talk shows, quiz shows and soap operas. The feminized content matches the increasingly 'pink-collar' nature of the workers in the industry. 'The mass media' therefore are highly diversified and it is difficult to make generalizations about content.

 *This section has dealt with representations of women in film and television fiction. Studies of representations of men are harder to find (though there is an interesting analysis of* Boys From the Blackstuff *in Curran 1987.) What comments would you make about the way men are represented in film and TV fiction?*

## Music

Medved is very critical of popular music in general and 'rap' music in particular for its often highly sexist lyrics and promotion of promiscuity. In the former category he quotes lyrics from Guns and Roses albums *Appetite for Destruction* (especially the song 'Anything Goes') and *Use Your Illusion I* and *II* to illustrate the contemptuous attitude towards women they often convey. Heavy metal bands such as Motley Crue are also well known for their sexist songs too. In the rap category he cites lyrics from Niggers With Attitude (NWA) and their album *Niggas4life* while the Geto Boys songs are described by Medved as 'violent and pornographic'. 2 Live Crew's album *As Nasty as They Wanna Be*, which sold 1.7 million copies, contained fairly graphic lyrics about mutilating their girlfriends' genitals. That album was ruled legally obscene by a judge in Fort Lauderdale, yet according to Provenzo is typical of this genre of music. Provenzo tells us that the album contains:

226 uses of the 'F' word;

81 uses of 'shit';

163 uses of 'bitch';

87 descriptions of oral sex;

117 explicit terms for male and female genitals.

Karen Saucier analysed the lyrics of the top 40 country songs of 1981. She describes the words of these songs as a 'three-minute soap opera' and was concerned to analyse the gender representations within them. What she found was that:

● 95% presented a male/female relationship theme (getting together or breaking up);

● 8% concentrated on male sexual prowess;

● 8% gave advice about love relationships;

● women are usually portrayed in terms of 'her man' (as in the famous 'Stand By Your Man'), having no status in terms of property or economic role in the community or workplace;

● the only acceptable role for a woman in this genre of music is as a housewife, mother or lover;

● men are commonly depicted as using alcohol to deaden the pain of loss or failure;

● women are often depicted as using their sexuality as a resource in a situation where men have the power.

She concludes that 'the symbolic world offered by country music lyrics represents a rather bleak, limited world for both men and women in regard to status, role and power. The only aspect of their lives that is somewhat under their control is the relationship between themselves and their lover' (p. 163).

 *Consider the sort of music you prefer. Is it possible to say anything about the symbolic world it creates in terms of gender roles?*

### Video games

Eugene Provenzo in *Video Kids* notes that games designed for Nintendo and other video games have very starkly stereotyped representations of both males and females, probably more so than other media. After analysis of a number of these games he reaches the following conclusions.

● Women are acted upon rather than being initiators of action. In *Double Dragon II*, for example, Billy has to rescue Marian, his kidnapped girlfriend. The cover of the game depicts him supporting Marian, her dress in shreds and her tank top ripped.

● Women are often not named, being referred to as someone's girlfriend or 'the princess'.

● Video games are very macho in orientation, depicting boxing, football, car racing and so on. The roles of both males and females in such scenarios are very limited.

● Women are often depicted in poses of what Goffman calls 'ritual subordination'.

● Males and females are usually depicted as young and physically 'ideal'.

Such grossly stereotyped images are accepted mainly because video games are part of what Provenzo calls an 'invisible culture' which receives little attention from the adult world. A second explanation is that they are exclusively located in the private sector; the video game market is largely controlled by the consumer rather than vetted by teachers, librarians and others.

*Spend ten minutes in a shop which sells video games. Examine their covers and the summary of their story-lines. Later, write short notes on your observations. If you are working in a group, compare your findings.*

### The news and weather

TV journalist Allison Pearson states that following the use of US consultants by ITN the re-modelled news on commercial channels began to have an 'obsession with surface'. She says:

> Just watch the news today and count the number of reporters who look like Sindy's boyfriend. With their heavy jaws and medium tans, the Bens and Toms could pass for celebrity hosts on any afternoon game show … I asked a senior BBC current affairs man who had just finished recruiting this year's graduate trainees if they were all good looking. He grinned and said, 'Funny, come to think of it they are. In fact one or two are real stunners.'

Pearson believes that there will be no place in the new world of infotainment for people like the BBC's political correspondent John Sergeant. She describes him as having a 'squashed cabbage face and sad rheumy eyes'. His problem is that he is liable to give viewers the impression that they are not supposed to be enjoying themselves.

Newsreaders are increasingly likely to be women and P. Holland argues that this trend can be linked to the new growing 'intimization' of television news. This opened a space for traditional female values of intimacy and emotionality whereas the earlier 'rationalistic' approach to the news was more clearly linked to male values. Women too are perhaps 'easier on the eye' according to Holland.

However, while news and weather presenters are much more likely to be female these days, they are usually young and attractive. Especially for young viewers, this may lead to the expectation that women need to be attractive if they are to be in a position of authority and that the normal holders of such positions are men.

Figure 9.3    Is it true that female presenters are chosen for their looks?

For feminist writers, news values (that is, what is considered newsworthy) are male in orientation. Women's issues are treated frivolously. For example, the famous bra-burning by 'women's libbers' never happened; it was an invention of the press. Women's sports are rarely featured on television sports roundups. The special problems women face are either ignored or trivialized. Feminism is treated in terms of the loss of femininity which is thought to occur to its proponents.

*Watch the next edition of* Sportsnight. *How many women appear in it? Do your findings suggest to you that any action needs to be taken?*

Rape and the murder of women is treated in an evocative way, and given so much over-reporting that the public generally overestimate the level of sexual crimes in society. The official statistics record sex offences as only 0.59% of all recorded crime in the UK in 1993, and rape as only 0.086% (though there are between four and ten times as many rapes committed as there are reported). Despite this sex offences in general and rape in particular figure largely in most crime reporting. The victim of rape attacks is viewed, it is claimed, with almost as much hostility as the aggressor in many of these reports.

*Conduct a survey asking people a series of questions about news readers (you supply a list of names). Questions could include:*
- *From this list, who is your favourite news reader?*
- *Who presents the news most convincingly?*
- *Who do you trust most? and so on.*

*Use the results to compare people's reactions to female and male presenters.*

### Print media

While in general there is greater awareness of gender representation in the mass media, the existence of 'the classics' in all forms of the media means that old approaches to representation are continued. For example, Kenneth Grahame, the author of *The Wind in the Willows*, wrote the blurb about it for his publishers, describing it as 'clean from the clash of sex'. There are only three female characters: the washerwoman; the bargewoman and the gaoler's daughter. Toad is described as 'being ordered about by female nurses' when he spends time in hospital after a car crash, and has been 'jeered at, and ignominiously flung in the water - by a woman, too!' Toad (although probably less sexist than Rat, Mole and Badger) says to the bargewoman 'You know what *girls* are, ma'am. Nasty little hussies, that's what *I* call 'em.' All the main characters are bachelors, and we get the impression happier for it.

*Go to your local library to conduct an analysis of sexism in the young children's books available. Prior to your visit you should prepare a scheme to help organize your research, perhaps by listing possible sexist criteria so that points can be given, contributing to an 'index of sexism'. Make a note of the date of publication of each book so that any trends can be identified.*
- *Note the date, author and title of the book.*
- *Note the number of male and female characters in it and assess the centrality of each to the story.*

Strong and dynamic women can also be quite stupid in the mass media as the Lois Lane example above demonstrates. This is equally true in the printed media:

Supergirl, a being of strength approximate to that of Superman himself and thus able to push planets out of orbit without working up a sweat would spend her time either frolicking with Supercat or Superhorse, or maybe falling in love with the young men from the bottle city of Kandor who would always turn out to be villains who wanted to use her in order to revenge themselves of Superman.

Somehow she never realized this until it was too late, no matter how many times it happened, not even when all her Kandorian boyfriends had names like E-Vill and Nars-Tee and the like.

(Moore 1983)

'Women's media' are of a quite different type from others. Women's pages in daily newspapers deal with soft news, the family, fashion and other material which is considered too trivial for the general media. Advertisements figure very highly, indeed such pages could be seen as merely a vehicle for advertising. Budgets are very low for them, and there seems now to be a certain amount of embarrassment about their nature. The *Observer* has a supplement called *Weekend* which is clearly designed to be for women. Other papers, too, feel it necessary to find some euphemism for 'women's page', normally something like *Living*.

 *Examine the 'women's pages' of a range of newspapers this week. How are they described at the top of the page?*

A detailed study of women's magazines was conducted by Marjorie Ferguson and published in *Forever Feminine: Women's Magazines and the Cult of Femininity*. As a woman, a journalist of ten years' experience and a PhD student of sociology she was particularly well qualified to study the treatment of women in women's magazines. She conducted a content analysis study of the three largest-selling women's magazines: *Woman*, *Woman's Own* and *Woman's Weekly*. In this she concentrated on only some parts of their content:

- features (which cover many subjects, including the life of the stars, real life drama etc.);

- the problem page;

- beauty;

- fiction.

Two studies were made, the first taking a random sample of issues for the period 1949–74. The second took issues between 1979 and 1980 to see what, if any, changes had occurred in the 1970s. In addition, she interviewed 34 women's magazine editors about their role, beliefs and professional practices. Additionally, 97 journalists, artists, publishers and managers were interviewed about their perceptions of the editorial processes, publishing organizations and market context of women's periodical production. The dominant themes identified by the content analysis of the magazines of 1979-80 are summarized in Table 9.2.

Table 9.2    Dominant themes, all subjects[1], all titles, 1979–80 (%)

| Order | | W | WO | WW | Total |
|---|---|---|---|---|---|
| 1 | Self-help: overcoming misfortune | 35 | 32 | 40 | 36 |
| 2 | Getting and keeping your man | 11 | 10 | 15 | 12 |
| 3 | Self-help: achieving perfection | 13 | 14 | 6 | 11 |
| 4 | The happy family | 9 | 12 | 12 | 11 |
| 5 | Heart versus head | 12 | 8 | 12 | 10 |
| 6 | The working wife is a good wife | 9 | 13 | 7 | 10 |
| 7 | Success equals happiness | 11 | 8 | 8 | 9 |
| 8 | Female state mysteries | – | – | – | – |
| 9 | Gilded youth | – | – | – | – |
| 10 | Other | – | 3 | – | 1 |
| | *n* | 24 | 24 | 24 | 72 |

[1] Excluding beauty
*n* = 1 per item, 3 items per issue, 4 issues per year;
*W = Woman; WO = Woman's Own; WW = Woman's Weekly*

*Source:* Ferguson (1983)

*Between 1949 and 1974 the relative positions of these themes were quite different. The 1979–80 'winner', self-help (overcomes misfortunes), came a poor second then (only 10% of items), while the top theme then was today's number 2; it appeared in 59% of items. The rest were as follows: 3rd heart versus head (9%), 4th the happy family (8%), 5th the working wife is a bad wife (3%), self-help (achieving perfection) (3%), female state mysteries (2%), gilded youth (1%), success equals happiness (1%), other (3%).*
*Account for these changes.*

---

### The cult of femininity

Women's magazines convey what Ferguson calls a 'cult of femininity'. This is: 'a set of practices and beliefs: rites and rituals, sacrifices and ceremonies, whose periodic performance reaffirms a common femininity and a shared group membership'.

These magazines instruct women in values and attitudes about being a woman. They tell women what to do and how to think about themselves, about their men, colleagues, children, neighbours and bosses. The novice is instructed in how to achieve her chosen ends: what to wear, how to act, and what to buy to be a *femme fatale*, super cook or office boss.

---

Ferguson notes that the cult of femininity is unique among women's magazines; magazines for men do not instruct them in 'how to be a man'. It is assumed, she says, that men know everything there is to know about being masculine. Moreover, though the *content* of the instruction has changed over the years, the instructional nature of women's magazines has not changed. However this part, at least, of her study is now dated. There is now a new breed of 'men's magazines' which do not cater for a specific interest and are different from the old-style men's magazines like *Mayfair* and *Fiesta*.

Figure 9.4    Men's magazines

Examples include *OM* (Options for Men), *Unique*, *Arena* and *Q* are becoming more numerous, despite the scepticism of observers who point to the failure of similar ventures in the past (who now remembers *London Gentleman*, or *Sportsweek*?). *Arena* tends to concentrate on fashion, *Q* on music, *OM* on both as well as other traditionally male concerns. They tend to sell between 40,000 and 60,000 copies each. Their rationale is that, with the increasing segmentalization of advertising, there is now room for 'men's magazines' of this type.

 *What common characteristics can you identify in Figure 9.4?*

Recent work on women's magazines has tended to move away from a position which purely criticizes them for their sexist images and ideology and their negative effects in the socialization of women. Joke Hermes (1995), for example, shows that people derive a lot of pleasure from reading these magazines and that they can be useful to them. After conducting 80 in-depth interviews with a socially and ethnically mixed sample of women and men she is able to analyse the different ways in which readers construct meaning from the text.

Readers find them relaxing and educative, both in terms of practical and emotional learning, and they also feel that the magazines connect them to the wider world.

Hermes notes how readers tend to change in the way they use these magazines during their life and also how the magazines tend to change over time as their readers do. Hermes contrasts this approach to magazines in particular and the media in general to earlier approaches. Hers is a postmodernist one, seeing readers as intelligent, diverse and active in their approach to the text. Modernist approaches, like Ferguson's, see readers as passively consuming ideological messages. We will return to these newer, audience-centred, approaches at the end of this chapter.

### Television advertisements

TV advertisements in particular have traditionally treated women in a stereotyped way. Early studies typically found results like those of Dominick and Rauch (1972):

- Women were seven times more likely to appear in ads for personal hygiene products than not to appear.
- 75% of all ads using females were for products for use in the kitchen or bathroom.
- 38% of females in ads were pictured inside the home, compared to 14% of males.
- Men were significantly more likely to be shown out of doors or in business settings than women.
- Twice as many women were shown with children than were men.
- 56% of women in ads were judged to be (only) housewives.
- 43 different occupations were coded for men, 18 for women.

However, a recent survey of trends over 15 years in the portrayal of women and men in US TV advertisements found that while these sorts of findings were typical of the beginning of the early 1970s, quite different results were being obtained by studies in the mid-1980s (Bretl and Cantor 1988). By then, typically:

- Males and females occur approximately equally as primary characters in prime-time TV adverts.
- Females have become more equal to men in the kind of arguments they use to promote a product. Males and females now tend to use scientific and nonscientific arguments with equal frequency.

But:

- Males were still significantly more likely than females to be shown having an occupation (though the depiction of males as spouses or parents only seems to be on the rise).
- Males were more often shown in occupations of a higher status than females' occupations (though this was not a statistically significant finding).
- Males are more likely than females to be depicted away from home and out of doors.
- Male and female characters continue to differ in the degree of credibility assigned to them. Males are still more likely to be depicted as authorities and females as consumers, though less so than in the past.

- Male and female characters continue to be associated with different types of products, especially in terms of those used inside or outside the home.

- 'The most striking and persistent inequality in the data continues to be with regard to the sex of the narrators: advertisers have continued to use male narrators approximately 90% of the time.' The few female narrators are typically used to promote products associated with care of the body.

*What reasons can you think of for the last point?*
*Does it matter?*

Sex role stereotypes are confirmed and supported in more subtle ways, however, than just the portrayal of roles. Commercials for girls' products have soft and melodious music, those for boys have loud and dramatic music. And it is easy not to notice the fact that the voice-over is almost always a male voice.

*Study the advertisements on commercial TV for the next few days. Note any examples which confirm or refute this criticism of them.*

Finally we should note that women's bodies continue to be exploited in advertisements as sexual commodities to sell anything from after-shave to motor cycles and ice-creams.

*Many media types have been omitted from the above account.*
*What are they?*
*How would you study the representation of gender in them?*

## 3. Gender, media and feminisms

During the time I was working on this book, a Dutch radio journalist called me one day to invite me to take part in a round table discussion on Madonna. Her CD and book *Erotica* had just come out and had incited considerable uproar in the Dutch media, as it did elsewhere. I told the reporter I was a great admirer of Madonna's and that I would happily take part. This was not at all what he had in mind. He had been hoping for 'a feminist who would object to Madonna's exploitation of her body and to her ventures into pornography'. The feminist he had in mind would have to confront other cultural critics with a more favourable outlook on Madonna ... I had to disappoint him.

(van Zoonen 1994)

- *What arguments would a feminist like van Zoonen use to support Madonna's image?*
- *What ingredients, commonly found in the media news values, was this journalist trying to introduce to his radio programme?*

The following section gives a threefold distinction between types of feminism to discuss feminist approaches to explaining media representations of gender and their effects. The categories are liberal feminism, radical feminism and socialist feminism. In her later work Lisbet van Zoonen has objected to this categorization of feminisms, noting a number of problems with it:

- it sets up the feminisms as divided when there are many similarities between them;
- the political and the theoretical strands within the different feminisms become mixed up when these artificial distinctions are made;
- there has been a huge diversification of feminist positions over the last 20 years, and a threefold scheme does not reflect this;
- the distinctions between liberal and radical feminisms have become blurred over recent years;
- radical feminism in one country (e.g. Holland) is different from that in another (e.g. the UK);
- the classification centres on issues of importance to industrialized countries, not those of the third world where the issues are different;
- it ignores black feminism, which is itself very diverse;
- saying that one type of feminist tends to be interested in particular things (e.g. liberals interested in stereotypes and socialization) angers non-liberals looking at that area.

In some of her earlier work van Zoonen has used this typology because of its clarity and simplicity. This section will do so too for the same reasons while noting the objections above.

### Liberal feminism

Figure 9.5 Turning the tables? This advert followed on from a TV commercial featuring a glamorous woman on a gondola in Venice. The mood is shattered when she gulps from a glass of Boddingtons bitter and announces, in a broad northern accent with a beer moustache on her lip: 'By heck, I was dying for that'.

Journalists have learned to portray the female world in a particular way; as classless and home-and-family based. They can easily unlearn this and begin to portray women differently. Indeed, this process has already begun, some feminists argue. The old stereotypes of women belonging to one of two types: *Waiting to Wed* and *Wife and Mother* have now been joined by a third; *Independent Woman*. A new breed of magazines has grown up for working women which deal with far wider issues than just home and man.

> ### Liberal feminism
>
> Liberal feminists argue that individuals are trained by the mass media and other social institutions into patterns of behaviour which are performed unconsciously. Sex roles, in particular, have been built-up over a long period of time and have become embedded in our culture. They can, however, be changed by a conscious process of rooting out those elements in society which perpetuate them. Clearly the media are one of the most important targets in this process.

Recent TV series and films have moved away from the old machismo approach and recognize the emancipation of women in a way which is both realistic and unafraid. Women in positive and non-sexist roles include the actresses playing the title roles in the film *Thelma and Louise*, Sigourney Weaver in the Alien series, the two American policewomen in *Cagney and Lacey* and Helen Mirren in *Prime Suspect*.

Despite this, there is much to be done. Media images of women change only slowly in response to real social changes. This 'culture lag' is due to the fact that ideas and attitudes change more slowly than material conditions. Women are still ignored and trivialized in much of the media and so their symbolic annihilation continues. However, we can expect a slow change in this as the media catch up and increasingly reflect the new social position of women. Tuchman in *Hearth and Home*, for one, believes that this is increasingly the case. The liberal feminist position, then, is quite close to the pluralist one – they both believe that the media largely reflect public attitudes and social realities.

### Radical feminism

> ### Radical feminism
>
> Radical feminists identify men as the enemy. They believe that men consciously and unconsciously manipulate social institutions for their own benefit and to the detriment of women. The family is a crucial site of this oppression, but the media are in the hands of men too, and are an important weapon against women. Men hold the dominant positions throughout the media and are able to use them to reflect the images of women which they desire.

For radical feminists the media consist of the powerful talking to the less powerful and men talking to women. The issues which affect women, such as discrimination at work and in education, sexual harassment, the problems of baby care, social isolation, attitudes of the police in rape cases and so on are not dealt with, or are trivialized. Meanwhile women are manipulated and duped into believing the Beauty Myth (Wolf 1990) by the mass media, the idea that they must slavishly imitate a particular image of what it is to be a woman.

D. Meehan argues in *Ladies of the Evening* that the Goodwife image, in particular, represents a male yearning for a time when the family was a woman's central concern. The popularity of programmes in which the Goodwife appears is due to men's fear of the women's movement and the increasing competition women are offering in the job market. The domesticity and submissiveness of the Witch was attractive for similar reasons. However, some of these characters appeal to women as well as men: the Imp because of her rejection of the boring domestic role, the Witch because of her implicit power over men. The radical feminist position, then, echoes the manipulative theory we examined in Chapter 2. Here, though, it is men who are manipulating both the content of the media and women's attitudes.

In fact, radical feminists adopt a mixture of the hegemonic and manipulative models described in Chapter 4. For example, R. Muir suggests that:

> If a film or television company is a mini sexist society, with women congregated in the lower paid service and support jobs, how can we expect the image of women that they produce to be anything but sexist?

The European Community was so concerned about the concentration of women in particular sorts of jobs in the media that it issued a directive in 1987 about the employment of women in television companies.

However some writers suggest that in the UK the media are becoming dominated by women – there has been a 'gender switch' so that the media are dominated by 'pink collar' workers (Creedon, 1989). While this may be so, it is clear that in the central fields of news, foreign reporting, economic news and current affairs, women are in a minority and still tend to be used for their attractiveness.

The media industries are, like others, also horizontally segregated. This means that the increasingly 'pink-collar' nature of media employment does not mean power and control for women, rather it reflects and produces a decline in status and salaries in the field.

---

### Horizontal and vertical segregation

Vertical: men in management areas, women in junior ones.
Horizontal: men in technical areas, women in administration.

---

## Socialist feminism

---

### Socialist feminism

Socialist feminists blame capitalism as an economic structure for the disadvantaged position of women in society. Women give their labour cheaply. They serve as a reserve army of workers who can be called on when the need arises and then sent back into the home. They are also useful to the capitalist class for breeding purposes; they bring the next generation of workers into the world. In addition, they help to sustain and pacify the male workers by providing a comfortable home, meals and sexual services for them. Finally, they are super-exploited by capitalism as consumers and as sex objects.

---

According to socialist feminists the role of the media is to sustain and perpetuate the capitalist system and the supporting role of women in it. Big business effectively controls editorial content of women's magazines in particular. That women are portrayed in traditional ways is in the interests of the capitalist class: it justifies using women as a reserve labour force. The pattern of ownership of the women's press would seem to lend some weight to this argument.

 *Socialist feminists point to the concentration of media ownership as part of the problem they are addressing. Taking the example of women's magazines, investigate how far there is concentration of ownership.*

Socialist feminists are inclined to adopt the manipulative model discussed in Chapter 2: for example K Davies says that:

> Since those who control the media are almost all (rich) men, there is every incentive for them to present the capitalist, patriarchal scheme of things as the most attractive system available – and to convince the less privileged that the oppression and limitations of their lives are inevitable.

However, crude capitalist manipulation of the media is not considered particularly important by most socialist feminists. What the media are doing is articulating the male-centred ideology of capitalism in an unconscious way. Editors, even female ones, interpret the wider world in terms of the 'woman's angle'; a trivial and home-centred one. Anything else gets little attention and, when it does appear, is treated dismissively or critically.

There is a clear opposition between the women's movement and the mass media. The women's movement defines the woman's position positively, the media define it negatively (ultimately around the concept of 'finding a male'). While it is true that 'Independent Woman' has become a feature of women's magazines recently, this is really only a new version of earlier stereotypes.

'Independent Woman' is expected eventually to become 'Wife and Mother'. The implication is that her career is only a temporary phase of her life. The dominant theme of women's magazines between 1949 and 1974 (getting and keeping your man) has been replaced by self-help instructions for the working woman. The message of 'get out there and win' has 'remember you also achieve as a wife and mother' added to it. This, then, is a variant on the hegemonic perspective we examined earlier. The dominant ideas and values reflected in the media are those of the men who control its content.

McRobbie (1991) notes how women's magazines now have to attract advertising and how the 'aditorials' are tied into this, with features on makeup surrounded by adverts for eyeliner, hair-mousse and lipstick. Fashion and the celebrity system, both prominent in the magazines, are also closely tied into the system of consumption. 'Looking at Wet, Wet, Wet and knowing about where they intend going on their holidays, is not completely divorced from listening to and buying their records.'

It is part of the 'inner logic' of these magazines that consumption is a natural feature of the readers' experience (p. 145) so that it is seen as extremely unusual not to be interested in 'hairstyles, cleansing and all the other intimate rituals which are an intrinsic part of being a woman in contemporary consumer culture' (p. 166). She

Gender and the mass media

Figure 9.6 Women's
magazines

notes that women and girls are concentrated in secretarial work and men play a
more active role in pop, rock, soul, funk and rap. Pop has a fast turnover, and groups
of good-looking young boys don't last long – because the phase of teenybopper
consumption does not last long. A new generation of girls must be catered to as the
last become young women.

 *What common characteristics can you identify in Figure 9.6?*
*How do they differ from the men's magazines in Figure 9.4?*

### The pluralists' response

From a pluralist perspective it is a pointless exercise to trade examples of partial
representations of gender roles across the media. For every lantern-jawed male
reporter or slender young actress there is a wise older woman or cabbage-faced
man. If the media portrayal of women and men is skewed in a particular direction,
this is only what the audience of particular media and their particular genres require.

Taking magazines as an example, the specialist groups involved in their production
merely cater to public demand. A *Women's Weekly* editor interviewed by M.
Ferguson said:

A lot of features actually come from readers' letters. The whole business about 'too scared to make love' was readers' letters. They were all still writing in about how, when, if – you know, all that sort of thing. I thought, 'Blimey, so a lot of them are doing it and don't know how to, and are scared stiff.'

There followed a frank series of articles about sex and sexual relationships. For the editor, then, this was not a propagation of any 'cult of femininity', merely a response to public demand.

Editors judge their success by total sales, advertising revenue and overall profitability. The best way to achieve these is to appeal to the tastes of the market they cater to. Magazines which appeal to women in traditional roles (*Good Housekeeping, Women's Weekly*) tend to thrive if they stick to the traditional format. By contrast many of the magazines for young working women adopt a different stance from the traditional ones and do not espouse the 'cult of femininity' or at least have a different, and popular, version of it. A variety of messages will be available for women, some rejecting the 'cult of femininity' entirely.

As far as advertisements are concerned, those portraying non-traditional roles are far more common than they were. Such changes in content as those described above are due to the work of the women's movement, women's greater spending power and changes in public attitudes according to David Lipsey (1987).

The pluralist believes that while the media *used* to be sexist, they no longer are. Public awareness of women's issues became so great in the seventies and early '80s that the problem no longer exists to any great extent. It is noticeable that many of the studies of sexism in the media are concerned with programmes shown in the past – even as far back as the 1950s. Attitudes among producers and writers, as well as among the audience, about what is and what is not acceptable have come a long way since then. This is particularly noticeable if one compares the children's books of today with those of the '50s, '60s and even '70s. The old sex-role stereotypes have now been purged from their pages (as have the racial ones).

This trend of 'liberalization' in the media is evident in the findings of research too. For example Signorelli (1989) analysed data from the 1975, 1977, 1978, 1983, 1985 and 1986 National Opinion Research Centre General Social Surveys in the USA as well as conducting content analysis of prime-time dramatic television programming. The idea was to establish the extent of gender stereotyping in TV content and to investigate whether there was a correlation between heavy viewing and sexist views of the role of men and women in society. Four questions in these surveys, similar to those asked by Gross and Jeffries-Fox (described below), were designed to highlight sexism in the respondent (sexist answer underlined):

- Do you <u>agree</u> or disagree with this statement: Women should take care of running their homes and leave running the country up to men?

- Do you approve or <u>disapprove</u> of a married woman earning money in business or industry if she has a husband capable of supporting her?

- If your party nominated a woman for President, would you vote for her if she were qualified for the job? Yes or <u>no</u>?

- Tell me if you <u>agree</u> or disagree with this statement: Most men are better suited emotionally for politics than are most women.

While Signorelli found a positive correlation between sexist attitudes and heavy viewing in the earlier surveys, in the 1983, 85 and 86 surveys there was a slight *negative* correlation which he suggests may be the result of the increased number of portrayals of dominant and successful women which his content analysis revealed.

 *Prepare a table that will enable you to analyse advertisements for the degree of sexism in them. The following example may help.*

| Product | Voice-over (M/F) | Dominant person (M/F). | With children (M/F) |
|---|---|---|---|
| 1. Com flakes (brief description of the ad) | | | |

*(You will need to think of more categories; these are just an indication.) Watch commercial TV for as long as possible, filling in the table when the adverts appear. The aim is to test whether the pluralists are correct about the representation of women in advertisements or whether critics of it are right.*

As far as the radical and socialist feminists' manipulative theory is concerned, there is very little evidence for it. Despite the potential for manipulation of content that the ownership patterns suggest, pluralists believe it has never actually occurred, apart from in the past to a very limited extent. Throughout the Second World War, women's magazine editors, government ministers and civil servants met regularly at the offices of the Periodical Proprietors Association. The aim was to teach women the practicalities of what to do and what not to do in wartime Britain for the national interest. The only peacetime equivalent to be discovered by researchers, however, was the agreement among cookery editors to adopt metric measurements in their recipes to help the process of metrification! As for the media reflecting bourgeois hegemony, the dominant ideas in society, to the pluralist this means only that they give a voice to what most people feel and believe. It is nothing more or less than the duty of the media to do this.

The example of the *Cagney and Lacey* police series demonstrates that though there may be a dominant set of values about gender within media organizations, as the hegemonic model suggests, the power of the market prevails. D'Acci's case study of this series shows that originally *Cagney and Lacey* was meant to be a feature film echoing male buddy movies like *Butch Cassidy and the Sundance Kid*. This film (provisionally titled 'Freeze') would have Cagney and Lacey uncovering a male brothel for women customers headed by a 'godmother'.

The characters and friendship of Chris Cagney and Mary Beth Lacey were based on those of the two women writers, Barbara Avedon and Barbara Corday, who were liberal feminists. However, no film studio would touch the script in the mid 1970s. CBS took it as a made-for-TV movie in 1980 but demanded that Cagney and Lacey be played by 'two sexy young actresses'. A compromise was reached, with Loretta Swit (from *MASH*) playing Cagney for CBS and the writers' choice Tyne Daly playing

Lacey (who continued in that role). The movie got high ratings and CBS decided to press ahead with the series idea. However CBS was uncomfortable:

> The evidence points to an extreme discomfort on the part of the network with 'woman' represented as non-glamorous, feminist, sexually active and working class and single (d'Acci).

This discomfort was irrelevant once it was shown that the series was popular and likely to be a great success. Moreover, the kinds of attitudes in high places revealed by d'Acci's research are quickly being broken down as women achieve important positions within the media. To take cinema as an example, the number of women directors and producers of high-profile films has increased dramatically in recent years. Some examples are:

Gale Anne Hurd, producer of *Terminator*;

Kathryn Bigelow, director of *Blue Steel* (1990), *Point Break* (1991) and *Strange Days* 1995);

Sally Potter, director of *Orlando* (1992);

Alison Ander, director of *Gas, Food and Lodgings* (1992);

Gurinda Chadha, director of *Bhaji on the Beach* (1993);

Penny Marshall, director of *Awakenings* (1990) and *Big* (1988)

Jodie Foster, director of *Little Man Tate* (1990);

Jane Campion, director, and Jan Chapman, producer, of *The Piano* (1993).

The feminization and liberalization of the media are moving hand in hand to produce a very different mass media from even five years ago.

## 4. Gender and media effects

Reviewing media representations of gender roles it is all too easy to agree with those feminists and others who argue that the socialization of girls and boys becomes distorted by the media. The first part of this section reviews some of the evidence and argument which argue for strong media effects. Simple views about media effects should be treated with some caution, though, and the second part of this section gives some reasons for caution.

### Part 1: Media Effects

> **Sex roles**
>
> Social guidelines for sex-appropriate appearance, interests, skills, behaviours and self-perceptions

One of the main effects of partial media portrayal of men and women is thought to be the reinforcement of sex roles. Girls are led to have a low self-evaluation and limited ambition in life. They may grow up with a 'victim mentality', seeing themselves as helpless without a man around. Boys, particularly those with little contact with females, grow up with a very strange view of what women are like. This can have unpleasant consequences, especially for the females with whom they come into contact.

Some specific claims about the consequences of media representation of sex roles are as follows:

1. L. Gross and S. Jeffries-Fox found that boys who watched a considerable amount of TV more often gave the sexist answer to the following questions (the sexist answer is underlined):

(a) True or <u>false</u> – Women have less chance than men to get the education for top jobs.

(b) <u>True</u> or false – Men are born with more drive to be ambitious and successful than women.

(c) <u>True</u> or false – By nature, women are happiest when they are making a home and caring for children.

(d) True or <u>false</u> – Our society discriminates against women.

(e) <u>True</u> or false – Women have just as much chance to get big important jobs, they just aren't interested.

The implication is that men's attitudes to women become limited to seeing them not as people but as representing one of a limited number of stereotypes. Provenzo says about video games that their effects are important not only for women but for men too:

> who come to assume from the images provided by the games (as well as other sources from the media and the general culture) that women are indeed the 'weaker sex' and constantly in need of aid or assistance. Thus the games not only socialize women to be dependent, but also condition men to assume dominant gender roles.

These prejudiced *attitudes* will then become translated into discriminatory *behaviour*. Male employers whose attitudes towards women have been affected by the media will be disinclined to give them jobs ('their place is in the home'), promote them ('they're only interested in babies really'), give them responsibility ('too emotional'), and so on. Teachers and others in positions of power will be affected in the same way. The media are partly to blame, then, for the continued disadvantaged position of women in British society.

2. Frueh and McGhee interviewed children in American kindergarten and asked them about the amount of time they spent watching TV, testing the extent and direction of their sex-typing. Traditional sex-role stereotyping was positively correlated with heavy viewing. According to this research women are persuaded to accept and collude in their role and women undergo the process of 'modelling', that is, imitating a role model seen on the TV.

3. A study conducted by Beuf (1974) was based on 63 interviews with boys and girls between the ages of three and six. Some girls had abandoned their ambitions even by this early age:

> Several girls mentioned [that their ambition] … could not be realised because of their sex. One blonde moppet confided that what she really wanted to do when she grew up was fly like a bird. 'But, I'll never do it', she sighed, 'because I'm not a boy.' Further questioning revealed that a TV cartoon character was the cause of this misconception.

The implication is that because of the small number of high-status female models in the media available for girls to model themselves on, the *ambitions* of real women are limited. The power of the media in this respect is thought to be very strong. This is not surprising, as the average American girl will have spent more time in front of the TV by the time she is 15 than she will have spent in the classroom.

4. Beuf also argues that women suffer anxiety and stress as a result of the above, and because advertising and soap operas create concerns in women particularly about:
    – their body image (which rarely lives up to those on the screen)
    – the constant need to spend money on products to make them more attractive and desirable for *males*
    – competition with other women in the fight to get *and* keep *a man*.

5. Steeves uses a version of cultivation theory (see p. 131) which shows that heavy viewers of TV begin to adopt a TV view of the world and quite peculiar views of 'normal' male and female roles.

### Part II: a cautionary note – reception analysis and media effects

It is too easy to fall into the 'hypodermic' view of the media when considering these issues. Van Zoonen (1994) points out that we cannot generalize about 'media effects' in such a simple way. The nature of the medium, message senders, types of effects, processes involved and so on are all important variables which make generalization impossible. Table 9.3 gives some examples

| Table 9.3 | Models of communication in feminist media theory | | | | |
|---|---|---|---|---|---|
| | Sender | Process | Message | Process | Effect |
| Stereotypes | Men | Distortion | Stereotype | Socialization | Sexism |
| Pornography | Patriarchy | Distortion | Pornography | Imitation | Oppression |
| Ideology | Capitalism | Distortion | Hegemony | Familiarization | Common sense |

A second problem for simplistic 'effects' research is that women enjoy many of the forms that are supposed to oppress them.

---

### The politics of pleasure

Radway's study (below) illustrates a crucial issue: whether we should interpret the pleasure the women get as an unliberating and temporary 'escape' from a limiting situation or a genuinely pleasurable and liberating experience which the women themselves see it as. As Ang (1985) puts it: 'Is *Dallas* good or bad for women?'

---

Again, van Zoonen's (1991) work is relevant here. She writes:

> the pleasure women derive from watching soap operas [makes it increasingly difficult] to find moral justifications for criticizing their contribution to the hegemonic construction of gender identities.

Janice Radway (1994) used a combination of content and audience research. She asked, 'How do women interpret Mills and Boon-type romance novels?' and sent questionnaires to 30 women, interviewing 20 living in 'Smithton', mid-West USA. Most read one romance a day. She asked them what makes a good and a bad novel, finding that heroes should be intelligent, and tough with a hint of tenderness which is later led to blossom by the irresistibly beautiful but sexually innocent heroine for whom he falls. The readers identify heavily with the heroine and the books provoke an emotional response in them.

While the story-line of a 'good romance' casts the heroine in a traditionally feminine passive role, the author tells the reader that she is independent, modern and in control. Radway interprets this contradiction as appealing to the women because they live very traditional lives and have a suppressed feminism. The author is reassuring the reader that the two things are compatible. The women get a number of things from these romances:

1. An escape from domestic responsibilities: 'I am reading my book, don't disturb me.'

2. Leisure and relaxation that is difficult for a housewife to achieve otherwise.

3. A fantasy world that reverses the 'real' one and gives vicarious pleasure. Here men care for women, locations are exotic, often in different historical periods.

4. Education: the women learn things about other times and places. The novels act as a substitute for travel. This enables the women to construct a self-image of self-improvement.

5. Reading the novels creates a community of readers and authors that provides real emotional support that is now lacking with the decline of the extended family.

Radway claims that the love of romance should be seen as a hidden protest against patriarchal culture, a form of ritualistic resistance: 'critical power ... lies buried in the romances as one of the few widely shared womanly commentaries on the contradictions and costs of patriarchy', though she recognizes the danger of the romances making a bad situation easier to cope with. The feminist critic has to help the reader exploit the elements of the novel which articulate their own implicit feminism and understand that a better world is possible in which it wouldn't be necessary to escape into fiction.

However, in taking this position she separates herself (feminist critic) from popular pleasures and puts herself in a superior position. This is not post-modernist. Ang (1985) suggests that watching *Dallas* has little if anything to do with feminist utopias or feminist politics. Brown (1990) takes a position closer to Radway's, arguing that the gendered reception of popular culture resists hegemony by privately making fun of definitions of masculinity and femininity.

For Elizabeth Frazer (1987) there are only limited effects. After conducting interviews with teenage girls she suggests that:

a self-conscious and reflexive approach to texts is a natural under-standing, not only of fiction, but of the genre of publications for girls of which *Jackie* is an example ... Ideology is undercut ... by these readers' reflexivity and reflectiveness.

However Martin Barker (1989) has criticized this approach. He says that there are different types of readers of *Jackie* (and other mass media). Some are casual readers and *Jackie* probably has little influence on them. However some readers form a 'contract' with *Jackie*:

A contract involves an agreement that a text will talk to us in ways we recognize. It will enter into a dialogue with us. And that dialogue, with its dependable elements and form, will relate to some aspect of our lives.

For these readers *Jackie* does exert a power and influences those aspects of their social lives which its stories relate to. Barker is in agreement with Morley's approach outlined in Chapter 2, p. 29. For Barker and Morley writers such as Frazer and Radway are effectively saying, 'relax, be happy: the media have no bad effects'. In fact the structured interpretation approach says they do.

*Imagine a feminist single parent watching* Blind Date *with her two teenage daughters. At each point she steps in to criticize the action and the dialogue, offering a running feminist interpretation of what is happening.*
1. *What is the dominant message as far as the daughters are concerned?*
2. *What influence will* Blind Date *have on the mother?*
3. *What influence will the experience tend to have on the daughters?*

*Re-read pp 202–204 then critically evaluate the following argument:*

Some may argue that simply classifying the content of television com-mercials says little about the *meanings* that people obtain from these portrayals, or the *effects* the differing portrayals of males and females have on their perceptions, beliefs, and attitudes.

On the other hand, while individual and idiosyncratic reactions to media stimuli must be taken into account, there is a good deal of research evidence indicating that sex-role stereotyped portrayals and heavy exposure to mass media in general are associated with more sex-typed views of the world. For example, Gerbner and Signorielli (1979) correlated adults' television-viewing patterns with their answers to questions measuring attitudes towards the sexes and found a positive relationship between the amount of television viewing and the belief that a woman should not work if her husband is able to support her.

Kimball (1986) studied the sex role attitudes of children in three separate communities; one receiving no television, one receiving one channel, and one receiving four channels. The survey revealed that children in the com-munities with television were more stereotyped in their sex role attitudes than were those in the town without television. Moreover, after television was introduced to the no-television community, the attitudes of children in that town became more stereotyped ...

(Bretl and Cantor 1988, pp. 607–8)

*Conduct a content analysis (see p. 40) on a few episodes of one particular soap opera. If you can legally video-record them in advance this would be helpful. Your aim is to examine the representation of women in that soap. You will need to identify in advance precisely which elements of this you will be looking for. For example: the number of women and men in each episode; the amount of time they each spend on screen; what occupations the men and women have; how long they are seen in traditional roles (baby-care, in the kitchen etc.) and so on.*

*The aim of the project is to test whether the criticisms made of the media portrayal of women are true of soap operas. It may be that nowadays women are often portrayed in important jobs exercising considerable power.*

*If you are working in a group it would be useful to conduct the same exercise on two quite different soap operas (say Roseanne and Coronation Street) so that a comparison of the results can be made.*

### Examination question

'Subordinate groups in society tend to be represented by the media in ways which reinforce their subordination.'

Examine this view with reference to *two* of the following groups: black people; the young; strikers; the poor; women.

(AEB AS, Sociology, June 1992, paper 2, question 8)

*An outline answer to this question can be found in the skeleton answers section at the end of the book.*

## Further reading

Baehr, H. and Dyer, G. (eds) (1987) *Boxed In: Women and Television*, London: Pandora.

Beasly, M. in Creedon, P. (1989) *Women in Mass Communication: Challenging Gender Values*, London: Sage.

Beuf, A. (1974) 'Doctor, lawyer, household drudge', *Journal of Communication*, 24(2), 142–5.

Bretl, D. and Cantor, J. 1988 'The portrayal of men and women in US television commercials: a recent content analysis and trends over 15 years (1971–1986)', *Sex Roles*, 18(9/10), 595–609.

Brown, M. (1990) *TV and Women's Culture*, London: Sage.

Davies, K. *et al.* (1987) *Out of Focus: Writing on Women and the Media*, London: The Women's Press.

Geraghty, C. (1991) *Women and Soap Opera*, Cambridge: Polity Press.

Gray, A. (1992) *Video Playtime*, London: Routledge.

Gunter, B. (1995) *Television and Gender Representation*, London: John Libbey. This gives an up-to-date account of research on the portrayal of gender on television and its effects on children and adults.

Hermes, J. (1995) *Reading Women's Magazines*, Cambridge: Polity Press.

Radway, J. (1994) *Reading the Romance*, University of North Carolina Press.

van Zoonen, L. (1994) *Feminist Media Studies*, London: Sage.

van Zoonen, L. (1991) 'Feminist perspectives on the media', in Curran and Gurevitch (eds), *Mass Media and Society*, London: Edward Arnold.

Wolf, N. (1990) *The Beauty Myth*, London: Vintage.

# Minority ethnic groups and the mass media

Figure 10.1 Waiting for a glimpse of Princess Diana in South London. What message might this picture put across if used by a tabloid newspaper?

This chapter is divided into the following sections:

1. Representations of minority ethnic groups in media content, which explores the regularities that have been found in the way ethnicity is represented in the output of different media and genres.

2. Theorizing ethnicity and the media, which looks at the different theories about the relationship between ethnicity and the mass media.

3. Ethnicity and media effects, which considers how far it is possible to make general statements about the effects the media have on attitudes and behaviour related to these issues.

---

### 'Race' and 'ethnicity'

'Race' is popularly thought to be a valid scientific concept which describes and explains the division of humankind according to physical characteristics (such as skin colour and facial characteristics). However although there are observable differences between people, there are no clear-cut dividing lines between one 'race' and another. Rather there are gradients

---

206

of difference. Some researchers use the word 'race' in inverted commas to indicate that they do not accept its validity but do recognize its social significance. By doing this they acknowledge that 'race' is a socially constructed not scientifically objective concept.

'Ethnicity' means the sense of shared cultural identity which binds a community together. It is used to distinguish one community from another and can be the basis for collective action by, and conflict between, communities. Ethnicity is often expressed through religious values and practices, language, dress, cuisine, and other cultural traditions and beliefs.

Minority ethnic group refers to a group of people in a particular context who have a cultural identity which is different from that shared by most people there. It is now considered correct to talk of 'minority ethnic group' rather than 'ethnic minority group'.

See Billingham (1995) for more details.

 *Why should we use 'minority ethnic group' rather than 'ethnic minority group'?*

## 1. Representation of minority ethnic groups in media content

Any discussion of media representations of ethnicity needs to start with the qualification that this area is one in which is very unwise to generalize about 'the media'. Some problems with trying to do this are as follows:

- Representations found in some parts of the tabloid press would rarely if ever be found on television or in the broadsheet press. The differences between them can lead to explicit conflict within the media, for example the *Sun* accused television channels of acting as a 'fifth column' (i.e. of being traitorous) in their unsympathetic account in *Death on the Rock* of the Gibraltar shootings of IRA suspects by the SAS in 1988.

- Some parts of the media are oriented to particular ethnic communities and representations of those communities (and the wider culture in which they exist) will be very different from those found in the wider media. For example *The Voice* describes itself as 'Britain's Best Black Newspaper'.

- We saw in Chapter 6 that while there is much concern about violence in the media, the prosocial intent of many television programmes, for example, is ignored. The positive role of the media in the context of 'race' is often ignored too. For example Desmond Wilcox recounts (in Pines 1992) his and fellow journalists' concern to report bigotry and intolerance in programmes like *This Week* and *Man Alive* and in his subsequent work on 'fly on the wall' programmes like *Black in Blue* (1990) which revealed racial prejudice in the Metropolitan Police.

- The same medium with very similar content can approach it, and be received, in very different ways in different countries. Ellis Cashmore (1994) shows how Londoner Alf Garnett in *Till Death Us Do Part* invited the audience's derision for his racist bigotry. His character was used to show the shallowness of the arguments used by racists like him. However when the series idea was exported to the USA under the title of *All in the Family* the Garnett character (now called Archie Bunker) was largely seen in a positive light, even becoming a model for some Americans. Although the character had been altered to remove some of the more ridiculous attitudes, this was not the whole explanation for the different reception. In America under President Reagan 'standing tall' and being proud to be American became acceptable again. This created a context which legitimized strident nationalism and obscured internal divisions such as 'racial' ones. The racial problems of the nation were contained 'all in the family' in the American context, but exposed for debate in the British one by these two almost identical programmes.

For these reasons, rather than tackle the question of representations by looking at different media types, as we did in the gender chapter, it is more appropriate to summarize the claims that have been made about the representation of minority ethnic groups by looking at the type of distortions which have been identified. These can be summarized as follows.

### Negative representations of cultural values

In this category we can include depictions of Muslim attitudes towards women. For example the *Daily Mail* carried a front-page story, *Scandal of Brides for Sale*, which claimed that parents of young girls of Asian descent sold them to strangers seeking the right to live in the UK. The paper could not provide any evidence for what it claimed to be a widespread practice.

Laziness and a culture of dependency leading to abuse of the immigration and welfare systems has been another common theme in reporting ethnicity:

## Visa Curb for Migrant Fiddlers (*Sun*, 2 December 1986)
## Visa Plan to Beat Immigrant Cheats (*Star*, 2 December 1986)
## Jobless Abdul on £470 a Week (*Mail*, November 1984)

Stories about events abroad can have implications for perceptions of the values of immigrants to the UK. For example Teun van Dijke argues that news reporting of the Ayatollah Khomeini's *fatwa* against Salman Rushdie for his book *The Satanic Verses* led to a hardening of attitudes towards Muslims in the UK and France. The reports cast both Khomeini and, by implication, the Iranian people as bigots. Similarly reports about Saddam Hussein before, during and after the Gulf War can have important implications for perceptions of Iraqis and, perhaps, Arabs generally.

Occasionally a kind of oblique racism operates. By making statements about 'British' cultural values there is an unstated assumption being made about non-British values. For example on September 9 1995 the *Daily Telegraph* carried a front-page story about a train crash near Maidenhead, Berkshire in which one person was killed and several were put in hospital. The train caught fire and smoke filled several carriages. The headline was:

## Through the Smoke a Voice Said: We're British, Let's Be Sensible

The headline implies that if 'we' were, for example, Indians, there would be irrational panic. While this phrase was actually spoken on the train (other passengers reported it being used), the important point is its selection by the *Telegraph* as a headline, surrounded by pictures of the burned-out train.

### Racial reductionism and cultural racism

Racial reductionism means reducing an explanation of people's behaviour down to their 'race' – saying 'they behave like that because they are Japanese/Italian/English' – it is 'in their blood'. Found rarely in the mass media now, it was more common in the past, especially during wartime.

Cultural racism involves explaining behaviour in terms of cultural traits. Effectively it is the modern version of racial reductionism. Hebdige (1992) notes that the English heritage industry involves a kind of institutionalized cultural racism, setting up a fictional model of English culture and effectively saying 'this is how the English are (and should be)'.

## Negative representations of norms of behaviour

Depictions of black people as criminals are very common in the media in general and the press in particular. Teun van Dijk's 1991 review of previous studies and his own extensive research based on a content analysis of tens of thousands of news items in many newspapers in several countries over several decades shows that the category of crime and violence is 'always among the five most frequent issues in ethnic coverage'.

The generally negative evaluation of minority groups is demonstrated by van Dijk's data on newspaper headline depiction of minority and majority groups (see Table 10.1).

Table 10.1   Frequencies of headline depictions of minority and majority groups, August 1985–January 1986

|  | The Times | Sun | Telegraph | Mail | Guardian |
|---|---|---|---|---|---|
| **MEC: neutral** | 22 | 11 | 20 | 15 | 26 |
| **MEC: negative** | 19 | 25 | 32 | 16 | 14 |
| **MEC: positive** | 4 | 1 | 4 | 4 | 5 |
| **Majority: neutral** | 23 | 0 | 9 | 6 | 20 |
| **Majority: negative** | 9 | 1 | 14 | 6 | 7 |
| **Majority: positive** | 3 | 0 | 10 | 2 | 7 |
| **State/parties: neutral** | 26 | 4 | 11 | 10 | 21 |
| **State/parties: negative** | 2 | 0 | 4 | 2 | 2 |
| **State/parties: positive** | 4 | 1 | 3 | 1 | 3 |
| **Police/judiciary: neutral** | 31 | 2 | 13 | 12 | 34 |
| **Police/judiciary: negative** | 21 | 4 | 6 | 8 | 25 |
| **Police/judiciary: positive** | 4 | 1 | 13 | 4 | 2 |
| Neutral: MEC | 10 | 3 | 7 | 10 | 11 |
| Negative: MEC | 11 | 7 | 14 | 8 | 16 |
| Positive: MEC | 10 | 3 | 13 | 3 | 7 |
| Neutral: majority | 3 | 1 | 3 | 4 | 7 |
| Negative: majority | 5 | 7 | 6 | 5 | 2 |
| Positive: majority | 1 | 0 | 2 | 0 | 2 |
| Neutral: state/parties | 3 | 0 | 2 | 0 | 2 |
| Negative: state/parties | 1 | 1 | 3 | 0 | 0 |
| Positive: state/parties | 0 | 0 | 1 | 0 | 0 |
| Neutral: police/judiciary | 12 | 1 | 5 | 7 | 6 |
| Negative: police/judiciary | 6 | 11 | 23 | 21 | 13 |
| Positive: police/judiciary | 2 | 2 | 2 | 3 | 3 |

*Source*: van Dijk (1991), p. 60.

MEC = individual/s from the minority ethnic community;
Majority = individual/s from the majority community;
Emboldened section = individual or group was the active agent;
Non-emboldened section = individual or group had actions done to them.

1. Summarize what the table tells us about the portrayal of minority and majority groups by different newspapers.
2. Which categories would the following headlines be placed in?

## Black Brixton Looters Jailed (*Telegraph*, 14 December 1985)

## Mob Protest fails as Race Storm Head [Honeyford] Goes Back to School

(*Mail*, 17 December 1985)

## Beaten-Up Asian in Fire Terror

(*Mail*, 20 August 1985)

## MP's Ready to Greet Dubious Immigrants

(*Telegraph*, 3 December 1985)

3. What problems can you identify with this approach to the study of ethnicity in the media?

The beating up of the black American Rodney King by policemen on 30 April 1990 gives an interesting insight into media representations of norms of behaviour. The beating was videoed by a passer-by and the tape was given repeated international airing on news programmes. This led to an outcry about racism in the police force. However, when the rioting by black Americans began in Los Angeles following the acquittal of the four policemen involved, the media depictions of black Americans again followed the usual stereotypes – violent, criminally inclined, angry, aggressive, emotional and irrational. This case demonstrates the danger of generalizing about media representations but also the persistence of particular frames of reference in reporting ethnicity.

Figure 10.2 Coronation Street - a fair reflection of society? The only non-white character is a hairdresser. Do any of the British soaps succeed in including minority ethnic groups in a convincing way?

Figure 10.3   Age and
gender of people from
minority ethnic groups
(percentages of total
people from that minority
ethnic group represented;
the total numbers of
people represented were
275 Africans, 81 Asians
and 64 others)

*Source*: adapted from
BSC 1995, p. 136,
table 35.

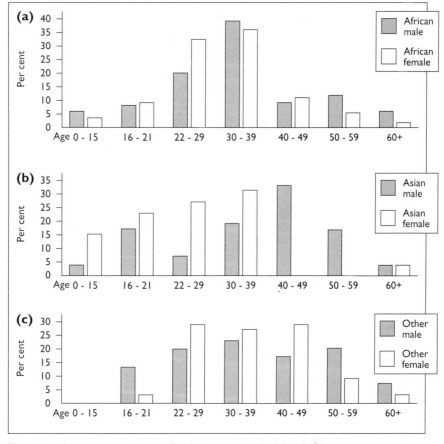

### Restricted representations of ethnic groups in social roles

A 1985 study by Preethi Manuel conducted a content analysis of Africans, Indians,
Pakistanis and Afro-Caribbeans in British drama and concluded that in more than 600
drama programmes only 2.25% of the total actors involved came from these groups.
Those who did appear were mostly cast as low-paid workers, students, law breakers
or background figures. Women from these groups hardly appeared at all. More
recently work done for the Broadcasting Standards Council has shown how ethnicity,
age, gender and genre are all important when considering media representations of
social roles. Their methodology is explained on p. 41. Some of their findings are
reproduced in Figures 10.3 (a), (b) and (c), Figure 10.4 and Table 10.2.

*Each pair or small group should take one figure or table and summarize
the important information it gives us ready for a presentation to the whole
group. Any problems you note in the data you have should also be noted.*

The problem with content analysis studies like this one is that we are left to infer the
effects of these limited representations of social role, and this is far from easy. We
can illustrate the difficulty by looking at a programme where black people are shown
in a *positive* light, *The Cosby Show*, the most popular TV comedy in history. Here a
successful upper middle class American black family (the Huxtables) are presented
extremely favourably in a variety of comedy situations. The lead actor, Bill Cosby, is
himself extremely popular, rich and successful in real life and in the show the

boundaries between the real Cosby and the fictional Dr Huxtable are blurred (as the title of the show illustrates).

Figure 10.4 People from minority ethnic groups by type of profession (percentages)

*Source*: adapted from BSC 1995, p. 135, table 34.

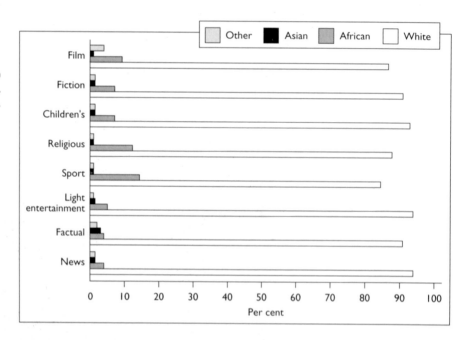

Table 10.2    Occupational status of people from minority ethnic groups (percentages)

|  | African | Asian | Other | Total |
|---|---|---|---|---|
| Arts and entertainment | 21 | 16 | 3 | 18 |
| White collar | 4 | 3 | 9 | 5 |
| Educationalist, academic | 1 | 1 | 2 | 1 |
| Travel and leisure | 4 | 4 | 13 | 5 |
| Health and caring | 4 | 20 | 6 | 7 |
| Legal | 1 | 0 | 2 | 1 |
| Police, inc. private detectives | 3 | 0 | 5 | 2 |
| Other uniformed services | 8 | 0 | 5 | 6 |
| Domestic staff | 4 | 0 | 5 | 4 |
| Blue-collar worker | 2 | 1 | 6 | 2 |
| Sports person | 6 | 0 | 0 | 4 |
| Clergy, religious leader | 1 | 0 | 2 | 1 |
| Politician/spokesperson | 6 | 3 | 0 | 4 |
| Shop/stall owner/assistant | 1 | 8 | 0 | 2 |
| Pensioner/retired | 1 | 0 | 0 | 1 |
| Student | 4 | 16 | 8 | 7 |
| Under 16 | 6 | 8 | 0 | 5 |
| Unemployed | 1 | 0 | 2 | 1 |
| Criminal | 3 | 0 | 2 | 2 |
| Others | 2 | 0 | 6 | 2 |
| Cannot code | 16 | 21 | 27 | 18 |
| Totals | 99 (N=275) | 101 (N=80) | 103 (N=64) | 98 (N=419) |

*Source*: BSC (1995), p. 137, table 36

The question is, however, should the Huxtable family (and Bill Cosby) be seen as positive representations of what American black people could become, positive role models (as John Downing 1988, believes). Alternatively, should they be seen as depicting an extremely unrepresentative group of black people who are isolated from, and ignore, the problems of racism, deprivation and underachievement that disproportionately affect black people in the US (as Jhally and Lewis 1992, suggest)? Similarly, the positive presentation of black sportsmen and sportswomen such as Frank Bruno, Linford Christie and Tessa Sanderson can be interpreted as propagating restricted stereotypes or as depicting members of MEG's in a favourable way.

Figure 10.5    Jhally and Lewis state that the overall effect of *The Cosby Show* is a negative one: 'a representation of the American dream which masks persistent division of race and class in that country.'

*What do you think?*

*This project uses content-analysis to establish the degree of exposure given to minority ethnic groups on TV and to compare different channels on this. Prepare a time sample sheet which you will be able to tick as you watch broadcast TV, recording the time devoted to representatives of MEG's and details of their portrayal. Table 10.3 gives some very basic ideas for you to develop:*

Table 10.3 Content-analysis of ethnic minority portrayal on TV: time sample sheet

| Occasions | Minutes of exposure | Main subsidiary character | Positive/ negative portrayal | Programme type | Etc. |
|---|---|---|---|---|---|
| 1 | | | | | |
| 2 | | | | | |
| 3 (etc.) | | | | | |

*On successive nights watch the output of just one channel for a predetermined amount of time, completing the sheets as you do so and supplementing this with notes where necessary. You will need a stopwatch to time each occasion when a representation of ethnicity appears.*

> *Having done this for all four channels, collate and write up your material,*
> *including an assessment of the method used and suggestions for improvement as*
> *well as an analysis of the results.*

### Ethnic minorities as a 'threat'

The representation of MEG's as a threat is best exemplified through an account of the reporting of MP Enoch Powell's speeches. In April 1968 Powell was given extensive publicity for the famous speech in which he declared that 'the black man will have the "whip hand" over the white man' because of excessive immigration and the large families of immigrants. He declared he could see a time when Britain would become like the 'River Tiber, foaming with much blood'. According to Seymour-Ure, Powell deliberately timed the speech – made to only 85 people – so that it would get extensive media coverage and shaped its content to make it newsworthy (it quickly became known as the 'rivers of blood' speech). He included anecdotes about constituents afraid to go out because of 'grinning piccaninnies' jeering at her and excreta being pushed through letter boxes to frighten white residents out of their homes.

Surveys at the time showed that 96% of the population had heard about the speech and there were marches by London dockers and LSE students in support of and protesting against the speech. Those who supported Powell's view were concerned, like him, that immigrants and their children presented a threat to their jobs, houses, living standards and, ultimately, their very culture. Since then Powell has been able to count on the press for a sympathetic hearing of his views on race according to Seymour-Ure and Gordon and Rosenberg. In 1983, 15 years later, the *Sun* ran a major article headed 'Was Enoch Right?' and in 1985, following riots in Handsworth, Powell's view that black people should be paid to leave Britain was given extensive publicity. His views were again given prominence in 1988 for no other reason than the 20th anniversary of the 'rivers of blood' speech. Gordon and Rosenberg suggest that:

> Virtually every utterance by Powell on race or immigration has been
> given extensive publicity. Yet, newspapers were not obliged to treat
> Powell in this way; they chose to.

Seymour-Ure agrees:

> Powell's speech, by its very attractiveness to the media in terms of
> their traditional news values, at least confirmed existing prejudices
> and possibly invigorated them by its emotive style.

---

### Primary definers

Primary definers are individuals or groups who set the agenda of issues to
be discussed in the media and, as a result, more broadly. They also set the
terms of the debate: the frame in which the topic is cast. Thus Powell
helped put 'race' issues on the agenda and framed the debate in terms of
numbers and conflict.

---

The Dutch researcher Teun van Dijk's cross-national content analysis study of newspapers confirms the view that the press, at least, gives priority to issues that Powell brought up in 1968: immigration, competition for resources and ethnic conflict. It shows that immigration and residence issues have historically been a major concern of the press over time. In the 1980s and '90s there began to be an increasing emphasis on 'conflict' subjects.

Two examples van Dijk cites are the Rushdie affair and the Honeyford case. Head teacher Ray Honeyford was suspended and eventually removed from his post for apparently racist remarks in a right-wing journal. He was defended by his professional association and much of the media treatment of the case was very sympathetic towards him. Similar 'conflict' issues have recently centred on education, particularly the desire of Asian parents to educate their children (especially girls) separately or white parents withdrawing children from schools over race issues. This arose in 1987, for example, when parents in Dewsbury withdrew their children from a school in which the pupils were predominantly Asian.

### Devaluing the lives of foreigners and minority ethnic group members

Implicit within much news reporting is the view that the life of a non-white, in the UK or abroad, is worth less than that of a white, and that therefore its loss is less newsworthy.

The treatment of Argentina and its people during the Falklands conflict of 1982 is a case in point:

WE'LL SMASH 'EM

(*Sun*, 6 April, 1982)

Argentines quickly became stereotyped into Gauchos (Latin American cowboys) or simply Argies:

STICK THIS UP YOUR JUNTA!

A Sun Missile for Galtieri's Gauchos

(*Sun*, 1 May 1982)

PANICKY ARGIES FLEE BAREFOOT

(*Sun*, 3 June 1982)

Their lives were not really worth considering:

GOTCHA!

(*Sun*, 4 May 1982, after the sinking of the *General Belgrano* with nearly 400 lives lost)

On television news the loss of Argentinian life was treated with as little gravity. Reports of the *Belgrano*'s sinking concentrated on the numbers rescued, not how many had been killed. The word 'dead' was replaced by 'lost' or 'missing':

*Newscaster*: The Argentines say there were around 700 survivors from the 1,082 men on board the *General Belgrano* which was torpedoed on Sunday.

*Newscaster*: The first group of survivors from the Argentine cruiser *General Belgrano* have been brought ashore. The General Belgrano was torpedoed by a British submarine on Sunday; 800 men have been rescued and the searches still continue for others.

(ITN, 5 May 1982 and BBC News, 5 May 1982 respectively)

The sinking of *The Sheffield*, a British warship, was treated quite differently. Casualties and deaths were the main focus, and emotive words like 'dreadful news' and 'terrible news' were used by newscasters and presenters.

It is worth noting, in ending this section, that *places* as well as people can be represented in a consistently distorted way. The coup-war-famine syndrome is the view (propagated by media coverage) that in the Third World the main things that happen are coups, wars and famines. The implication underlying this syndrome is that these 'facts' are largely due to black stupidity, barbarism, laziness, corruption, unstable political regimes and/or climatic disaster. Other sorts of news from the Third World rarely get access to Western media and so our impressions are highly distorted. It appears that the government and people of these countries are somehow inadequate because they cannot solve these problems. Such countries are pictured as having an ever-extended begging bowl held out to the rich countries. More sophisticated views, such as the idea that the Third World's poverty may be due to its dependency relationship with the West, are ignored.

### Examination questions

'With reference to sociological studies, assess the claim that the mass media are biased against ethnic minorities.'

(AEB, June 1993, A level sociology, question 8)

'Discuss the media representation of one social group.'

(AEB Media Studies, 1997 examination, specimen questions, paper 2, question 1)

## 2. Theorizing ethnicity and the media

This section examines theoretical approaches to explaining relationships between the mass media and ethnicity, primarily media representations of minority ethnic groups. Four theoretical approaches can be identified: pluralism, postmodernism, Marxism (which adopts a view close to the manipulative model described in Chapter 4) and neo-Marxism (which adopts a view close to the hegemonic model described in the same chapter).

For *pluralists* the poor media representation of minority ethnic groups in the past reflected the disadvantaged position of these groups in society. However, this has improved over the years as the media images have started to become more positive and the stereotyped images used less often.

In support of this claim, pluralists can point to members of ethnic minorities in authoritative positions in British television. Well-known examples are presenters like Moira Stewart and Trevor MacDonald, but there are many others in both local and national media. Programmes for ethnic minorities such as *Eastern Eye* and *Black Bag* are increasingly given airtime. The obligation placed on BBC and ITV as well as Channel 4 to commission programmes from independent companies (see p. 5) means that commissioning editors have an opportunity to give contracts to the black independent sector. Farrukh Dhondy (in Pines 1992), Commissioning Editor of Multicultural Programmes at Channel 4, explicitly followed this policy.

Furthermore, there is an increasing amount of time given to black and Asian culture in general in the broadcast media, while in the publishing world there has been a rapid growth in recent years in the number of magazines catering especially for minority ethnic groups as their presence and their spending power has come to be recognized. This view is confirmed by those at the top. Michael Grade said in an interview on *The Black and White Media Show* that:

> There are more minority faces in positions of responsibility in the factual area as presenters, reporters, newscasters and so on, and that's a tremendous step forward.

(Though he did go on to say that there are still many problems in fictional programmes and comedy.)

> I'm disappointed ... by the sense in which [black issues] ... are ghettoised into what amounts to travel documentaries. It's very interesting to see a documentary about corruption in Pakistan or about politics in Trinidad for example. But as a black person living in this country, trying to construct a life or another identity for myself and my children, it is not particularly useful. I would like to see a policy directed more towards talking about what we are, giving us the sense to emerge from what I call the kind of dumbness that is imposed on us ... An increasing gap has been developing in the representation of black experiences in minority programming – between the sense of black people as media images on the one hand, and a sense of black people as real people on the other ... black people are being presented more and more as 'ethnic', as 'Third World', as alien to the concerns of people in this country.

> (Mike Phillips, academic, journalist and freelance writer for newspaper and
> TV in Pines (1992), p. 173)

*There is considerable debate over TV programming for black and Asian people. Some argue that programmes for them are essential because of the inferior treatment they receive in mainstream broadcasting. Others argue that making such separate programmes is a form of televisual apartheid and tokenism. The answer is to involve black issues and black presenters in normal programming. Where do you stand in this debate?*

In the United States both the representation of minority ethnic groups in the media and their roles within media organizations have improved since the 1960s. According to R. D. Colle (1973) this has resulted from the following factors.

- Key organizations in the mass media espoused a non-discriminatory policy from the mid-1960s onwards.

- Positive action (demos etc.) became more forceful.

- Minority groups became stronger and more articulate.

- Legal action was taken where employment policies etc. did not conform to new, liberal laws.

- Marketing conditions changed so that films were being sold abroad to countries which wanted black and Asian people seen on the screen in important roles.

- Industry training programmes began to provide talented black actors, writers and so on.

- Independent producers became more important as the power of the monolithic picture houses such as Paramount began to decline. These producers were much more willing to use black actors in realistic roles.

- Pioneering black actors such as Sidney Poitier served as examples for others to follow.

- The social climate changed so that racial discrimination and overtly stereotyped representations of blacks became unacceptable.

The same argument applies to American advertisements. In the US today people from minority ethnic groups are portrayed in positive roles in advertisements, but this was not the case in the past. The change is due to the affluence of the minority market now and to political strength, exemplified by the success of the campaign by Jesse Jackson to get Coca-Cola to change its advertising and employment practices. He asked black people to drink Pepsi instead until Coke did so; it soon did! In Britain, though, the old racial stereotypes still linger in some advertising because of the lack of black political power and limited spending power black people have. Pluralists argue that the same processes have happened or are happening in the UK too.

As far as the British press are concerned, the pluralist would say that they cannot be expected to analyse the underlying socio-economic causes of the problems minority ethnic groups have. Their role is the day-to-day reporting of events as they occur. News values call for reporting of conflict. Readers would quickly switch allegiance if the *Sun* or the *Star* had long and detailed analyses of discriminatory practices in employment and housing. Media reporting of race, as with other issues, is in line with what the public want. This is identified by news editors, revealed by newspaper sales and disclosed by public opinion research.

In *The Mass Media and Racial Conflict* Paul Hartmann and Charles Husband suggest two main reasons for the biased representation of minority ethnic groups in the British media, the press in particular:

1. That portraying black people as a 'problem' coincides with journalists' ideas about what is newsworthy, i.e. their news values. Fear, tension, conflict etc. are words which make the audience sit up and take notice. Coexistence, harmony and peace are words which just don't get into the news. One possible exception is the Notting Hill carnival with the obligatory picture of the smiling policeman joining in, though even this has a frisson provided by the ever-present threat of trouble.

2. That in providing these images of black people in the media, journalists and others responsible for them are merely reflecting back to society the derogatory attitudes and negative symbols concerning foreigners and blacks which are inherent in the British culture.

Hartmann and Husband therefore partly subscribe to the pluralist model of the media; the media don't shape society, they are shaped by it. Racism is stamped onto the consciousness of whites brought up in a racist society. Their assumptions, judgements and feelings are permeated with attitudes inherited from centuries of colonialism and racism, and are hence untrustworthy.

Figure 10.6 A slogan daubed across a billboard advertising skin-whitening cream in the U.S.

Postmodernist theory has much in common with pluralism. It suggests that social identities have become fragmented and less stable. With the acceleration of mass communications and the compression of space and time associated with this, people begin to have a less fixed idea of who they are. Mercer (1990), for example, suggests that in a postmodern age people are more displaced and disenchanted than they were. Traditional sources of authority are eroded and people no longer collectively identify with class and community. For most postmodernists this 'casting adrift' means that individuals are empowered to create their own identities, including ethnic identities. Several studies, including Hebdige (1988 and 1989) have concluded that British working-class youth have used fashion to create an original public identity, thus challenging the power of organized commercialism (see Gillespie's study, below).

---

### Bricolage

This refers to the creative use of the products of consumer culture through unusual combinations and/or alterations to create distinctive subcultures and identities, including of course ethnic identities. James Lull (1995) gives a simple example from the London underground system where he saw two London punks changing a sign which said:

**Do not obstruct the door. It causes delay and can be dangerous**
into:
    **obstruct the door. cause delay. be dangerous**

A fuller discussion of bricolage can be found in Nava (1992).

---

Angela McRobbie argues in *Postmodernism and Popular Culture* that in a postmodern society the power of 'primary definers' is much reduced, even to the point of making the concept redundant. No sooner is an issue raised by a primary definer than interested pressure groups jump into the argument and take it in unpredictable directions. An example comes from the summer of 1995, the time of writing. It concerns London's Metropolitan Police Commissioner's statement that a large proportion of the capital's criminals are young black men. The reporting of this immediately led to the mobilization of opinion by pressure groups on the issue through the media and a debate quickly ensued around a number of issues. These included questioning the factual basis of the statement and the Chief Constable's wisdom in saying such a thing, the economic and social circumstances of young black males which might lead them to crime and so on. The reporting of the issue went through a number of phases and was multi-dimensional.

Marxists and neo-Marxists in particular are very dismissive of this approach. Marxists feel that pluralism and postmodernism do not really address why the ideology of racism persists, or why news values are as they are. Nor do these perspectives appreciate the importance of power and ownership and the way they are concentrated in a few hands. A more radical approach sees the reasons for the unique treatment of minority ethnic groups as based in the nature of British capitalism. This says it is in the interests of British capitalism to set white worker against black and Asian workers (who can be easily scapegoated because of their skin colour) for a number of reasons:

● black and Asian workers are blamed for unemployment (too many blacks taking jobs), this diverting attention from the inevitable crises in capitalist production;

● unions will not defend black and Asian workers and so low wages and poor conditions prevail where black workers predominate; they can be 'super-exploited' by the capitalist class;

● workers will be disunited and, therefore, not put forward an effective opposition to capitalism;

● white workers will feel relatively privileged compared to blacks and their militancy will be correspondingly reduced.

 *Would you agree or disagree with this perspective? What evidence or argument can you bring to bear to support your point of view?*

This perspective can be found in books such as *The Empire Strikes Back* (Hall) and *Immigrant Workers and Class Structure in Western Europe* (Castles and Kosack). In them it is suggested that the role of the media is to shape the views of white workers, encouraging them to blame black immigrants for problems which are really the inevitable consequences of the capitalist system. These include unemployment, low wages, lack of decent housing, inner-city deprivation, violence on the streets, and poor schooling ('they're taking our jobs/homes', 'they're turning inner cities into no-go areas', 'schools can't teach in English any more', etc.). In this way, those who suffer most from bad conditions are blamed for them. Such *fractionalization* of the working class is clearly in the interests of the capitalist class, and the media are their tool in this.

Most Marxists, and many others, would argue that racism in the media is not the result of a *deliberate* attempt to manipulate attitudes. Rather, those who hold powerful positions and can decide what does and does not get into the media have racist attitudes themselves, often more so than the population at large because of their particular social background and training. This is a version of the hegemonic perspective (see p. 65). One of the ways this hegemony is reinforced is through the selective employment practices that go on in the media. There are very few representatives of minority ethnic groups working in the media, particularly not in the more senior positions. Thus, the 'black' perspective on issues is rarely voiced. This is reflected in the comments of black and Asian journalists, artists and managers who have been involved with the British media:

> The BBC is a very white institution. At practically all the meetings I attend, I'm the only non-white face present ... we tend to get most of the non-white faces down in the canteen, and that's not good enough. Changes have to be made everywhere, right up to Board level.
>
> (Samir Shah, head of BBC TV's current affairs output from 1987, quoted in Pines (1992), p. 162)

> I personally think that British broadcasting is a stuffy little establishment that needs its backside kicked. For me, the main problems still are that black production can only be done via comedy, or you see black faces via singing and dancing, for instance ... It's about time that we actually had more actors doing drama and showing off their skills. As for multicultural programming, I think this effectively lets everybody else off the hook.
>
> (Trix Worrell of production company Writers Ink, quoted in Pines 1992).

Juliet Alexander, who was once a reporter on the *Hackney Gazette* in East London, tells how in her initial interview for the job her editor told her that he was 'killing two minorities in one'.

Alex Pacall relates the difficulties he had as one of the few black people working for Radio London in the 1970s and '80s. His programme *Black Londoners* caused particular difficulties with the BBC management. He writes:

> The programme was in fact intended for the white liberal element who sponsor what passes for black culture, black programmes made for white people from a white point of view, as part of the contribution to the anti-racist struggle. Hence they expect us to be in a state of high exultation, and gracefully receive the crumbs from the master's table.

The prejudiced views of some editors are illustrated in the following account of the handling of a story by a London radio station. A black journalist on the station gained an interview with the black victim of unlawful arrest and malicious wounding by the Metropolitan Police. He had suffered a broken leg in the back of a police van and was awarded damages by the High Court for this and the arrest. The journalist wrote the story along the lines of 'aggrieved man wins victory over bullying cops'. But the editor changed it so that the bulletin eventually reported how the man's neighbours thought he was a bit mad because he wore African clothes in the winter. There was very little background about the events or the case. The editor's explanation was that he was making a heavy story lighter so it would be more acceptable to a wider audience. This racist approach resulted from his ideas about black people as colourful characters not to be taken seriously and from his concept of 'news values'.

In television the same sort of thing occurs. In fiction programmes there are very few actors from minority ethnic groups. *It Ain't Half Hot, Mum* used some white actors to play Indians. Tony Freeth, a freelance producer, was told by someone in the BBC that 'the leading actor [in that series] loves Indians, in fact he thinks the British should never have left India'. It is not surprising that few black people are seen in TV advertisements when we learn from a senior executive of Saatchi and Saatchi that only one copywriter out of its 800-odd employees is black.

Stuart Hall and the other authors of *Policing the Crisis* subscribe to a neo-Marxist explanation of media racism, though they are perhaps more radical than many in their interpretation of it. They consider that the primary definers of what is 'important news' and what the 'correct' perspective on that news should be, such as politicians, police and business leaders, are in fact very important. The ideas of such people have hegemony in society and in the media, the latter because their ideas become integrated into concepts of news values, professional journalism and so on.

Hall (1986) says the media constitutes a 'machinery of representation', determining 'what and who gets represented and what and who routinely gets left out [and] how things, people, events, relationships get represented … the structure of access to the media is systematically skewed towards certain social categories', and away from others, including minority ethnic communities. South American novelist Manuel Puig recalls, for example, that watching American films in Argentina as a boy led him to believe that 'reality was spoken in English and came sub-titled' (quoted in Morley and Robins 1989).

Similarly, once race relations in Britain have become defined by the primary definers in the media as 'a problem of numbers', this is picked up by the media. Other viewpoints (such as the multiple disadvantages suffered by minority ethnic groups) do not see the light of day and even liberal spokesmen and women are forced to conduct the debate on this ground.

Another example of the operation of hegemony is NBC's attempt to remove an anti-apartheid sign on Theo Huxtable's bedroom door in *The Cosby Show*. Bill Cosby, by now a powerful and rich media figure, insisted that the sign should stay, and it did. Jhally and Lewis note that what is important about this example is not Cosby's triumph but 'the almost pathological fear of certain kinds of political discourse by executives in charge of TV entertainment'. Their view of what was appropriate in a programme like *The Cosby Show* did not include what they saw as inappropriate political statements: such shows should only seek to entertain. It was only Cosby's popularity, and therefore power, that made them overcome their initial reluctance to put the show on the air.

The problem lies not only *within* media institutions, according to this view, but also with the sources used by them. Crime reporters lean heavily on 'official sources' such as Scotland Yard and the police in general for their crime reporting. Checking it against other sources or looking for other angles on a story would undermine the hotline to a valuable source of news. Thus, journalists are fed the official, white and police version of events. One effect of this is that the socio-political causes of events such as the 'riots' in Brixton in 1981, and others like them, are ignored. The 'criminal angle' is the one that gets the attention in the news. This cosy relationship between the police PR departments and the media is evident in stories like the marriage between an Asian PC and a white policewoman (a splash story in both the *Express* and the *Mirror*) and a TV news item showing black sixth formers visiting New Scotland Yard.

*Examine as many sources of news as possible in one day. Identify those items which appear to emanate from police PR departments or similar sources (for example companies, universities etc.).*

The Dutch researcher Teun van Dijk also adopts the hegemonic perspective. Analysing the data from his long-term multi-disciplinary and multi-methodology study of the racism and the press (1991) he argues that there is a very close relationship between the press and the other major institutions and élite groups in society. Access is denied to minority group members, even when issues directly concern them. The dominant ideology shared by members of the press and the élite intimately affects how stories are selected (or ignored), interpreted and put into words by the press. The press and éite mutually affect and reinforce each other's interpretations of the world and together their ideological work helps reproduce consensus: 'ethnic affairs coverage in the press rather closely reproduces, confirms and legitimates prevailing ethnic ideologies as well as the power relations based on them'.

All this is not to deny that the media 'on occasion' may *deliberately* manipulate the presentation of race issues. B. Parekh, Professor of Political Theory at Hull University, recounts how the press distorted two stories (one about Brent's appointment of 177 staff to deal with the underachievement of minority ethnic children and the other about a change in the visa requirements for Commonwealth countries). Parekh concludes that

> the press twists facts, tells lies, declares a cold war on a section of the community, uses editorials as party political broadcasts and subjects its readers to a daily breakfast of raw prejudices …

The reasons for the lies and twisting of the truth are not explored by Parekh, but it is clear that he believes that there is a very deliberate attempt to manipulate people's attitudes towards ethnic minorities in Britain.

### Exam question

'Subordinate groups in society tend to be represented by the media in ways which reinforce their subordination.'
Examine this view with reference to *two* of the following groups: black people; the young; strikers; the poor; women.

(AEB Sociology, AS, June 1992, question 8)

## 3. Ethnicity and media effects

### The hypodermic model

It is easy to think that media representations of ethnicity have immediate and direct effects. Anecdotal evidence at the individual level appears to support this view. For example Chris Searle, who in the mid 1980s was the black chairperson of a community association in the St Paul's district of Bristol, found himself attacked by the *Sun, Star* and *Mail* for his outspoken stand on issues affecting black people. The papers ran stories about him, accusing him of orchestrating the 'race riots' which were affecting the city at the time:

Mr Nasty of St. Paul's

(*Western Daily Press*)

## MARIJUANA ON THE RATES!

(*Sun*)

The Face of Hate

(*Mirror*)

## RASTA RATBAG

(*Star*)

The *Sun* offered to pay him £667 for a one-way ticket to Zimbabwe as long as he promised never to come back. The *Star* printed his address in full. All the papers made use of the fact that he had a criminal record.

The effects of this on Mr Searle were immediate and unpleasant. He received letters addressed to 'Chief Nigger, Monkeyville, Bristol'. Some contained razor blades, others excrement and many suggested he should go back to the jungle.

In a similar vein, Carmen Proetta was dubbed 'The Tart' by the *Sun* after she stated in *Death on the Rock* that she saw SAS marksmen shoot suspected IRA terrorists Mairead Farrell and Daniel McCann *after* they had put up their hands in the 1988 Gibraltar operation against the IRA. Because of this Ms Proetta had her past dragged up and, like Searle, she became a foreign folk devil (her Spanish origin was emphasized by the report that she had been among only 44 Gibraltarians to vote for the island to become Spanish in a referendum 11 years previously). As a result of this vilification Ms Proetta was beaten up and she found her car daubed in red, white and blue paint.

Figure 10.7

Moving from the individual to the social level, Hartmann *et al.* in a UNESCO study (1974) conducted a survey to find out whether there was any correspondence between media content and people's views of race relations. They discovered that there was such a correspondence. Many of their respondents claimed to have obtained most of their ideas about race from the media.

A study by Hartmann and Husband (1974) on the attitudes towards race of children aged 11–12 and 14–15 years yielded similar results. Part of the sample selected for study lived in the West Midlands and Yorkshire (where there is a high density of Asian groups particularly) and a second part lived in Teesside and Glasgow (where there is not). Hartmann and Husband found that children in the latter areas were more likely to view race relations in terms of 'conflict', 'threat' and 'numbers' because they were gaining virtually all of their information on the issue from the media rather than from actual experience.

van Dijk reports the initial results of a study of the effects of the press reporting of 'race' on people's perceptions of race issues. Based on interviews designed to reveal how people recall and re-tell press stories, the conclusions are that:

● people recall stories even from years ago – time is not a major factor;

● where an event is massively reported, individuals can integrate the story about it into their understandings of reality and their more general knowledge about, for example, a particular group of immigrants (van Dijk concentrated on stories about Tamil immigration);

● where the reader has a good understanding of the issues already, the stories are more likely to be recalled and integrated into their ideas.

According to van Dijk virtually no reader challenges the interpretation of immigration issues put forward in the press (and which come from the élite groups in society). The possibility that different audiences will interpret the text in different ways as the 'reception analysis' approach would suggest, is discounted by van Dijk.

For someone who believes that the media representations of minority ethnic groups do have a direct effect it would not be a surprise to learn from the British Social Attitudes Survey of 1984, therefore, that:

● 91% of people think Britain is a racially prejudiced country;

● 33% of people are prepared to state openly that they are prejudiced against black people;

● 40% think that racial tensions will worsen in Britain in the future.

The fear which the hypodermic model gives rise to is that attitudes which are 'injected' into the audience will quickly be converted into actions: that media-inspired racial prejudice will turn into racial discrimination, or worse, that race hatred will turn into race killings.

### Reception analysis

Reception analysis, by contrast, alerts us to the fact that cause and effect are usually more complicated than the hypodermic model would suggest. bell hooks's reflections on her own past show us why:

> When we sat in our living rooms in the fifties and early sixties watching those few black folks who appeared on television screens, we talked about their performance, but we always talked about the way white folks were treating them. I have vivid memories of watching the Ed Sullivan show on Sunday nights, of seeing on that show the great Louis Armstrong. Daddy, who was usually silent, would talk about the music, the way Armstrong was treated and the political implications of his appearance. Watching television in the fifties and sixties, and listening to adult conversation, was one of the primary ways many black folks learned about race politics … The screen was not a place of escape. It was a place of confrontation and encounter.
>
> (bell hooks 1990)

Reception analysis means that we need to look not so much as the message, but at the audience. Fiske gives another example to illustrate the importance of the audience. When young Australian Aborigines watch old American TV westerns they ally themselves with the Indians and 'cheer them on as they attack the wagon train or the homestead, killing the white men and carrying off the white women' (Fiske 1989).

An in-depth audience study was conducted by Marie Gillespie, a lecturer at Cardiff University, which showed how television and video are used to recreate the culture of South Asians in London and how these media are also leading to cultural change. Her study is an ethnographic account of young Punjabis (14–18 years old) living in Southall, west London (more details of her methodology are given on p. 51). Punjabis there comprise the largest single Asian community outside the Indian subcontinent. Though the 'community' is cross-cut by class, caste, linguistic and regional differences, Gillespie feels it is appropriate to refer to them as 'London Punjabis'.

She conducted her ethnographic fieldwork between 1988 and 1991, a period during which the Berlin Wall fell, the *fatwa* was pronounced against Salman Rushdie, the Gulf War occurred and communism in Eastern Europe collapsed. Gillespie finds that the young people use television and video to redefine their ethnicity. A range of choices are available to young Punjabis, from *Dirty Dancing* and *Neighbours* to Indian sacred soaps like *The Mahabharata*. This gives the young people a cosmopolitanism and encourages them to compare, contrast and criticize cultural forms, including those of their parents. The young people dream an essentially American dream represented in advertisements for Coca-Cola and Levi jeans. However, they are not being duped or living in fantasy:

> the visit with friends to McDonald's in Hounslow is an entirely real 'escape' into a new social and communicative space, in which young people can actively redefine their culture. (p. 206)

They have a reflective awareness of cultural difference even when they are drawn into a programme and identify with its characters, as tends to happen with *Neighbours*. For example one young girl, Amrit, uses *Neighbours* as a kind of looking glass to reflect on gender roles:

You can see that families in *Neighbours* are more flexible, they do things together as a family, they don't expect that girls should stay at home and do housework and cooking, boys and girls are allowed to mix much more freely … Indian families do go out together to eat … but most of us can only go out with the family, they can't go out with their mates like the boys do … Boys live on the outside and girls on the inside.

The news reporting of the Gulf War had the same function, though this time relating to religion and national and international affiliation. Here the young people were placed in an ambivalent position: to identify with Iraqi Muslims being attacked by the Americans or not; to adopt the parents' position (based on the experience of colonialism) on the conflict or not; to take a critical stance to the reporting of the war or not and so on. This event, totally mediated by television's account of it for these young people, again threw into sharp relief their sense of hybrid national and cultural identity, but at the same time gave them the freedom to make choices. It gave them a sense of risk and uncertainty, but also of global interconnectedness.

TV and video thus enables the young people to 'stand outside' their parents' culture and to judge it against a large number of alternatives. The next step is to change it, to construct new and original versions of ethnicity and to define what it is to be a young British Asian. These young people are informed and active 'readers' of media text, not just passive receivers of it. The effect of the media is, on the whole, to empower them.

*Gillespie convincingly argues that television and video enable young Punjabis to take a critical stance on a variety of cultures, including their parents'. What is less well presented in the study are details of the new ethnicity these young people create from the mix they are presented with (the McDonald's example above is a rare one).*

- *What sorts of things might this re-creation of ethnicity involve?*
- *How convincing do you find her account in general?*

Miller's (1992) study, *The Young and the Restless in Trinidad*, confirms this view. His analysis of Trinidadians' reception of American television concludes that viewers there do not just receive the messages incorporated in the soap in a passive way, they incorporate them into their own culture and interpret it in terms of that culture also.

Jhally and Lewis also demonstrate the importance of understanding social differentiation within the audience and the need to distinguish between types of response to media messages. They conducted a study to determine the audience's response to *The Cosby Show* in an attempt to answer the question, 'Is its overall effect positive or negative with regard to attitudes towards ethnicity?' They used a discussion group method (see p. 37) using 52 small groups, 23 black, 3 Hispanic and 26 white. Most groups included both men and women. Each was shown a single episode of *The Cosby Show* and this was used as the basis for subsequent discussion, though all participants were required to be frequent or occasional viewers (not difficult in America, where the show is extremely popular). Discussion began by the interviewer asking very open questions such as 'What do you think the show was about?' or 'What do you think of Clair Huxtable?'

One interesting finding of the study was the degree to which respondents viewed *The Cosby Show* as real. Both black and white respondents had no difficulty making statements about black people based on their experience of the Huxtables. The authors note that:

> The line between the TV world and the world beyond the screen has, for most people, become exceedingly hazy. We watch at one moment with credulity, at another with disbelief. We mix scepticism with an extraordinary faith in television's capacity to tell the truth. We know that the Huxtables are not real yet we continually think about them as if they were.

However, the overall response to the Cosby show was heavily conditioned by the ethnicity of the person watching it. Black interviewees tended to discuss the show in terms of the TV racial stereotyping. Generally they contrasted the portrayal of the Huxtables very favourably with earlier programmes containing representations of minorities, and even contemporary ones, saying, in effect, 'for this relief, much thanks'. *The Cosby Show*, however, places black viewers in a bind. Do they go along with the Cosby fiction that 'there are black millionaires all over the place', thus ignoring the deep racial divisions in the US. On the other hand do they subscribe to a picture of the socio-economic position of American blacks which their own experience tells them is more realistic, and then leave themselves open to charges of stereotyping and fatalism? For white viewers there is no such problem. They tend to be

> seduced partly by television's fictions [into believing] that this is how [the world] could be. We learn to live in the dreams sold by network executives.

White respondents come to believe that there is room for minorities to get ahead without affirmative action. This, for Jhally and Lewis, is simply a more sophisticated form of racism. Other blacks have failed to succeed where the Huxtables have not and their lack of success must, therefore, be their own fault. Jhally and Lewis' conclusion is that the overall effect of *The Cosby Show* is a negative one, a representation of the American dream which masks persistent divisions of race and class in that country.

## Conclusion

Dennis McQuail (1987) suggests that we should be aware of the different ways in which the mass media can 'mediate' reality. There are a number of possibilities of the relationship between the audience, the media and 'reality':

● the media between us and those things we have not directly experienced in reality (as was the case for half of the sample in the Hartmann and Husband study, above);

● the media as a link with institutions with which we deal (for example the law or industry);

● the media as a channel of communication between us and others;

● the media as a source of material for us to form perceptions of other groups.

The various forms of mediation mean that the media can perform different functions and, therefore, have different effects. These are best described through a series of metaphors:

Figure 10.9

## The media as . . .

a window, extending our vision

an interactive link

a platform or carrier for information

a filter

a signpost

an interpreter, making sense of otherwise puzzling events

a screen or barrier

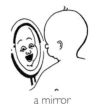

a mirror

In the study of the mass media and ethnicity it is wise to keep these multiple models of the media in mind. There are many types of media and a huge variety of content which is received in very different social contexts. A sophisticated understanding of the media should make us wary of over-simple generalizations about cause and effect.

### Examination questions

'With reference to sociological studies, assess the claim that the mass media are biased against ethnic minorities.'

(AEB Sociology (with coursework), June 1993, paper 2, question 8.)

*See the skeleton answers section at the end of the book for an outline answer to this question.*

*You were asked to attempt this question in Chapter 2. Try it again now concentrating on ethnicity:*

'Assess the sociological evidence for and against the view that the effects of the mass media vary according to the social characteristics of the audience.'

(AEB Sociology A level (with coursework), June 1992, paper 2, question 8.)

'How far do you feel it is possible for minority audiences to read against the intended meanings of media texts?'

(AEB Media Studies, 1997 examinations specimen questions, paper 2, question 12.)

## Further reading

Colle, R. D. (1973) 'Negro image in the mass media: a case study in social change', in R. F. Hixon (ed.), *Mass Media: A Casebook*, NY: Thomas Y. Crowell, pp. 71–80.

Gillespie, M. (1995) *Television, Ethnicity and Cultural Change*, London: Routledge. This is both a fascinating read and raises many interesting sociological issues.

Gordon, P. and Rosenberg, D. (1989) *Daily Racism:*

*The Press and Black People in Britain*, London: The Runnymede Trust.

Hartmann, P. (1974) 'Race as news: a study in the handling of race in the British press for 1963–70', in J. D. Halloran, *Race as News*, Paris: Unesco Press.

Hartmann, P. and Husband, C. (1974) *Racism and the Mass Media: A Study of the Role of the Mass Media in the Formation of White Beliefs and Attitudes in Britain*, London: Davis-Poynter.

Jhally, S. and Lewis, J. (1992) *Enlightened Racism: the Cosby Show, Audiences and the Myth of the American Dream*, Oxford: Westview Press. Again, a good read on a subject many will be familiar with,

raising many general sociological issues about class and ethnicity, culture and the power of the individual.

Millwood Hargrave, A. *et al.* (1992) *The Portrayal of Ethnic Minorities on Television*, London: Broadcasting Standards Council.

Pines, J. (1992) *Black and White in Colour: Black People in British Television since 1936*, London: BFI.

Searle, C. (1989) *Your Daily Dose: Racism and the Sun*, London: CPBF.

van Dijk, T. (1991) *Racism and the Press*, London: Routledge.

## Useful addresses

**The Campaign Against Racism in the Media (CARM)**
BOX 50
London N1

**The Campaign for Press and Broadcasting Freedom**
8 Cynthia Street
London N1 9JF
tel: 0171 278 4430
(They will supply a catalogue of their publications)

**Runnymede Trust**
11 Princelet Street
London E1 6QH
(Publishes books and information on ethnicity issues, including *The Runnymede Bulletin*)

#  Media representation of age and class

Figure 11.1   Harry Enfield and Paul Whitehouse as *The Two Old Gits*

This chapter gives an account of the ways in which age and social class have been represented in the media as this has been researched by sociologists. It makes only a limited attempt to address the effects that such representations may have. Therefore, while reading this chapter it is best to keep in mind the complex nature of the relationship between 'media cause' and 'social effect' discussed elsewhere in the book. It would be unwise to jump to hasty conclusions about the effects of patterns of representation discussed here.

It is important, too, to remember that both age and class are cross-cut by other forms of social stratification, especially gender and ethnicity. A few examples illustrate the importance of seeing representations as interleaved by different aspects of stratification rather than only one:

● The mass media often portray teenagers as 'a problem'. But they almost exclusively refer to males, and predominantly to working-class males, especially black working-class males.

● Mass media representations of poverty and affluence are often simultaneously representations of 'race' within the social structure.

● The images of ageing that are portrayed are often different for men and for women.

For any individual, whether real or fictional, then, aspects of social structure come together in a particular way, as Figure 11.2 illustrates.

Figure 11.2   The individual embodying aspects of social structure

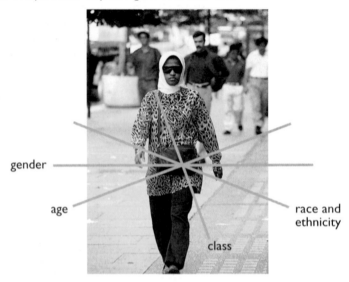

gender

age

race and ethnicity

class

## Representations of age

In considering media representations of age, it is useful to make a distinction between images of the young and images of ageing. We begin with representations of the young.

### The young

Any analysis of media representations of age needs to begin with ideas about age categories found in society at large. These are both represented through the media and, at the same time, are influenced through media representations.

From a sociological point of view the important ideas about age categories are socially, rather than biologically derived. Phillipe Aries in *Centuries of Childhood*, for example, discusses the way in which conceptions of 'childhood' have changed over time in Europe. He argues, as we see below, that as a result 'childhood' in the Middle Ages was very different from 'childhood' today, though children were biologically identical. Similarly anthropologist Margaret Mead in *Coming of Age in Samoa* claimed that adolescence in the Pacific island of Samoa was quite different to our idea of it. Both authors argue that biology is of very limited significance.

> ### Social constructionism
>
> When we say something is 'socially constructed' (for example 'childhood') we mean that its important characteristics are defined by the attitudes, values and norms of behaviour that surround it in any given society or part of society, and that these actually shape the 'reality' of that thing.

This social constructionist view places the media in a very significant position. The media articulate current dominant perceptions of 'age'. At the same time they are involved in shaping and re-shaping these perceptions. Marie Gillespie shows the importance of the mass media in the construction of what it means to be a young 'Punjabi Londoner' (see p. 226). Dick Hebdige makes a similar point, saying that when we try to understand youth subcultures we have to take account of the fact that the mass media structure the way society is perceived by young people. Their subcultures are based both on the realities of their social situation and perceptions of it mediated by the mass media (see Figure 11.3).

Figure 11.3 Interaction between social structure and subcultures mediated by mass-media representations.

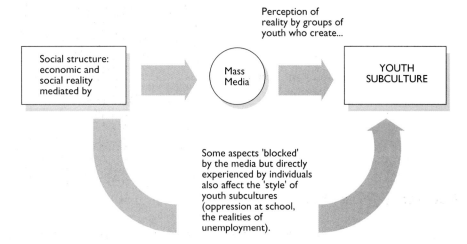

There are two distinct strands in sociological work on the social construction of youth. One concerns the social construction of childhood and the resulting images of childhood in the mass media. The other concerns the social construction of adolescence. We will deal with them each in turn.

*Children: little angels*

Phillipe Aries (1962) suggests that in the Middle Ages children were treated as miniature adults, while at the same time 'adulthood' was closer to our notion of childhood. He takes a number of aspects of social life to illustrate this:

*Leisure*

- Children dressed like adults (Aries uses evidence from contemporary art to demonstrate this).

- Games such as hide and seek, blind man's buff and snowball fights were played by adults and children (Aries uses evidence from contemporary art again).

- 'Nursery rhymes' were made by and for adults, not children

- There was discussion of sex and general ribaldry in front of children, no notion of childish innocence.

*Work*

- Children were sent to work early in life. They could join the army at 11 years and be a lieutenant by 14.

*Education*

- School was for all ages (if they could afford it), there was no distinction between adults and children.

*Family*

- Life was lived in public until the seventeenth century and even the house was open – the family was of secondary importance to the community, and children were not central to the family (evidence from contemporary art is used again).

According to Aries change began in the fifteenth century, but accelerated around 1700 with the rise of the bourgeoisie (urban industrialists) whose male children were the first 'children' in the modern sense. The eighteenth century saw the beginning of a market for children's literature. Games began to be differentiated between adults' and children's during this century, part of a general tendency at the time towards distinguishing and separating, according to Aries. The modern concept of childhood as an age of innocence had begun. By the twentieth century this notion of childhood had spread down through the class structure. In all aspects of society, including the mass media, childhood is now portrayed as a very special time, one of innocence and magic which must be protected by responsible adults: parents, teachers and others.

 *Raymond Briggs' book and film* The Snowman *encapsulates this approach to childhood. Hire the video and conduct a semiotic analysis of it (see p. 44). Listen carefully to the music as well as giving attention to the images and storyline (the singer, Aled Jones, was at the time of its production a very popular child soprano – a media favourite).*

Some critics of the media such as Michael Medved (1992) argue that they take the 'children as angels' image too far. Medved suggests that American television and films portray children as 'ultimate source of all wisdom, sanity, and sensitivity'. Parents in general and fathers in particular are seen as useless and stupid. *The Simpsons* is one example of this and films like *Home Alone* and *Honey I Shrunk the Kids* another.

 *Is he right?*

### Diversity in representations of children

Aries is not without his critics. The Marxist historian Peter Fuller in *Uncovering Childhood* (1979) makes the point that Aries's argument is without any view of significant groups in society wielding power in their own interests or any notion of economic change causing cultural change. If childhood has changed then it will have been as a response to technological and economic conditions; for example to differentiate the market to increase profitability by selling specifically 'children's goods' to that market. Aries has no real explanation of why conceptions of childhood changed. Moreover the evidence Aries has for his 'social construction' argument is also weak – mostly based on notoriously unreliable art of the time (which, for example, was almost entirely commissioned by and therefore concentrated on the rich, who wished themselves portrayed in a good light) and adds that the children of the rich were bargaining counters in the negotiation of political marriages.

Anthony Synnott in *Little Angels, Little Devils* (1988) suggests that Aries's view is too simplistic. During every period in history, including today, there have been a variety of beliefs about and representations of childhood. He identifies five in particular:

- There are two kinds of children, noble and savage, but all should be treated kindly.

- Children are sinful – they should be restrained and punished.

- Children have no distinctive character; they are a tabula rasa (clean slate) on which to write.

- Individual children are born each with their own nature, not easily altered.

- Children are naturally good.

Synnott's idea of diversity of views about childhood is confirmed by John and Elizabeth Newsom's survey in the 1950s with over 700 mothers. They found a huge variety of attitudes and behaviour towards the children.

Media representations of childhood do seem to reflect this diverse view rather than the Aries conception of modern representations of childhood. Media coverage of the James Bulger murder case illustrates the first category (two-year-old James was murdered by two children). Coverage of drugs and bullying in schools illustrates the second. There is, in short, great diversity in representations of childhood, especially if one looks across the different types of mass media.

 *Buy the current edition of the* Beano. *What kinds of representations of childhood are found there?*

### The social construction of childhood: a new paradigm

Arguing from what is basically a postmodernist position, James and Prout in *Constructing and Reconstructing Childhood* suggest that previous ways of understanding childhood fell into the trap of seeing children only as underdeveloped adults, as individuals going through a period of apprenticeship. In this (mistaken) view children gradually move from simplicity to complexity of thought, from irrational to rational behaviour, from empty to full, undeveloped to developed. They note the similarities between these kinds of understandings of childhood and early theories about Third World development (which were basically evolutionary – 'these countries will eventually be like us'). Children are just another low-status group whom academics have treated rather shabbily.

James and Prout propose a new approach to the understanding of childhood. Instead of a view, like Aries', which interprets the 'social construction of childhood' as adults doing the constructing we should see children as active agents in the construction of their own cultures. These authors say that children's social relationships are worthy of study in their own right, independent of the concerns and perspectives of adults. They are social actors with their own (constructed) forms of social reality. We should, effectively, take children on their own terms and reject what was essentially a type of 'racism' which previously informed our ways of thinking about childhood. However, in doing this we must also see childhood as only one social variable. It can never be entirely divorced from other variables such as class, gender and ethnicity.

What this new approach means for the study of the mass media, then, is:

- the reality of childhood is that there are innumerable cultures of childhood; this may or may not be reflected in media representations;

- children may use the media in the construction of their own social reality in much the same way as Gillespie suggests London Punjabis do;

- whereas in the past children's mass media, especially television programmes, were made from an adult perspective in an educative, even patronizing format, we can expect the media increasingly to represent the child's view of the world as adults achieve new understandings of this social group.

 *How far do children's programmes such as* Byker Grove, Grange Hill *and the modern* Blue Peter *operate within 'childhood culture'?*

### Images of adolescence

Harry Hendrick (1990) shows how the modern concept of 'adolescence' was shaped and came to prominence in late Victorian and Edwardian times (he examines the period 1880–1920). Initially the idea gained ground with social scientists, educationalists and youth workers. The main idea was a clearly identifiable 'stage of life' during which biological changes led to extremes of emotion, quarrelsomeness, general unpredictability and anti-social behaviour. Stanley Hall, in his book *Adolescence* (1904), sums this up:

> [During adolescence] important functions previously non-existent arise. ... Every step of the upward way is strewn with wreckage of body, mind and morals ... Sex asserts its mastery in field after field, and works its havoc in the form of secret vice, debauch [and] disease ... There are new repulsions felt towards home and school, and truancy and runaways abound ...

Of course, it is clear that although the nature of adolescence was supposed to be determined by universal biological forces, the attention of the middle class was exclusively on working-class boys. No-one seemed to seriously ask why such powerful forces concentrated their attention on this one group.

Adolescents, then, were seen as potentially dangerous, ready to go on the rampage unless kept gainfully employed. It is not surprising then that many youth organizations (boys' clubs, the Boys' Brigade, the Scouts etc.) were set up around the turn of the century. The worry was that unemployment or dead-end jobs would lead working-class boys to express their worst characteristics, so other ways must be found to 'keep them off the streets'. The music hall and the cinema were seen as offering opportunities to go astray too, and these important contemporary forms of mass media received the same sort of criticisms as 'video nasties' do today (see p. 105).

John Davis (1990) argues along the same lines as Hendrick. He says that:

> a process has been in motion since at least the nineteenth century whereby adolescence/youth has increasingly been separated out as a distinct phase of the human life-cycle. The process has been given additional impetus in the post-war period through such factors as the rise of the teenage consumer and the spread of secondary and higher education.

Just one Ecstasy tablet took Leah Betts.

Figure 11.4 Leah Betts - a solemn reminder of the perils of Ecstasy. But will media coverage of her death deter teenagers from taking the drug?

This has been reflected in media representations of youth, particularly youth subcultures, during this century. In the 1950s, for example, Teds were portrayed in the media as outcasts, frequently in trouble and wandering the streets. Rock and Cohen (1970) have argued that the image of the Ted in the press can be understood as the personification of evil:

> He seems to stalk like some ... monster through much of the otherwise prosaic newspaper reporting of the fifties.

Similar portrayals of mods and rockers have been extensively documented by Stan Cohen in *Folk Devils and Moral Panics*. Here Cohen argues that youth subcultures should be seen largely as a media creation, born largely of the need to create news if there was none. The mods and rockers subcultures were only made up of groups of youth with different clothing styles before the exaggerated claims of the press began the process of their formation into the subcultures we know about today.

Press editorials and comment exaggerated and distorted events, using words like 'riot', 'battle' and 'siege' to describe what were in reality minor events. There were no gangs as such; the mods and rockers polarization did not exist. Newspapers predicted that these 'riots' would happen again and this produced a self-fulfilling prophecy as youths descended on seaside resorts where they expected something interesting to happen. By now they had learned, through the press, what the expected styles of dress, forms of behaviour and attitudes were.

However, John Davis notes that there are periodic attempts to 'institutionalize' youth cultures. For example he quotes a *Daily Mirror* piece by journalist Tony Miles:

> There's hope among the teacups in the Teen Canteen where the boys in Slim Jim ties find they belong ... As a class the Teddies are often branded as trouble makers through the headline antics of a few. Individually I found the boys I met in the canteen personable, friendly and responsive to trust – given the chance.

The image here has changed from troublemakers to one where Teds are seen as 'redecorating the premises, forming self-governing committees and themselves taking care of any trouble that might occur' (Davis 1990, p. 143).

From a neo-Marxist point of view, Dick Hebdige sees this attempt to incorporate threatening youth subcultures into mainstream society as a capitalist response to resistance to the dominant system which these youth subcultures represent. Instead of allowing young people to resist capitalist society through their oppositional styles, the capitalist world attempts to neutralize them through incorporation. The mass media are centrally important in this process. They portray members of youth subcultures as 'just normal kids underneath', the sons and daughters of Mr and Mrs Average, just going through a phase. Davis's quote from the *Daily Mirror*, above, is an example of this happening. Hebdige calls this 'ideological incorporation'.

A second method of neutralizing youth resistance is what Hebdige calls the commodity form of incorporation. Here youth cultural signs (dress or music for example) are converted into mass-produced objects and sold on the high street. In this process they lose their threatening and oppositional meaning. The capitalist market is effectively taking the artefacts of the culture away from the young people, alienating them from their own subculture. Furthermore the market 'normalizes' the symbols of resistance by turning them into a 'leisure-time only' style. Hebdige quotes the headline of an article in *Cosmopolitan* which illustrates the point nicely:

### To Shock is Chic

Davis shows how, by 1960, the dangerous and deviant image of youth that had been associated with the emergence of rock and roll had been replaced by a safe, conforming image of 'the teenager', summed up in the person of Cliff Richard.

Geoffrey Pearson in *Hooligan* (1983) takes a different view, arguing that while contemporary images of youth are predominantly in the 'youth as problem' category, this is usually contrasted in the media with a Golden Age (usually 20 years ago) where young people knew their place, there was little crime and people respected the police. His fascinating account of his search through press archives reveals that, no matter what period of time we look at, this same story is told. The Golden Age is *always* 20 years previously. The media are in a permanent panic about whatever manifestation of 'youth as a problem' is current: the Hooligans of Victorian times, the Teds of the 1950s or the Travellers of today. So, the youth of today are bad, those of 20 years ago good.

Davis goes further than Hebdige in his view of the power of the mass media. While Hebdige sees the media as 'merely' mediating reality for young people, Davis argues that film and the content of pop music and magazines for the young was effectively *creating* the teenager and simultaneously exploiting them:

> Early singles by the Coasters ..., Paul Anka ..., Eddie Cochran ... and many others provide a comprehensive picture of the concerns, limitations and problems of (American) teenage life. Similarly the stances of Elvis Presley ... Tommy Steele and the rest embraced and projected the various possibilities, some deviant but most largely conventional, inherent in the general notion of 'being a teenager'. Rock 'n' roll music – and later pop – helped to provide a model, or a range of models, for the various self-images of 'the teenage generation'.

Whatever their respective views on the *power* of the contemporary mass media, however, most authors see media representations of teenagers as linked to economic and social change. For Harry Hendrick, periods of unemployment and economic depression led to worries about young people with time on their hands, and representations of youth in the media reflected this. For John Davis, images of youth are a kind of index of concern about social change and 'the state of the nation'. These images can swing between presenting youth as an active force for social regeneration and the equally distorted image of youth as a new and particularly threatening social problem.

For the Birmingham Contemporary Cultural Studies group, writing in the mid 1970s (most famously in *Resistance Through Rituals*) the form that youth subcultures take is directly tied to changing socio-economic circumstances, though these are then presented in the media in distorted ways, as Hebdige shows. For Geoffrey Pearson media panics about youth represent a recurring preoccupation about social change, while for Hall *et al.* in *Policing the Crisis* these panics represent a manufactured opportunity for the control culture to increase and exercise its power to stem the tide of opposition to the status quo during times of economic and social crisis.

### Images of ageing

Keep young and beautiful
If you want to be loved.

(From the film *Roman Scandals*, 1933, Samuel Goldwyn)

The cautionary note at the beginning of the chapter about simplistic thinking about social stratification has a special significance in thinking about media representations of the old. Unlike gender and 'race' disadvantages, old age is something that comes to us all if we stick around long enough. Moreover, there is a 'double standard of ageing' (Sontag 1978) where women are required to try to match up to an youthful ideal all their lives but men are not. For men there can be very positive images of ageing. Lambert *et al.*'s 1984 content analysis study of British TV over a two-week period showed that 50% of programmes included people over the age of 60. Most images of the elderly were those of 'world leaders': politicians, businessmen, experts, administrators and judges. These were almost exclusively men. Similarly anchor men and quiz masters tend to be older and portrayed as having gravitas. Suzanne Moore (1993) asks:

> Do John Simpson or Jon Snow or Peter Sissons worry about their lines, their paunches or their greying hair? Do their editors feel these old boys should not be inflicted on the rest of us any longer? Do we worry about the emptiness of their private lives as we seem to do with [Kate] Adie?

*Consider the following representations of older women in the mass media:*
*Germaine Greer*
*Joanna Lumley*
*Thora Hird*
*Joan Collins*
*Anna Ford*

*Is the maintenance of beauty in later life really more important for women than men?*

Simon Biggs has summarized the recent research on age stereotyping in British television, entertainment and other non-current affairs broadcasting. He finds that:

- Soap operas are dominated by those in middle age or older people.

- Sitcoms tend to present older people as enfeebled, vague and forgetful or cantankerous battleaxes.

- There are examples of 'reverse stereotyping' in which older people are portrayed as unrealistic exceptions to the rule.

- Recently the media have promoted an active image of ageing.

- But there is a lack of concern for the problems of age and ageing (enduring problems are not newsworthy because they occur over a long period of time and cannot be fixed).

Signorelli reports on a content analysis of over 14,000 American TV characters between 1969 and 1981. She found that the very old and the very young were under-represented in prime-time dramatic fiction. Older characters were less likely to be presented as 'good' but less likely to be involved in violence than younger characters. Seventy per cent of older men and 80% of older women were treated as being of low status and treated discourteously. However, the representation is patchy. For example Dail (1988) found that older women in soap operas were likely to be portrayed in a positive way.

 *Consider and make a list of representations of older men and women in:*
*(a) films,*
*(b) television fiction.*

*Do the sorts of images found in your list confirm these findings?*

This patchiness is found across the media too. On Radio 4, for example, there is a preponderance of older men. Featherstone and Wernick (1995) cite programmes such as *Gardeners' Question Time* and *Just a Minute* to illustrate the point. In sports broadcasting too there is a tradition of the positively portrayed older man 'moving on' into semi-retirement (with a bit of commentating on the side). Examples are Ian Botham, Viv Richards, Ted Dexter and Graham Taylor. One or two examples of women in the same position exist (Virginia Wade) but their numbers are far smaller. However, there is evidence to suggest that this may be changing:

> Peter Hobday, the longest-serving presenter on Radio 4's *Today* pro-gramme, is being squeezed out because he is 'middle-aged, middle-class and male' . . . Hobday is a victim of *Today*'s search for younger and female listeners . . . Hobday's indirect replacement is Anna Ford . . . Ford is noted for playful on-air spats with the *Today* sports team. 'And now for some items of interest to boys only – here's Gary Richardson.' With her modulated vowels Ford may be middle class and middle-aged like Hobday. But she is not male.
>
> (*Observer*, March 1996)

Stuart Ewen (1976) studied interwar American advertising and demonstrated the existence then of a 'cult of youth'. Older people were under-represented to a remarkable extent at that time. He explains this in terms of the workings of the capitalist system and ties it to a general celebration of 'the new' at that time. The work society was based on production and income-generation. Retired people no longer earned and so were not seen as potential consumers. They no longer had status in the field of production either, hence their under-representation.

Today, however, things have changed. The over-50 age segment now holds over 50% of the discretionary income in the United States. In industrialized countries the world over they are becoming a larger and larger part of the population as the birth rate declines and longevity increases. Moreover they are increasingly likely to be affluent in retirement as a result of changes to the socio-economic structure and generally improved pension provision. Mike Featherstone and Mike Hepworth (1995) show how the magazine *Retirement Choice* is one aspect of the mass media which presents positive images of ageing in recognition of the new, large market. Despite this they are still critical of representations of age within its pages. Ageing is represented as

Figure 11.5

> an extended plateau of active middle age … a period of youthfulness and active consumer lifestyles.

The message *Retirement Choice* propagates is that the ageing process can be constructed and reconstructed by making the right lifestyle (and hence consumer) decisions. The difficult issues around ageing such as decay and dependency are avoided. This is another aspect of modern culture's hostility to these kinds of images.

Featherstone and Wernick point out that even images of death in the mass media concentrate on death of the young in accidents or through disease. The death within *Love Story* is an example. Recently, though, there have been some exceptions to this as a result of the articulation of the process of death of famous people such as Dennis Potter, François Mitterrand and Derek Jarman, for example.

## Representations of class

### *Images of the class structure*

*There is insufficient space to consider what is meant by 'class' here. As you read this section ask yourself how these authors are defining class, what problems there are with their approach and what alternatives there might be.*

Content analysis studies of television representations of class tell a consistent story: that the middle class are over-represented and working-class under-represented.

Glennon and Butsch (1982) studied television representations of social class lifestyles in family contexts between 1941 and 1978. They collected information about 218 family series. All of these were American prime-time programmes, mostly (86%) situation comedies but there were also family dramas, adventure serials and cartoons. The uniting feature was that the main characters were members of a family and most of the interactions portrayed were within the family. The findings were that:

● working-class families were under- and middle class families over-represented;

- almost half had professional heads of household (two-thirds of these either managers or proprietors – actually a quarter of the American workforce in 1970);

- blue collar workers were portrayed as head of household in 4% of the series (36% in reality);

- glamorous and successful families were portrayed most: many of the families were portrayed as *extremely* wealthy;

- in the few working-class families represented, some were represented as upwardly mobile; others were portrayed with an unintelligent father (Glennon and Butsch argue that these two themes undermine the dignity of the working class family lifestyle);

- the effort of moving from a working-class to a middle-class family lifestyle is underplayed.

 *Make a list of television programmes today in which the main characters are members of a family and most of the interactions portrayed are within the family. Do these findings still apply?*

Moving now to more recent representations of social class and ethnicity; data from the cultural indicators project at the Annenberg School in Philadelphia supplemented by a one week content analysis study by Jhally and Lewis demonstrate that the vast majority of American TV characters (around 90% constantly from 1971 to 1989) are middle-class and that the representation of clearly lower-class characters declined in that period from 4% to 1% while the number of black characters rose from 7% to 10%, with many of them representing positions at the higher end of the social scale.

The problem with merely conducting a content analysis of the number of characters from different social classes is that this tells us nothing about the way they are portrayed (e.g. positively or negatively). Glennon and Butsch made some attempt to do this. For example they note that:

- in the middle-class families, parents were usually portrayed as being able to cope effectively with problems;

- many working-class fathers were portrayed in a comic way – being laughed at by the rest of the world.

However, large content analysis studies like theirs are not methodologically appropriate to make these kinds of judgments. They don't tell us anything, either, about how these images are received by the audience. They merely tell us how the researchers interpret them. Jhally and Lewis's study of *The Cosby Show* (see p. 227) is a more rounded analysis of TV representations of class and ethnicity, and audience response. However this has, necessarily, had to limit itself to one show.

Studies of representations of social class in television non-fiction have been conducted by the Glasgow Media Group (particularly 1976, 1980 and 1982). Their findings are summarized in detail on pp. 151–153. It is interesting to note that for the GMG the working class are generally portrayed as 'trouble' on television news in very much the same way as working-class youth are (see above). From a neo-Marxist perspective such as Stuart Hall's or Dick Hebdige's this is no surprise: the media are simply acting against counter-hegemonic groups in an effort to sustain ideological dominance.

## Further reading

Davis, J. (1990) *Youth and the Condition of Britain: Images of Adolescent Conflict*, London: Athlone Press.

Featherstone, M. and Wernick, A. (eds) (1995) *Images of Ageing*, London: Routledge.

Gunter, B. and Svennevig, M. (1987) *Behind and in Front of the Small Screen*, London: John Libbey.

Hendrick, H. (1990) *Images of Youth*, Oxford: Clarendon Press.

Jhally, S. and Lewis, J. (1992) *Enlightened Racism:* The Cosby Show, *Audiences, and the Myth of the American Dream*, Oxford: Westview Press.

Pearson, G. (1983) *Hooligan: A History of Respectable Fears*, London: Macmillan.

# Appendix: Skeleton answers

The examples of answers below are not meant to be definitive, only to set out what a good answer might contain. For contrast, the typical sorts of things a bad answer (fail grade or minimal pass) might contain are also set out. In each case you are invited to fill out the skeleton of the 'good' answer with the flesh and blood of a complete essay.

The author and the publisher would like to thank the Associated Examining Board for permission to reprduce exam questions. However, the skeleton answers are wholly the responsibility of the author and are not provided or approved by the Board.

## 1. (Chapter 2, p. 32)

'Any sociological explanation of the influence of the mass media needs to take into account the social situation of the audience.'
Explain and evaluate the view expressed in this statement.

(AEB A, Sociology, November 1993, paper 2, question 8)

| Good | Bad |
|---|---|
| *Intro*: Distinguishes between sociological and other approaches (psychological, media studies\*, cultural studies\*\*). Notes that borders are fuzzy (social psychology, interactionism on the sociology/psychology border). Explains what distinguishes a sociological explanation. Defines mass media, problematizes 'social situation' – does it mean micro (eg the social context you watch TV in) or macro (your social status, socio-economic position eg class, ethnicity, gender)? 'Maps' the rest of the essay. | *Intro*: Ignores question and goes straight into an answer. Answers the question in the first paragraph before reviewing evidence or setting out the argument. Says something trite like 'there have been many studies of the mass media'. Does not give the reader a clue about the structure of the rest of the essay. |
| *Body*: Explains the development of media theory from hypodermic through to reception analysis approaches. Gives examples of some studies to illustrate change and comments critically on them. Explains that studies of media 'influence' have covered many substantive areas – violence, gender roles, voting behaviour, social interaction etc. Goes into detail on two or three studies which take the 'social situation of the audience' into account, looking both at micro situation and macro situation. Gives brief critical evaluation of them, particularly how well the audience's social situation has been taken | *Body*: Gives a few sketchy examples of studies of media influence. Doesn't categorize them or relate them to the question about the social situation of the audience. Hazy about authors and dates. Describes but does not evaluate. Uses the title as an (inappropriate) opportunity to rant about the evil influence of the mass media. |

into account. Notes that some studies do not (eg Baudrillard) but these tend not to be sociological. Glasgow Media Group have changed focus to take audience into account now, McRobbie claims to have done, but hasn't.
*Conclusion:* Concludes by agreeing with title and suggests that a study which did not do so today would not be sociological. Finishes with appropriate quote.

*Conclusion:* Repeats question and agrees (or disagrees) without reference to the discussion.

\* A helpful text on media studies is Price (1993).
\*\* A helpful text on approaches to research in disciplines other than sociology is Berger (1991). However for the purposes of this answer little detail is necessary.

## 2. (Chapter 4, p. 90)

'Examine the relationship between ownership of the mass media and control over the media's output.'

(AEB AS Sociology, June 1993, paper 2, question 7)

| Good | Bad |
| --- | --- |
| *Intro:* Defines mass media. Distinguishes between ownership and control. Maps essay, which will range across a variety of media types and categories of output, examining three models. | *Intro:* Ignores question. Uses 'bias' instead of 'biased'. Uses 'media' as a singular noun. Does not distinguish between types of media or types of output. |
| *Body:* Gives a detailed account of reasons behind worries about media ownership, particularly monopolization in the media. Examines the three models and their views on the relationship between ownership and control of output. Integrates an understanding of Burnham's 'managerial revolution' thesis into discussion of pluralist approach. Uses balance of theoretical ideas, sociological studies and empirical examples to support and refute aspects of the models and build a case. | *Body:* Gives sketchy accounts of patterns of ownership. Does not structure answer but gives a few disjointed examples of where ownership has, or has not, influenced output. |
| *Conclusion:* Returns to the question and summarizes what can be said about the relationship. Criticizes the simplistic nature of conspiracy theory and notes the other influences on media content: | *Conclusion:* Comes to a confused and simplistic conclusion, for example that media ownership does, or does not, influence media output (always, on all subjects, in all types of media). |

● market
● pressure groups
● public opinion
● news values
● technical abilities and constraints
● ideological factors.

Concludes by noting that media output is contested terrain, as is its reception. We need to adopt a much more sophisticated multi-causal approach.

## 3. (Chapter 5, p. 104)

'Evaluate the sociological arguments surrounding the claim that the mass media have created a mass culture in society.'

(AEB Sociology A level (with coursework), June 1992, paper 2, question 7)

| Good | Bad |
|---|---|
| *Intro*: Defines mass media and mass culture, with examples. Distinguishes between culture and mass culture. Distinguishes between 'sociological arguments' and other sorts. States the structure of the essay to come. | *Intro*: Ignores the question and jumps straight into an answer without defining terms or clarifying the question. |
| *Body*: Establishes the nature of the arguments from both the left and the right that lead to the conclusion that the mass media have created a mass culture. Clarifies the differences between the left and the right argument. Criticizes the assumptions underlying the notion of 'mass culture', particularly the judgements it entails. Gives examples of what might be considered 'mass culture' and explores them critically. Puts the pluralist and postmodernist viewpoints. Discusses the relativism of the latter. Examines evidence which may support the various arguments put forward by each side. Critically addresses the hypodermic model of media influence implicit in the word 'created' and discusses why the mass media may not be so powerful. Shows that different sorts of media have different content and, if they have any influence, different directions of influence. | *Body*: Tackles the question from a one-sided point of view (either agreeing or disagreeing with the title) without exploring the arguments or evidence put forward by other positions. Gives a limited account of the little argument and evidence that is used. Sticks to one aspect of the mass media. |
| *Conclusion:* Concludes by making an evaluation of the arguments and evidence presented in the main body. Makes a statement about 1) whether a mass culture can be said to exist and 2) how far the mass media can be said to have created it (if one exists). | *Conclusion:* Repeats earlier material and ignores the question (again). Makes no attempt to evaluate. |

## 4. (Chapter 6, p. 130)

'Explain and evaluate the role of the mass media in the social construction of "moral panics" in society. Illustrate your answer with reference to at least two examples of "moral panics".'

(AEB A Sociology, Winter 1994, paper 2, question 8)

| Good | Bad |
|---|---|
| *Intro*: Defines mass media and moral panics. Explains what is meant by 'social construction'. Identifies the two (or more) examples that will be used in answering the question. 'Maps' the answer to follow. | *Intro*: Goes straight into a rather weak account of Stan Cohen's theory about moral panics. |
| *Body*: Explains Stan Cohen's argument about moral panics and the role of the mass media in them. Explains how Stuart Hall and the CCCS adapted this theory to include an | *Body*: Continues the Cohen account and uses a large number of current examples of 'folk devils' to fill out the rest of the essay, uninformed by any other sociological |

| Good | Bad |
|---|---|
| account of the control culture and ideological hegemony. Makes clear the slightly different role of the mass media in the two accounts. Explains McRobbie's critique of the Cohen/Hall account from a postmodernist position and articulates the role of the mass media as put forward in this theoretical position. Uses throughout the examples identified in the introduction and distinguishes between the roles of the different forms of mass media. | theory or concepts. Sticks only to the press in the discussion of the mas media (because this is what Cohen concentrated on). |
| *Conclusion:* Summarizes the role of the mass media as it is theorized in these accounts. Evaluates the theoretical and empirical quality of the various accounts. Identifies any changes in the role of the mass media in respect of moral panics over time. | *Conclusion:* Makes a weak attempt to evaluate Cohen's study, but probably finds it difficult to find fault. |

## 5. (Chapter 9, p. 205)

'Subordinate groups in society tend to be represented by the media in ways which reinforce their subordination.'

Examine this view with reference to two of the following groups: black people; the young; strikers; the poor; women.

(AEB AS Sociology, June 1992, paper 2, question 8)

| Good | Bad |
|---|---|
| *Intro:* Explores the different aspects of subordination and gives some evidence to demonstrate that the groups chosen are subordinate in the ways identified (and perhaps not in other ways). Defines the mass media. 'Maps' the rest of the essay, explaining which two examples are chosen. | *Intro:* Identifies the two groups to be discussed and goes straight into the discussion. |
| *Body:* Women: gives an account of the different ways women are represented in the mass media, distinguishing between different types of media, different genres and showing how this has changed over time. Informs the discussion with appropriate theory (types of feminism, pluralism). The young: distinguishes between children and adolescents. Shows how media representations of them are different. Concentrates on one (because of lack of space) and gives examples of media representations, distinguishing between different types of media and different genres. Informs the discussion with appropriate theory (moral panics etc. if discussing adolescents, Aries, Prout and James etc, if discussing childhood.) | *Body:* Gives anecdotal examples from a limited range of types and genres to illustrate representations of the two types. Very little or no sociological theory is used. |
| *Conclusion:* Summarizes the findings about representations across the media in the two groups chosen. Uses the conclusion to address the issue about 'reinforcement'. Notes that reception analysis approaches make it difficult to come to such clear conclusions as the essay question suggests: the social context of reception must be addressed. | *Conclusion:* Repeats the other material and does not problematize (or perhaps even address) the 'reinforcement of subordination' issue. |

### 6. (Chapter 10, p. 216)

'With reference to sociological studies, assess the claim that the mass media are biased against ethnic minorities.'

(AEB Sociology (with coursework), June 1993, paper 2, question 8)

| Good | Bad |
| --- | --- |
| *Intro:* Defines mass media and makes qualifications relevant to this discussion about the different types and genres. Defines ethnic minorities and makes the point about the assumptions in that phrase. Problematizes the phrase 'biased against' – both in terms of the assumptions it contains about 'reality' and accounts of it and the different ways that 'bias' may occur. 'Maps' the rest of the essay. | *Intro:* Does not problematize the words in the title or 'map' the essay. |
| *Body:* Gives an account of a number of ways in which the mass media could be said to be 'biased' against minority ethnic groups, eg. in representations in different genres, in access to the media etc. Puts the more positive view about the media and minority ethnic groups – for example the postmodernist social constructionist view, the positive interpretations of programmes like *The Cosby Show*. Critically addresses these. Uses detail from sociological studies throughout. | *Body:* Gives a limited account of one or two memorized sociological studies in this area without drawing out their significance for this question. Uses extended accounts of representations of minority ethnic groups to fill out the essay. Draws these from a limited range of mass media types and genres. |
| *Conclusion:* Uses the conclusion to assess the claim of 'bias'. Makes general observations about the relationship between the mass media and society, particularly 1) the role of ideology as it is reflected in and reinforced by the media and 2) the social situation of minority ethnic groups and representations of it in the media. | *Conclusion:* Agrees that the media are biased and says that something should be done about it. |

# Bibliography

Adams, V. (1986) *The Media and the Falklands Campaign*, London: Macmillan.

Adorno, T. and Horkheimer, M. (1991) *The Culture Industry*, London: Routledge.

Agee, W. K., Ault, P. H. and Emery, E. (1982) *Introduction to Mass Communications*, 7th edn, London: Harper & Row.

Alvarado, M., Gutch, R. and Wollen, P. (1987) *Learning the Media*, London: Macmillan.

Anderson, J. (1987) 'Commentary on qualitative research', in T. Lindlof (ed.), *Natural Audiences*, Ablex.

Ang, I. (1985) *Watching Dallas*, London: Methuen.

Ang, I. (1991) *Desperately Seeking the Audience*, London: Routledge.

*Annual Review of BBC Broadcasting Research*, London: John Libbey.

Aries, P. (1965) *Centuries of Childhood*, London: Vintage Books.

Atkin, C. K. (1980) 'Effects of television advertising on children' in E. L. Palmer and A. Dor (eds), *Children and the Faces of Television: Teaching, Violence, Selling*, New York: Academic Press.

Atkinson, M. (1984) *Our Masters' Voices: The Language and Body Language of Politics*, London: Routledge.

Baehr, H. and Dyer, G. (eds) (1987) *Boxed In: Women and Television*, London: Pandora.

Bandura, A., Ross, D. and Ross, S. A. (1963) 'The imitation of film-mediated aggressive models', *Journal of Abnormal and Social Psychology*, 66(1), 3–11.

Barker, M. (1989) *Comics: Ideology, Power and the Critics*, Manchester UP.

Barker, M. *et al.* (1994) *The Video Violence Debate: Media Researchers Respond,* press release reacting to the Newson report signed by 23 leading media researchers.

Barlow, G. and Hill, A. (eds) (1985) *Video Violence and Children*, London: Hodder & Stoughton.

Barthes, R. (1973) *Mythologies*, St Albans: Paladin.

Baudrillard, J. (1985) 'The ecstasy of communication', in H. Foster (ed.), *Postmodern Culture*, London: Pluto.

Bauman, Z. (1988) 'Is there a postmodern sociology?', *Theory, Culture and Society*, 5, 217–37.

Beasly, M. (1989) in P. Creedon, *Women in Mass Communication: Challenging Gender Values*, Sage.

Beharrell, B. and Philo, G. (1977) *Trade Unions and the Media*, London: Macmillan.

Belfield, R. and Hird, C. (1991) *Murdoch: the Great Escape*, Time Warner.

Bell, D. (1976) *The Coming of Post-Industrial Society*, New York: Basic Books.

Belson, W. (1978) *Television Violence and the Adolescent Boy*, Aldershot: Gower Press.

*Benn's Media Directory,* Benn's Business Information Services Ltd (annual).

Berger, A. (1991) *Media Analysis Techniques*, London: Sage.

Berger, P. and Luckmann, T. (1973) *The Social Construction of Reality*, Harmondsworth: Penguin.

Berle, A. A. and Means, G. C. (1968) *The Modern Corporation and Private Property*, New Brunswick, NJ: Transaction Books.

Beuf, A. (1974) 'Doctor, lawyer, household drudge', *Journal of Communication*, 24(2), 142–5.

BFI (1983) *Selling Pictures: The Companies You Keep*, London: BFI.

Biggs, S. (1993) *Understanding Ageism*, Milton Keynes: Open University Press.

Bigsby, C. (ed.) (1976) *Approaches to Popular Culture*, London: Edward Arnold.

Billingham, S. (1995) 'Racism, ethnicity and education', in P. Trowler, *Investigating Education and Training*, London: HarperCollins.

*Black and White Media Shows* (two programmes) available from the NUT, Hamilton House, Mabledon Place, London WC1 9BD or from their producer, John Twitchin, Villiers House, Ealing Broadway, London W5 2PA.

Blumler, J. G. and D. McQuail (1968) *Television in Politics: Its Uses and Influence*, London: Faber & Faber.

Bouchier, D. (1983) *The Feminist Challenge*, London: Macmillan.

Bower, T. (1991) *Maxwell the Outsider*, London: Mandarin.

Boyd-Barrett, O. and Braham, P. (1987) *Media. Knowledge and Power*, London: Croom Helm.

Bretl, D. and Cantor, J. (1988) 'The portrayal of men and women in US television commercials', *Sex Roles*, 18(9/10), 565–609: Plenum Publishing Corp.

British Film Institute *Film and TV Handbook* , London: BFI.

Broadbent, S. (1979) *Spending Advertising Money*, London: Business Books.

Broadbent, S. (1984) *20 Advertising Case Histories*, London: Holt, Rinehart & Winston.

Broadcasting Standards Council *Annual Reviews*, London: John Libbey.

Brown, C. (1984) *Black and White Britain: The Third PSI Survey*, London: Heinemann.

Brown, C. and Gay, P. (1985) *Racial Discrimination: Seventeen Years After the Act*, London: PSI.

Brown, M. (1990) *TV and Women's Culture*, London: Sage.

Brunsdon, C. and Morley, D. (1978) *Everyday Television: Nationwide*, London: BFI.

Bryson, B. (1994) *Made in America*, London: Minerva.

BSC (1995) *Broadcasting Standards Council Monitoring Report 3*, London: BSC.

Buckingham, D. (1993a) *Children Talking Television*, Lewes: Taylor and Francis.

Buckingham, D. (ed.) (1993b) *Reading Audiences: Young People and the Media*, Manchester University Press.

Burgess, A. W. and Holmstrom, L. (1979) *Rape: Crisis and Recovery*, London: Brady Co.

Burnham, J. (1942) *The Managerial Revolution*, Harmondsworth: Penguin (most sociology textbooks contain a section on the notion of managerial, as against capitalist, power; see Haralambos 1990, pp. 160–2, for example).

Busby, L. (1975) 'Sex role research in the mass media', *Journal of Communications*, 25(4), 107–31.

Butcher, H. *et al.* (1974) *Images of Women in the Media*, Birmingham: Centre for Contemporary Cultural Studies.

Cantor, M. and Pingree, P. (1983) *The Soap Opera*, Sage.

Cashmore, E. (1994) *... And There Was Television*, London: Routledge.

Castles, S. and Kosack, G. (1973) *Immigrant Workers and Class Structure in Western Europe*, Oxford: Oxford University Press.

CBI (1981) *The Headline Business*, London: CBI.

Centre for Contemporary Cultural Studies (1982) *The Empire Strikes Back*, London: Hutchinson.

Chapman, S. (1986) *Great Expectorations: Advertising and the Tobacco Industry*, London: Comedia.

Chibnall, S. (1977) *Law and Order News*, London: Tavistock.

Chippindale, P. and Horrie, C. (1990) *Stick It Up Your Punter*, London: Mandarin.

Cline, S. and Spender, D. (1987) *Reflecting Men (At Twice Their Natural Size)*, London: André Deutsch.

Clutterbuck, R. (1983) *The Media and Political Violence*, London: Macmillan.

Cockburn, C. and Loach, L. (1986) 'In whose image?', in J. Curran *et al.*, *Bending Reality*, London: Pluto.

Cockerell, M., Hennessy, P. and Walker, D. (1984) *Sources Close to the Prime Minister*, London: Macmillan.

Cohen, P. and Gardner, C. (1985) *It Ain't Half Racist Mum*, London: Comedia.

Cohen, S. (1971) *Images of Deviance*, Harmondsworth: Penguin.

Cohen, S. (1980) *Folk Devils and Moral Panics*, 2nd edn, Oxford: Martin Robertson.

Cohen, S. and Young, J. (1973) *The Manufacture of News: Social Problems, Deviance and the Mass Media*, London: Constable.

Colle, R. D. (1973) 'Negro image in the mass media: a case study in social change', in R. F. Hixon (ed.), *Mass Media: A Casebook*, NY: Thomas Y. Crowell, pp. 71–80.

Congdon, T. *et al.* (1995) *The Cross Media Revolution*, London: John Libbey.

Corner, J. (1991) 'Meaning, genre and context', in Curran and Gurevitch (1991).

Creedon, P. (1989) *Women in Mass Communication: Challenging Gender Values*, London: Sage.

Crouse, T. (1972) *The Boys on the Bus*, New York: Random House.

Cudlipp, H. (1980) *The Prerogative of the Harlot*, London: Bodley Head.

Culf, A. (1995) 'Tide of television is declining', Tuesday, 22 August, p. 5 (*Report of the Sheffield Study of Media Violence*, Gunter and Harrison).

Cullingford, C. (1984) *Children and TV*, Aldershot: Gower Publishers.

Cumberbatch, G. and Howitt, D. (1989) *A Measure of Uncertainty: The Effects of the Mass Media*, London: John Libbey.

Cumberbatch, G. *et al.* (1993) *Children and Video Games: An Exploratory Study*, The Communications Research Group, Aston University, Aston Triangle, Birmingham B4 7ET.

Curran, J. (1986) 'The impact of advertising on the British mass media', in R. Collins *et al.* (eds), *Media Culture and Society*, London: Sage, pp. 309–36.

Curran, J. *et al.* (1986) *Bending Reality*, London: Pluto.

Curran, J. *et al.* (1987) *Impacts and Influences*, London: Methuen.

Curran, J. and Gurevitch (1991) *Mass Media and Society*, London: Edward Arnold.

Curran, J. and Seaton, J. (1991) *Power Without Responsibility*, 4th edn, London: Methuen.

Curtis, L (1984) *Ireland: The Propaganda War*, London: Pluto.

Dahrendorf, R. (1968) *Homo Sociologicus*, London: Routledge.

Dail, P. W. (1988) 'Prime time portrayals of older adults in the context of family life', *The Gerontologist*, 28(5), 700–6.

Davidson, A. (1993) *Under the Hammer: The 1991 ITV Franchise Auction*, London: Mandarin.

Davies, K. *et al.* (1987) *Out of Focus: Writing on Women and the Media*, London: The Women's Press.

Davis, J. (1990) *Youth and the Condition of Britain: Images of Adolescent Conflict*, London: Athlone Press.

Davis, M. (1989) *Television is Good For Your Kids*, London: Shipman.

Diamond, E. and Bates, S. (1992) *The Spot*, 3rd edn, MIT Press.

Docker, J. (1994) *Postmodernism and Popular Culture*, Cambridge: CUP.

Dominick, J. R. and Rauch, G. E. (1972) 'The image of women in network TV commercials', *Journal of Broadcasting*, 16(3), 259–65.

Dorr, A. (1988) *Co-operation with Broadcasting Applied Social Psychology Annual 8: Television as a Social Issue.*

Dowmunt, T. (ed.) (1993) *Channels of Resistance*, London: BFI.

Downing, J. (1975) 'The (balanced) white view', in Husband (1975).

Downing, J. (1980) *The Media Machine*, London: Pluto.

Downing, J. (1988) '*The Cosby Show* and American racial discourse', in G. Smitherman-Donaldson and T. van Dijk, *Discourse and Discrimination*, Michigan: Wayne State University Press.

Dutton, B. (1986) *The Media*, London: Longman.

Dyer, G. (1982) *Advertising as Communication*, London: Methuen.

Dyer, R. (1973) *The Dumb Blonde Stereotype*, London: BFI.

Edgar, P. (1977) *Children and Screen Violence*, St Lucia: University of Queensland Press.

Eldridge, J. (ed.) (1993) *Getting the Message: News, Truth and Power*, London: Routledge.

Epstein, D. (1993) 'Too small to notice? constructions of childhood and discourses of 'race' in predominantly white contexts', *Curriculum Studies*, 1(3), 317–34.

Evans, H. (1994) *Good Times, Bad Times*, Phoenix.

Ewen, S. (1976) *Captains of Consciousness*, NY: McGraw-Hill.

Eysenck, H. J. and Nias, D. K. (1978) *Sex, Violence and the Media*, London: Maurice Temple Smith.

Fairclough, N. (1989) *Language and Power*, London: Longman.

Featherstone, M. (1990) (ed.) *Global Culture*, London: Sage.

Featherstone, M. (1991) *Consumer Culture and Postmodernism*, London: Sage.

Featherstone, M. and Hepworth, M. (1995) 'Images of positive ageing', in Featherstone and Wernick (1995).

Featherstone, M. and Wernick, A. (eds) (1995) *Images of Ageing*, London: Routledge.

Ferguson, B. (1986) 'Black Blue Peter', in L. Masterman (ed.), *Television Mythologies*, London: Comedia.

Ferguson, M. (1983) *Forever Feminine: Women's Magazines and the Cult of Femininity*, London: Heinemann.

Ferguson, M. (1978) 'Imagery and ideology: the cover photographs of traditional women's magazines', in Tuchman *et al.* (1978).

Festinger, L. (1957) *A Theory of Cognitive Dissonance*, Stanford: Stanford University Press.

Feuer, J. (1987) 'Genre Study and Television', in R. C. Allen (ed.), *Channels of Discourse*, London: Routledge.

Fiske, J. (1982) *Introduction to Communication Studies*, London: Comedia.

Fiske, J. (1989a) 'Moments of television', in E. Seiter *et al.* (eds), *Remote Control*, London: Routledge.

Fiske, J. (1989b) *Understanding Popular Culture*, Boston: Unwin Hyman.

Fiske, J. (1988) *Television Culture*, London: Methuen.

Fiske, J. and Hartley, J. (1978) *Reading Television*, London: Methuen.

Forrester, M. (1987) *Everything You Always Suspected Was True About Advertising (but were too Legal, Decent and Honest to Ask)*, London: Roger Houghton Press.

Franklin, B. (1994) *Packaging Politics*, London: Edward Arnold.

Franklin, B. and Murphy, D. (1991) *What News? The Market, Politics and the Local Press*, London: Routledge.

Frazer, E. (1987) 'Teenage girls reading Jackie', *Media, Culture and Society*, 9(4), 407–25.

Fuller, P. (1979) 'Uncovering childhood', in Hoyles (1979).

Gans, H. (1974) *Popular Culture and High Culture*, NY: Basic Books.

Garnham, N. (1986) 'The media and the public sphere', in P. Golding *et al.*, *Communicating Politics*, Leicester University Press.

Geraghty, C. (1991) *Women and Soap Opera*, Cambridge: Polity Press.

Gerbner, G. (1970) 'Cultural indicators', *Annals of the American Academy of Political and Social Science*, 338, 69–81.

Gerbner, G. and Gross, L. (1976a) 'Living with TV', *Journal of Communication*, 26, 173–99.

Gerbner, G. and Gross, L. (1976b) 'The scary world of TV's heavy viewer', *Psychology Today*, April, 89–91.

Gillespie, M. (1995) *Television, Ethnicity and Cultural Change*, London: Routledge.

Glasgow Media Group (1976) *Bad News*, London: Routledge.

Glasgow Media Group (1980) *More Bad News*, London: Routledge.

Glasgow Media Group (1982) *Really Bad News*, London: Writers and Readers.

Glasgow Media Group (1985) *War and Peace News*, Milton Keynes: Open University Press.

Glasgow University Media Group and Eldridge, G. (ed.) (1993) *Getting the Message: News, Truth and Power*, London: Routledge.

Glennon, L. M. and Butsch, R. (1982) 'The family as portrayed on television, 1946–1978', in D. Pearl *et al.* (eds) *Television and Behaviour*, Rockville MD: National Institute of Mental Health.

Glover, D. (1984) *Sociology of the Mass Media*, Ormskirk: Causeway Press.

Golding, P. (1984) *The Mass Media*, 6th edn, London: Longman.

Gray, A. (1987) 'Behind closed doors: women and video', in H. Baehr and G. Dyer (eds), *Boxed In*, London: Routledge.

Gray, A. (1992) *Video Playtime*, London: Routledge.

Greenslade, G. (1992) *Maxwell's Fall: The Appalling Legacy of a Corrupt Man*, London: Simon & Schuster.

Gross, L. and Jeffries-Fox, S. (1978) 'What do you want to be when you grow up, little girl?', in Tuchman (1978), pp. 240–71.

Gross, R. D. (1992) *Psychology: The Science of Mind and Behaviour*, London: Hodder & Stoughton.

Gunter, B. (1987) *Television and the Fear of Crime*, London: John Libbey.

Gunter, B. (1995) *Television and Gender Representation*, London: John Libbey.

Gunter, B. and Svennevig, M. (1987) *Behind and in Front of the Small Screen*, London: John Libbey.

Gunter, B. and Wober, M. (1992) *The Reactive Viewer*, London: John Libbey.

Gunter, B. *et al.* (1994) *Television: the public's view 1993*, London: John Libbey.

Gunter, B. and McAleer, J. L. (1990) *Children and Television: The One Eyed Monster*, London: Routledge.

Hagell, A. and Newburn, T. (1994) *Young Offenders and the Media*, London: Policy Studies Institute.

Hall, S. (1986) 'Media power and class power', in J. Curran *et al.* (eds), *Bending Reality*, London: Pluto.

Hall, S. *et al.* (1982) *The Empire Strikes Back*, London: Hutchinson.

Hall, S. and Jefferson, T. (1976) *Resistance through Rituals*, London: Hutchinson.

Hall, S. *et al.* (1978) *Policing the Crisis: Mugging, the State and Law and Order*, London: Macmillan.

Halloran, J. (1970) *The Effects of Television*, St Albans: Panther.

Halloran, J. D. (ed.) (1974) *Race as News*, Paris: UNESCO Press; see especially P. Hartmann, *et al.*, 'Race as news: a study in the handling of race in the British national press for 1963–1970'.

Handel, G. (1988) *Childhood Socialisation*, Hawthorne, NY: Aldine de Gruyter.

Handlin, O. (1994) 'Comments on mass and popular culture', in N. Jacobs (ed.), *Culture for the Millions?*, Boston: Beacon Press.

Haralambos, M. (1990) *Sociology: Themes and Perspectives*, 3rd edn, London: Unwin Hyman.

Harris, R. (1983) *Gotcha! The Media, The Government and the Falklands Crisis*, London: Faber & Faber.

Harrison, N. (1985) *TV News: Whose Bias?*, Berkshire: Policy Journals.

Hartley, J. (1982) *Understanding News*, London: Methuen.

Hartley, J. (1983) 'Ideology and organisational behaviour', *International Studies of Management and Organisation*, 13(3), 26–7.

Hartley, J. *et al.* (1985) *Making Sense of the Media*, London: Comedia.

Hartmann, P. (1974) 'Race as news: a study in the handling of race in the British press for 1963–70', in J. D. Halloran, *Race as News*, Paris: Unesco Press.

Hartmann, P. and Husband, C. (1974) *Racism and the Mass Media: A Study of the Role of the Mass Media in the Formation of White Beliefs and Attitudes in Britain*, London: Davis-Poynter.

Hebdige, D. (1988) *Subculture: the meaning of style*, London: Routledge.

Hebdige, D. (1989) 'After the masses', in S. Hall and M. Jacques (eds), *New Times*, London: Lawrence & Wishart.

Hebdige, D. (1992) 'Digging for Britain', in D. Strinati and S. Wagg (eds), *Come on Down: Popular Media Culture in Post-war Britain*, London: Routledge.

Hendrick, H. (1990) *Images of Youth*, Oxford: Clarendon Press.

Hennessy, P. (1985) *What the Papers Never Said*, London: Portcullis Press.

Hermes, J. (1995a) *Easily Put Down*, Cambridge: Polity Press.

Hermes, J. (1995b) *Reading Women's Magazines*, Cambridge: Polity.

Hetherington, A. (1985) *News, Newspapers and Television*, London: Macmillan.

Himmelweit, H. (1958) *Television and the Child*, London: Oxford University Press.

Hitchcock, G. and Hughes (1994) *Research and the Teacher*, 2nd edn, London: Routledge.

Hixon, R. F. (ed.), *Mass Media: A Casebook*, NY:

Thomas Y. Crowell; see especially R. D. Colle, 'Negro image in the mass media: a case study in social change', pp. 71–80.

Hobson, D. (1980) 'Housewives and the mass media', in Hall *et al. Culture, Media, Language*, London: Hutchinson.

Hobson, D. (1990) in Brown (1990).

Hodge, B. and Tripp, D. (1985) *Children and Television*, Oxford: Basil Blackwell.

Hoffman, A. (1968) *Revelation for the Hell of It*, NY: Dial Press.

Hoggart, R. (1957) *The Uses of Literacy*, London: Chatto & Windus.

Holland, P. (1987) in Baehr and Dyer (1987).

hooks, b. (1990) *Yearning: Race, Gender and Cultural Politics*, South End Press.

Hood, S. (1980) *On Television*, London: Pluto.

Horrie, C. and Clarke, S. (1994) *Fuzzy Monsters: Fear and Loathing at the BBC*, London: Mandarin.

Hoskins, C. and Mirus, R. (1988) 'Reasons for the US dominance of the international trade in TV programmes', *Media Culture and Society*, 10(4).

Hoyles, M. (ed.) (1979) *Changing Childhood*, London: Writers and Readers.

Husband, C. (1975) *White Media and Black Britain*, London: Arrow Books.

Husband, C. (1977) 'The mass media and the function of humour in a racist society', in A. J. Chapman and H. C. Frost (eds), *It's a Funny Thing, Humour*, Oxford: Pergamon Press.

Hutton, W. (1994) 'Moguls on the podium', *Guardian*, 30 March.

*It Ain't Half Racist, Mum* (an Open Door film), available from Concord Films, 201 Felixstowe Road, Ipswich, Suffolk.

James, A. and Prout, A. (1990) *Constructing and Reconstructing Childhood*, Lewes: Falmer.

Jencks, C. (ed.) (1982) *The Sociology of Childhood*, Batsford Academic.

Jensen, K. (1986) *Making Sense of News*, University of Arhus Press.

Jhally, S. and Lewis, J. (1992) *Enlightened Racism:* The Cosby Show, *Audiences, and the Myth of the American Dream*, Oxford: Westview Press.

Johnson, J. and Ettema, J. (1982) *Positive Images: Breaking Children's Stereotypes with Children's Television*, London: Sage.

Johnson, P. (1964) 'The menace of Beatleism', *New Statesman*, 28 February.

Jones, D. *et al.* (nd) *Media Hits the Pits*, London: CPBF.

Jones, N. (1986) *Strikes and the Media: Communication and Conflict*, Oxford: Basil Blackwell.

Katz, E. (1959) *Mass Communications Research and the Study of Popular Culture Studies in Public Communication*, vol. 2.

Katz, E. and Lazarsfeld, P. (1955) *Personal Influence*, NYFP.

Killick, M. (1991) *The Sultan of Sleaze: The Story of David Sullivan's Sex and Media Empire*, Penguin.

Knorr-Cetina, K. (1988) 'The micro social order', in N. F. Fielding (ed.), *Actions and Structures*, London: Sage.

Lambert, J. *et al.* (1984) *The Image of the Elderly on TV*, Cambridge: University of the Third Age.

Lang, K. and Lang, G. E. (1991) 'Theory development: studying events in their natural settings', in K. Jensen and N. Jankowski, *A Handbook of Methodologies for Mass Communication Research*, London: Routledge.

Lazarsfeld, P. and Merton, R. (1948) 'Mass communication, popular taste and organised social action', in W. Schramm and D. Roberts (1971) *The Processes and Effects of Media Communication*, University of Illinois Press.

Leapman, M. (1994) 'Lady Stephens: the hand that rocked the editor's chair?', *Independent on Sunday*, 28 August.

Lewis, J. (1991) *The Ideological Octopus*, London: Routledge.

Lewis, L. (1990) 'Consumer girl culture', in Brown (1990).

Liebert and Sprafkin (1988) *Sesame Street: Anatomy of a Success*, NYFP.

Lipsey, D. A. (1987) 'Black mark for advertisers', *New Society*, 21 August, 11–13.

Lodziak, C. (1987) *The Power of Television: A Critical Appraisal*, London: Pinter.

Lull, J. (1988) *World Families Watch Television*, London: Sage.

Lull, J. (1990) *Inside Family Viewing: Ethnographic Research on Television's Audiences*, London: Routledge.

Lull, J. (1995) *Media, Communication, Culture: A Global Approach*, Cambridge: Polity.

Lyotard, J. (1984) *The Postmodern Condition*, Manchester University Press.

MacKinnon, C. (1987) *Feminism Unmodified*, Cambridge, Mass.: Harvard University Press.

McQuail, D. (1972) *The Sociology of Mass Communications*, Harmondsworth: Penguin.

McQuail, D. (1987) *Mass Communication Theory*, 2nd edn, London: Sage.

McRobbie, A. (1991) *Romantic Individualism and the Teenage Girl*, reprinted in McRobbie, A. (1991) *Feminism and Youth Culture*, London: Macmillan.

McRobbie, A. (1994) *Postmodernism and Popular Culture*, London: Routledge.

Mander, J. (1980) *Four Arguments for the Elimination of Television*, Brighton: Harvester Press.

Manuel, P. (1985) 'Blacks in British television drama', *Media Development*, 4, 41–3.

Marx, K. (1965) *The German Ideology*, London: Lawrence & Wishart.

Mattelart, M. (1986) *Women, Media, Crisis: Feminists and Disorder*, London: Comedia.

Maynard, M. (1987) 'Current trends in feminist theory', *Social Studies Review*, 2(3), January.

Mead, M. (1943) *Coming of Age in Samoa*, London: Penguin.

Medved, M. (1992) *Hollywood Vs. America*, London: HarperCollins.

Meehan, D. M. (1983) *Ladies of the Evening*, NY: Scarecrow Press.

Mercer, K. (1990) 'Welcome to the jungle', in J. Rutherford (ed.), *Identity: Community, Culture, Difference*, London: Lawrence & Wishart.

Merton, R. (1946) *Mass Persuasion*, NYFP.

Miller, D. (1992) 'The young and the restless in Trinidad', in R. Silverstone and E. Hirsch (eds), *Consuming Technologies*, London: Routledge.

Millum, T. (1975) *Images of Women: Advertising in Women's Magazines*, London: Chatto & Windus.

Minority Press Group (1980) *Here is the Other News*, London: Minority Press Group.

Mitchell, G. D. (1968) *A Dictionary of Sociology*.

Moore, A. (1983) 'Sexism in Comics', *The Daredevils*, 4, April.

Moore, S. (1993) 'A certain ageism', *Guardian*, 2, 13 August, 11 (quoted in Featherstone and Wernick (1995), p. 108).

Morley, D. (1980) *The Nationwide Audience*, London: BFI.

Morley, D. (1986) *Family Television*, London: Comedia.

Morley, D. (1992) *Television Audiences and Cultural Studies*, London: Routledge.

Morley, D. and Robins, K. (1989) 'Spaces of identity', *Screen*, 20(4), 3–15.

Morley, D. and Silverstone, R. (1990) 'Domestic communication media', *Culture and Society*, 12, 31–55.

Morrison, D. (1992) *Television and the Gulf War*, London: John Libbey.

Muir, R. (1987) *A Woman's Guide to Jobs in Film and Television*, London: Pandora Books.

Myers, K. (1986) *Understains*, London: Comedia.

Nava, M. (1992) *Changing Cultures: Feminism, Youth and Consumerism*, London: Sage.

Nava, M. and Nava, O. (1990) 'Discriminating or Duped?' *Cultural Studies*, 1, 15–21.

Negrine, R. (1994) *Politics and the Mass Media in Britain*, 2nd edn, London: Routledge.

Negroponte, N. (1995) *Being Digital*, London: Hodder & Stoughton.

Nevett, T. R. (1982) *Advertising in Britain*, London: Heinemann.

Newson, E. (1994) *Video Violence and the Protection of Children*, London: Broadcasting Standards Research Monographs.

O'Mally, T. (1994) *Closedown? The BBC and Government Broadcasting Policy 1979–92*, London: Pluto.

O'Sullivan, T. *et al.* (1983) *Key Concepts in Communication*, London: Comedia.

*Observer* (1987), 'Chomp! Thatcher tucks into cow pie capers', 9 June, p. 5.

Owen, J. (1995) 'I'm not a prude but …', in D. Petrie and J. Willis, *Television and Household*, London: BFI.

Paletz, D. and Entman, R. (1981) *Media, Power, Politics*, NYFP.

Parekh, B. (1986) 'Prejudice and the press', *New Society*, 7 November.

Peak, S. (ed.) (annual) *The Media Guide*, London: Fourth Estate.

Pearson, G. (1983) *Hooligan: A History of Respectable Fears*, London: Macmillan.

Pecheaux (1982) *Language, Semantics and Ideology*, Macmillan.

Phelps, G. (1991) *A Student's Guide to Film Classification and Censorship in Britain*, London: BBFC publications.

Philo, G. (1990) *Seeing and Believing: The Influence of Television*, London: Routledge. Philo's reply to Harrison is taken from a letter from Greg Philo to the journal of NATFHE, April 1986, pp. 28–9.

Pines, J. (1992) *Black and White in Colour: Black People in British Television since 1936*, London: BFI.

Porter, H. (1984) *Lies, Damned Lies and Some Exclusives: Fleet Street Exposed*, London: Chatto & Windus.

Postman, N. (1984) *Amusing Ourselves to Death*, London: Methuen.

Potter, J. and Wetherell, M. (1987) *Discourse and Social Psychology*, London: Sage.

Press, A. (1990) 'Class, gender and the female viewer', in Brown, University of Pennsylvania Press.

Price, S. (1993) *Media Studies*, London: Pitman.

Provenzo, E. F. (1991) *Video Kids: Making Sense of Nintendo*, Harvard University Press.

Radway, J. (1994) *Reading the Romance*, University of North Carolina Press.

Rex, J. and Tomlinson, S. (1979) *Colonial Immigrants in a British City*, London: Routledge & Kegan Paul.

Richards, C. (1993) 'What young girls do with television', in Buckingham (1993b).

Rock, P. and Cohen, S. (1970) 'The Teddy Boys', in V. Bogdanor and R. Skidelsky, *The Age of Affluence*, London: Macmillan.

Rosenberg, B. (1965) *Mass Culture*, London: Macmillan.

Saucier, K. (1986) 'Healers and heartbreakers: images of women and men in country music', *Journal of Popular Culture*, 20(3), 147–66.

Schlesinger, P. (1978) *Putting Reality Together – BBC News*, London: Constable.

Schramm, W. *et al.* (1961) *Television and the Lives of Our Children*, Stanford University Press.

Seymour-Ure, C. (1974) *The Political Impact of the Mass Media*, London: Constable.

Signorelli, N. (1985) *Role Portrayal and Stereotyping on Television*, Westport, Conn.: Greenwood Press.

Signorelli, N. (1989) 'Television and conceptions about sex roles', *Sex Roles*, 21(5/6), 341–60.

Singer, J. L. and Singer, D. G. (1986) 'Family experience and television viewing as predictors of children's imagination, restlessness and aggression', *Journal of Social Issues*, 42(3), 107–24.

Skirrow, G. (1986) 'Hellivision: an analysis of video games', in C. McCabe (ed.), *High Theory/Low Culture*, Manchester University Press.

Smith, R. (1987) 'Black journalists and the white media in race and society', *New Society*, 2 October.

Sontag, S. (1978) 'The double standard of ageing', in V. Carver and P. Liddiard (eds), *An Ageing Population*, London: Hodder & Stoughton.

Sparks, R. (1992) *Television and the Drama of Crime*, Buckingham: Open University Press.

Spender, D. (1995) *Nattering on the Net; women, power and cyberspace*, London: Spinifex.

Steeves, L. (1987) 'Feminist theories and media studies', *Critical Studies in Mass Communications*, 4(2), 95–135.

Stevenson, W. (ed.) (1995) *All Our Futures: The Changing Role and Purpose of the BBC*, London: BFI.

Stoll, C. (1995) *Silicon Snakeoil*, London: Macmillan.

Swingewood, A. (1977) *The Myth of Mass Culture*, London: Macmillan.

Synnott, A. (1989) 'Little angels, little devils', in Handel (1988).

Tuchman, G. (1978) *Making News*, NYFP.

Tuchman, G. *et al.* (eds) (1978) *Hearth and Home: Images of Women in the Mass Media*, NY: Oxford University Press.

Tunstall, J. (1983) *The Media in Britain*, London: Constable.

Turkle, S. (1988) 'Computational reticence', in C. Kramarae (ed.), *Technology and Women's Voices*, London: Routledge.

Twitchin, J. (ed.) (1988) *The Black and White Media Book: Handbook for the Study of Racism and Television*, Stoke-on-Trent: Trentham Books.

van Dijk, T. (1991) *Racism and the Press*, London: Routledge.

van Zoonen, L. (1991) 'Feminist perspectives on the media', in Curran and Gurevitch (1991).

van Zoonen, L. (1994) *Feminist Media Studies*, London: Sage.

Vestergaard, T. and Schroder, K. (1985) *The Language of Advertising*, Oxford: Blackwell.

Wagg, S. (1987) 'Mass communications: the debate about ownership and control', *Social Studies Review*, March.

Walkerdine, V. (1993) 'Daddy's gonna buy you a dream to cling to', in Buckingham (1993b).

Wasco, J. *et al.* (1993) 'Hollywood meets Madison Avenue media', *Culture and Society*, April.

Waters, M. (1995) *Globalization*, London: Routledge.

Whale, J. *The Politics of the Media*, London: Fontana.

Whitaker, B. (1981) *News Ltd – Why You Can't Read All About It*, London: Comedia.

Whitehouse, M. (1967) *Cleaning Up Television*, London: Blandford Press.

Whitehouse, M. (1974) 'Mental pollution', *Viewer and Listener*, Spring.

Williams, G. (1994) *Britain's Media – How they are Related: Media Ownership and Democracy*, Campaign for Press and Broadcasting Freedom.

Williams, R. (1974) *Television, Technology and Cultural Form*, London: Collins.

Williamson, J. (1978) *Decoding Advertisements*, London: Marion Boyars.

Willings Press Guide, *British Media Publications (annually)*.

Willis, P. (1990) *Common Culture*, Milton Keynes: Open University Press.

Winship, J. (1987) *Inside Women's Magazines*, London: Pandora Press.

Wolf, A. (1990) *The Beauty Myth*, London: Vintage.

Wrong, D. (1961) 'The oversocialised conception of man', *American Sociological Review*, 26, April.

Young, B. M. (1990) *Television Advertising and Children*, Oxford: Clarendon.

# Index